W9-AAA-427

WHEN MAIN STREET WAS A PATH AMONG THE STUMPS

COMPILED AND EDITED
BY SALLY EUSTICE HUMPHERY

IMAGE RESEARCH AND EDITING
BY DOUGLAS B. DAILEY

The Historical Society of Cheboygan County, Inc.

Copyright 2012 by The Historical Society of Cheboygan, Inc.

All rights reserved. No part of this book may be reproduced or transmitted in any form or by any means, electronic or mechanical, including photocopying, recording, or by any information storage and retrieval system, without permission in writing from the publisher.

Published by The Historical Society of Cheboygan, Inc., P.O. Box 5005, Cheboygan, Michigan 48721-5005. Additional copies available at the Cheboygan History Center, 427 Court St., Cheboygan. E-mail: museum@cheboyganhistorycenter. org. Phone 231.627.9597

Publisher's Cataloging-in-Publication Data
Humphery, Sally Eustice
   When main street was a path among the stumps / edited by Sally Eustice Humphery
Cheboygan Mich., The Historical Society of Cheboygan County, Inc. 2012
         p.   cm.   ill.
   ISBN 978-0-9854811-0-0
   1. History–United States.

PROJECT COORDINATION BY BOOKABILITY OF MICHIGAN LLC

Printed in Canada

Front cover drawing by Shobar and Carqueville Litho.- Chicago

INTRODUCTION

The Historical Society of Cheboygan County has long felt the need for a comprehensive history of the county. To accomplish such a broad goal and ambitious undertaking, the Society's publication committee decided that a series of books chronicling the story of Cheboygan would be more appropriate than a single volume.

Much of the history of Cheboygan County lies buried in scrapbooks, newspaper articles, term papers, individual family histories and county records. Over the years various individuals have written books and articles that treat single historical subjects, but to date no comprehensive history has been published. In his long tenure at the *Cheboygan Daily Tribune*, Gordon Turner, kept alive a vibrant interest in local history and wrote many articles for the newspaper. Some of these have been compiled in book form. More recently, Ellis Olson and Matthew Friday have conducted research and contributed to the written history of the County and its industries.

This first volume in the Cheboygan County History Series chronicles the early years of Cheboygan's history. Rather than presenting the story of Cheboygan as a running narrative, I have chosen to let our earliest residents speak for themselves. Whether from first-hand accounts, newspaper articles, personal recollections or letters, our earliest residents tell their own story in their own words. Whether they are doctors or lawyers, farmers or fishermen, housewives or midwives, each person brings their own perspective to frontier life in rural Northern Michigan.

For those with roots in Cheboygan County, you will no doubt recognize the names and perhaps the faces of those whose stories are represented. If you are new to the county, you will quickly discover the great heritage of Cheboygan's founding families. So explore these pages, discover your connection to the past and imagine how you can help keep alive the common wealth that we all share.

Sally Eustice-Humphrey
Cheboygan, Michigan
April 1, 2012

*Dedicated to all those who walked along Main Street
when it was only a path among the stumps.*

CHAPTER AUTHORS

Sally Eustice Humphrey: native of Cheboygan, Michigan, retired school teacher, local genealogist and historian.

Phil Porter: a resident of Cheboygan and Executive Director of the Mackinac State Historic Parks, Mackinac Island, Michigan

Ellis Olson: retired teacher, former mayor of Cheboygan, and local historian who began the first Cheboygan Museum.

Dale France: local resident of the Black River area of Cheboygan, he writes of the history of the farming activity along the Black River.

Terry Pepper: Executive Director of the Great Lakes Lighthouse Keepers Association in Mackinaw City, Michigan.

Stuart R. Bell II: a resident of Cheboygan and descendent of the Bell fishing family.

Notice to the reader: In most instances, the punctuation and spelling within quotations used in this publication have been left as in the original. In other places, for better understanding, grammar and punctuation have been standardized.

TABLE OF CONTENTS

This downtown Cheboygan mural depicts the earliest written references to the Cheboygan River. The 8ft × 100ft mural was a U.S. bicentennial project and was first placed to cover the site of the burned J.C. Penny Store, located where the Citizen's National Bank parking lot is today. The mural was later moved to face the parking area of Straits Area Federal Credit Union.[1]

[1] The mural was a project undertaken by the Cheboygan Area Arts Council. Many locals were involved in securing funds, building the wood frame, and designing and painting the mural. Many local artists spent the summer painting the mural. Exposure to weather, through the years, has led to repainting, with the help of local art students.

CHEBOYGAN'S EARLIEST DAYS

The Inland Water Route from Cheboygan to Petoskey had been a well-established traveling route for Native Americans for hundreds of years prior to the first permanent settlement in 1844. The Ottawa (Odawa) and Chippewa Indians had seasonal migration patterns where they wintered in southern Michigan and spent the summers in the north. They came north to collect maple sap to turn to sugar, to gather whitefish and lake trout, to grow crops of corn, and to trade furs for trade goods. The Chippewa traditionally lived between the Cheboygan River and Lake Huron while the Ottawa lived between the River and Lake Michigan. They all gathered at Mackinac for trading and, in later years, to receive annuity payments. During the summer months they made many summer camps along the inland water route. Some of these areas included the old sawdust pile site opposite the paper mill, various points in Mullett Lake including Dodge's Point and the old Boy Scout camp on the east side, Topinabee, Indian River and Burt Lake.

Two traders, John Askin and James Barthe, were known to have had trading posts near the mouth of the Cheboygan River. Askin's son-in-law, Samuel Robertson, placed the ship *"Welcome"* in the Cheboygan River during some winter months.

To keep vessels in safety there during the Winter, the most safest place near Michilimackinac for wintering vessels is the River Shaboygan, there is six feet water upon the Barr, the river is about twenty yards wide at the entrance, & a Vessel of 6 feet draught of water cannot go up further than 200 or 300 yards, & then he can lay alongside of a Clay Bank, in two fathoms water, or she can be hove up two or three feet in mud & lay with all safety, I never saw the River freeze or any sea to hurt a Vessel, it is clear level marshy ground for half a mile around at the mouth so that there could be no danger of them being surprised from Indians & there is always good Fishing and shooting, there is plenty of fine pines both sides of the River, & other good wood, up to the little lake which is 3 Leagues [l league = about 3 Miles] from the mouth of it, I had a Dwelling House & Garden by the Edge of the wood and the Welcome wintered two winters there.[2]

Robertson served as Captain of Askin's ship, the *Welcome*. During the time of the American Revolution, John Askin was trying to protect his property. If he had left his ship in Detroit for the winter, it would have been confiscated by the British. If he left it at Fort Michilimackinac, where there was no safe harbor, chances are the ship would have been crushed by the winter ice in the Straits. Therefore, Askin turned to the "Shaboygan" river for safe harbor.

Established in 1715 as a fortified fur trading village, Michilimackinac had need for large quantities of firewood and timber for building. All of the nearby timber had been cut. The area around the Cheboygan River provided an ample supply of timber, close to the water, for easy transport to Michilimackinac. During the summer, Askin sent crews to Cheboygan to cut hay to supply the fort livestock with feed. The hay was cut and rafted from Cheboygan to Michilimackinac or else transported on board the *Welcome* or *Felicity*. The house at Cheboygan to which Robertson refers could have been used to house the crew. It could also have been used as a trading post with the Indians who traveled the Inland Route. Askin's 1778 inventory lists 285 bags of corn at Cheboygan.[3]

Welcome Logbook[4]

1779

The " Welcome" in the forenoon sailed to Sheboygan for hay

Govt's order about 10 A.M. sent the "Felicity" to Sheboygan for hay

. . . saw the "Felicity" on out weather quarter coming from Sheboygan—in the evening the "Felicity" and the "Welcome" arrived with hay

The troops embarked agreeable to the government's order under the command of Lieut. Clowes—at noon got underway from wharf—turned down to about a mile to the westward of Sheboygan by 7 PM then came to

Monday 23d July 1781 Took a Canoe on board for the hay Cutters-6 Canadians sent on board for the Raft. About 11 got underway & run to the Pinery. By 1 PM filled the vessel with Hay-in the evening brought the Raft off and moored it astern

Saturday, July 28 The "Welcome" in the forenoon Sailed to Cheboygan for hay—about 7 PM sailed also with the "Angelica" for the Pinery.

Sunday 29 July Having come to off the hay ground about 6 AM began to load with hay aboard & the "Welcome" arrived also for hay—took in both vessels about 500 bundles being all that was cut

Monday 30 July The "Felicity" to Sheboygan for hay-about noon the 'Welcome" also sailed there for hay

---

2 *Michigan Pioneer & Historical Collection (MPHC)*, Vol. 9: 642, Haldimand Papers, letter Samuel Robertson to Captain John Shank, April 26, 1781.
3 Kent, Timothy, Rendezvous at the Straits, Vol. II, p. 553.
4 Alexander Harrow Papers, Logbook of the Welcome, 1779-1782, Burton Historical Collection, Detroit Public Library, University Microfilms, Inc., 1967).

Photo © Ken Rochleau of reconstructed "Welcome" entering the Cheboygan River.

Another record of an early house on the Cheboygan River is unusual. Patrick Sinclair, Lieutenant Governor and Superintendent of Michilimackinac, employed Pierre Durand to dismantle a log house and move it from old Fort Michilimackinac (Mackinaw City) to the Chippewa village on the Cheboygan River. This was to reward Chief Matchekewis for his help in organizing raiding parties against the Americans who were threatening British rule in the Great Lakes Region. Durand took the house over the ice, in winter, on wood rollers and re-erected it on the river bank. The description Durand gave on his invoice was for the work.

March 5, For having pulled down a house of twenty four feet long by twenty deep and having transported it six leagues on rollers of white wood, having furnished the necessary wood for repairs and having put the key of the said house into the hands; the said house for the great Chief of the Sauteaux named Macquiquiovis for the price and sum of 4500 livres of expenses . . . For having been down the river besides the house of the Chief Macquiquiovis to examine & find the pineries of red and white pine to make a saw mill & to examine the different sorts of wood and land for the good of the King . . . . 250 livres[5]

There is no record of a mill being built in Cheboygan at that time. Instead, one was constructed at Mill Creek, between Cheboygan and Mackinac City.

An early map, by Gother Mann, dated 1788, was made of Mackinac Island and the Straits area. It named the "Sheboagan River." This map belongs to the Library and Archives of Canada and a copy of it has been published in Brian Dunnigan's book, "A Picturesque Situation."[6]

After the War of 1812, the Americans had control of the area and there seems to be no written reference to the Cheboygan area or river for many years. Settlement in the area centered on Mackinac Island, where the fishing industry was replacing the fur trade. Cheboygan was then part of the Northwest Territory until Michigan became a state in 1837.

The Treaty of Washington of 1836 was concluded between the U.S. government and the Chippewa and Ottawa Indians on May 27, 1836. Henry Schoolcraft was the Indian Commissioner for the United States. In the treaty, the tribes ceded 13,837,207 acres in the northwest portion of the Lower Peninsula of Michigan and the eastern portion of the Upper Peninsula. In return for this land they received the following promise.

An annuity of thirty thousand dollars per annum, in specie,

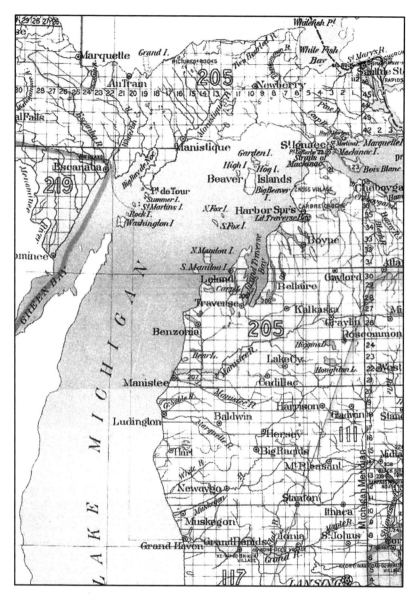

Map from Indian Affairs,: Laws & Treaties, compiled by Charles J. Kappler, Washington, Government Printing Office, 1904.

for twenty years; eighteen thousand dollars, to be paid to the Indians between Grand River and the Cheboigun; three thousand six hundred dollars, to the Indians on the Huron shore, between the Cheboigan and Thunder-bay river; and seven thousand four hundred dollars, to the Chippewas north of the straits, as far as the cession extends; the remaining one thousand dollars, to be invested in stock by the Treasury Department and to

5 MPHC Vol. 10, 365-66

6 Brian Leigh Dunnigan, A Picturesque Situation, Mackinac before Photography, 1615-1860, Wayne State University Press, 2008.

remain incapable of being sold, without the consent of the President and Senate, which may, however, be given, after the expiration of twenty-one years. 2nd. Five thousand dollars per annum, for the purpose of education, teachers, school-houses, and books in their own language, to be continued twenty years, and as long thereafter as Congress may appropriate for the object. 3rd. Three thousand dollars for missions, subject to the conditions mentioned in the second clause of this article. 4th. Ten thousand dollars for agricultural implements, cattle, mechanics' tools, and such other objects as the President may deem proper. 5th. Three hundred dollars per annum for vaccine matter, medicines, and the services of physicians, to be continued while the Indians remain on their reservations. 6th. Provisions to the amount of two thousand dollars; six thousand five hundred pounds of tobacco; one hundred barrels of salt, and five hundred fish barrels, annually, for twenty years. 7th. One hundred and fifty thousand dollars, in goods and provisions, on the ratification of this treaty, to be delivered at Michilimackinac, and also the sum of two hundred thousand dollars, in consideration of changing the permanent reservations in article two and three to reservations for five years only, to be paid whenever their reservations shall be surrendered, and until that time the interest on said two hundred thousand dollars shall be annually paid to said Indians.[7]

This treaty included a special provision for some of the "half breed" children. This included "To John A. Drew, for a tract of one section and three quarters, to his Indian family, at Cheboygan Rapids, at the rate of four dollars." John Drew was a partner with Edward Biddle on Mackinac Island.

Honorable William A. Burt

They both had Indian wives. The rapids area in this description is where the Cheboygan dam is now located.

Between 1840 and 1843 John Mullet and William Austin Burt surveyed Cheboygan County which was then part of Mackinac County. Access to northern Michigan by travelers was still by boat and was limited to the ice- free months when ships could navigate the Great Lakes. Although Burt and Mullett made survey trails, there was no road or path overland, except the Indian trails. One of the main Indian Trails went from Saginaw to Grand Traverse and then on to the Straits and was called the "Cheboigan Trail." Once this land was surveyed, it was opened for settlement. The next chapter will tell about some of the first to come and stay at Cheboygan.

In the next chapter we will meet some of the county's earliest families.

---

7 Article 4, of Treaty of Washington of 1936.

Our Founding Family and Their Neighbors

By Sally Eustise Humphrey

Did you ever wonder what life was like for those who first came and settled in Cheboygan? If you live in northern Michigan you are familiar with log cabins, hunting, fishing, cutting firewood and going for a boat ride. However, Cheboygan's homesteaders came before generators, chain saws, cell phone communication or even roads. What was their life really like?

This collection of biographical information about some of our founding fathers comes to us through their descendants, through oral histories printed in the newspapers of the times, and other sources. Enjoy their memories and next time you are fishing along the river bank, imagine seeing one of them paddle by, with a boatload of supplies, headed to their homestead.

Jacob Sammons[1]

Jacob Sammons was born June 11, 1804, near Syracuse, New York. He married Chloe Ann Dutton on January 13, 1833 and moved to Chicago after the birth of their son Francis in June of 1834. He was a captain on a canal boat and after their marriage, Chloe lived with him, aboard the boat, and was in charge of the cooking. From Syracuse, they moved to Joliet, Illinois, where Jacob bought a 300-acre farm and later homesteaded at Yellowhead, Kankakee County, about 30 miles outside of Chicago. They were doing well but,

because of the prevalence of fever and ague, they decided to move to a different area. Jacob, having also learned the coopering and barrel making trade, decided to give up farming, buy hoop timber and pine lands, and operate a cooperage.[2]

The Sammons moved to Mackinac Island in 1842. In the fall of 1844, Jacob came to Cheboygan in a small boat, accompanied by his eight year old son, Sylvester, with a description from Lansing of available homestead land in his pocket. The following day he located the land, which covered both sides of the river all the way from the Straits to the vicinity of what is now Lincoln Avenue. Jacob was issued the first conveyance of land within the present day boundaries of the City of Cheboygan in 1848. This was platted in 1851 and contained 45 lots.[3]

Jacob came to Cheboygan in a sail scow, called the *Bunker Hill* commanded by Captain Moses Nason. They went up the river and cut pine trees to make barrel staves which they took back to Mackinac Island.[4] Jacob returned to Mackinac Island, but soon came back with a load of bark for the roof of a cabin he had built, on the west bank of the river near the present day range light. In the spring of 1845, Jacob moved to Cheboygan with his family and went into the business of making fish barrels and boxes. The booming fishing industry on Mackinac Island created a large demand for

---

1 Biographical information provided by Mary Lou Miller, a descendent of the Sammons family. Much of it was written by or based on interviews of Lottie Sammons, daughter of Sylvester Sammons.

2 Jacob Sammons sold his farm to Jerry Chapman, his brother in law.

3 Jacob Sammons received the following three patents for his *"Original Plat of Cheboygan"* patent number 2210, section 29, T. 38 N., R. 1 W: number 2211, section 31, T. 31 N., R 1 W. and number 2212, section 31, T. 38 N., R. 1 W. all dated September 1, 1848. Information provided by Ellis Olson, local historian.

4 *Centennial History of Cheboygan County,* Rev. W. H. Ware, originally printed in 1876, reprinted by Historical Society of Cheboygan County in 1976, p. 15.

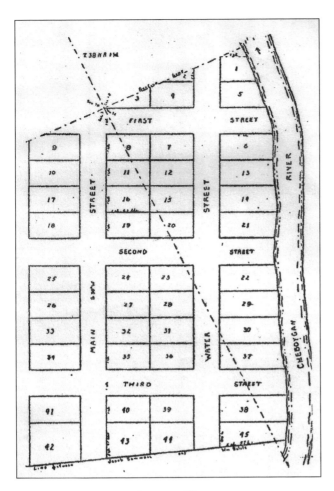

Sammons Plat

built of lumber from the mill. "It was a steam saw mill, built in the winter of 1847 and 1848, at the mouth of the river. It had two upright saws, capable of cutting from eight to twelve thousand feet of lumber in twenty-four hours. It was kept in running order for only a few years and then allowed to go into decay."[5]

Later Jacob Sammons and Alexander "Sandy" McLeod were partners in a mill at the watermill site (the dam). They later sold out to the McArthur Company, which went on to improve the mill and build and operate the dam, locks, lighting plant, lumber campstore, flour mill, and sawmill.

Jacob Sammons and Lorenzo Wheelock built a wharf for Medard Metivier in 1855. It was on the river, above First Street and was later owned by A. P. Newton.

Lottie's father, Sylvester Sammons, married Johanna Schwark in 1859 when he was 23 years

Jacob Sammons died, age 55, in Cheboygan. He is buried in Pine Hill Cemetery.

barrels to ship this fish to market. Cheboygan had a ready supply of timber to make the barrels.

To encourage others to come and settle, Sammons gave away parcels of land. Lottie Sammons, Jacob's granddaughter, said he gave land on the east side of the river to a cousin, whom she did not name. He gave land in the vicinity of the lighthouse to Lorenzo Backus. He also gave Backus land which is now part of Main Street.

Lottie said her grandfather, Jacob Sammons, started the first sawmill in Cheboygan. It was located across from where the USCGC *Mackinac* ties up. Jacob Sammons and Peter McKinley, who came here from New York, were partners in the mill, and Lottie said the first homes were

---

5 Ware p. 18.

old. "My father had to borrow the dollar and a half for the license, there being no money here at that time, all dealings being done by trading different commodities, even with Chicago, where their supplies were purchased and at Mackinac Island." Lottie's father was a carpenter and he built many of Cheboygan's early houses. He made fish and flour barrels and helped build boats. Lottie said "He also made the shingles that covered the roof of our log house by hand, and they lasted many years. He also helped build the piers for the first bridge."

Sylvester Sammons, Jacob's son, lived in a log house on the property that he homesteaded on Pine Hill Avenue, moving there in 1862. He had 160 acres. "He cleared 80 acres with his own hands, after his day's work at the cooperage shop," Lottie related. "With an ax, my father cut a path to Duncan from his farm, which was the trail for many years that people traveled to go to Thompson Smith's store to trade. He helped build a Catholic Church on land, part of which is now the Jewell Gravel Pit." Sylvester was a market gardener, for 28 years, growing vegetables for Duncan, Mackinaw City and Mackinac Island. He and Patrick Sullivan paved a large part of Pine Hill Avenue with broken bricks from the Sullivan brickyard which was located nearby.

When Beulah Miller, daughter of Fannie Hope and Charles Jacob Sammons, was about eight years old, she had the duty of calling on her grandfather, Sylvester Sammons, to see that he ate meals set out by her Aunt Lottie. She would sit with him at a table by a window, and he would often talk about earlier times. His wife was dead and he was in a wheelchair. He told her he was a small boy when the Sammons family left Chicago to come to Mackinac Island and later to Cheboygan. He told her that one of his first impressions was that the pines were so thick on both sides of the river that they seemed impenetrable. He remembered that

Patrick Sullivan
Courtesy of Darlene Holling.

when he was a boy he used to take a rowboat to cross the river and play with Indian children. They could not speak each other's language, but they got along wonderfully well.

Lottie also had memories of her Uncle Francis Sammons, oldest child of Jacob Sammons. Francis started the Masonic Lodge in Cheboygan and was the first Worshipful Master. He owned the land at the corner of the present day Court and Main Streets.

Francis M. Sammons, the oldest son of Jacob Sammons, the first settler in Cheboygan County, was born near Syracuse, New York, in the year 1834. He had moved with his family to Illinois and remained there with an uncle until his family was settled in Cheboygan in 1846. On July 4, 1857, he

CHEBOYGAN,   Hoskins, PHOTOGRAPHER.   MICHIGAN.

Lottie Sammons, age 14.

married Samantha R. St. John, of Cheboygan. She had been adopted and raised by the Lorenzo Backus family. Francis and his wife had nine children. "At an early day Mr. Sammons used to buy fur and in that pursuit traversed nearly the whole region between the Saginaw Valley and the Straits. His principal occupation was the mercantile business, lumbering and contracting. He was one of the contractors for building the old wharf in 1861, also the Third Street Bridge." [7]

There was a wharf at the mouth of the river. "It was constructed in 1861 by

F. M. Sammons, H. F. Todd, and Geo. Stevenson, contractors, for Harrison Averill. Sometime after midnight, a part of it floated off while full of wood, with Mr. Stevenson on it. . . He soon discovered a boat attached to his 'ark,' so he took it and made for the shore, and waked the people who went out and saved most of the wood. The remains landed at Duncan. The dock was rebuilt in 1863, by F. M. Sammons, and made somewhat larger. In the spring of 1876 it followed the example of its predecessor, floated off and went ashore at Duncan." [8]

"In company with Dr. A.M. Gerow, Francis Sammons opened the first drug store in the village. He was also one of the contractors for opening the route to Crooked Lake, he having been the first to conceive the idea of carrying the mail over that route. He held the offices of county clerk and town supervisor several terms and was school director and moderator about twenty years. In these capacities he rendered the public very valuable service in organizing the affairs of the town and establishing a prosperous school system. He has been from its beginning a prominent member of the Greenback Party, and was a candidate for representative to the state legislature in 1878." [9]

Francis Sammons moved to Tacoma, Washington by February 4, 1895, the date he applied for a passport. He listed himself as a merchant and permanent resident of Tacoma. He died in Hunter, Stevens County, Washington.

---

7 "*The Traverse Region, Historical and Descriptive, with Illustrations of Scenery and Portraits and Biographical Sketches of Some of Its Prominent Men and Pioneers*," Chicago: HR Page & Co., 1884,p. 113.

8 Ware, p. 26.

9 "*The Traverse Region, Historical and Descriptive, with Illustrations of Scenery and Portraits and Biographical Sketches of Some of Its Prominent Men and Pioneers*," Chicago: HR Page & Co., 1884, p. 113.

Sylvester L. Sammons

Francis M. Sammons

CHARLES SAMMONS—

MY FATHER STARTED CHEBOYGAN[10]

At 237 North Street resides Charles Sammons, 82 year old son of Jacob Sammons, first white settler in Cheboygan. He is the only one left here of the Jacob Sammons family. A little bent and a little deaf, he retains an amazing vitality. With the help of his cane, he walks up town regularly. He is surly and jolly, with a splendid memory. He enjoys life, especially fishing. He has retired from an interesting life that is an illustration of the experiences of Cheboygan pioneers.

(Comments by Gordon Turner, Cheboygan Daily Tribune Reporter)

I am the youngest of 11 children of Jacob Sammons and Chloe Ann Dutton Sammons. The family came here in 1846.

My father built a log house where Captain William Hall's range light station is now, and he made fish barrels in a shop there on the river.

I was not born until 11 years after the family came. He was appointed keeper of the first Cheboygan lighthouse, located on Lighthouse Point. I was born in the lighthouse on April 11, 1857. My father was keeper there from 1856 to 1857 and the lighthouse has since been replaced.

Only two of us children are still alive. Francis M. Sammons was the oldest of us. He died in Washington State. My brother Sylvester L. who came next was a cooper. Sarah was the oldest girl. Martha and Jane followed her. They died here when they were small girls from the black smallpox. My brother Myron served as Captain of the Second Michigan Cavalry, Company

---

10 The 1939 Golden Jubilee edition of the *Cheboygan Daily Tribune* includes this story told to Gordon Turner by Charles E. Sammons, the youngest of Jacob Sammon's children.

K, in the Civil War. He got his honorable discharge at 10 o'clock in the morning and died at 11 that morning from typhoid.

My father owned a lot of land here, including the property where the New Cheboygan Hotel is now. He laid out a lot for a family burying ground. When Martha and Jane died he buried them there. That was Cheboygan's first cemetery.[11] The first child to be born after they died was a girl so Father and Mother named her Martha Jane. She was the first white child to be born in Cheboygan. She is dead now. She grew up, married, had children of her own, and died in Grand Haven. Elsie was born after her, and she died here. John C. Sammons was the next of us. He is still living, at Muskegon. He will be 88 on the 7th of July. Jacob A. Sammons was the 10th child. He died in 1887 in Dr. Perrin's hospital, where the Court House stands now. I was the eleventh and last and I am here yet.

Charles Sammons

New Cheboygan Hotel was located on the SW corner of Water and State Street.

Collection of the Historical Society of Cheboygan County, Inc.

---

11 Remains from an early Indian Cemetery have been dug up during construction projects, just north of the Kingston Theater, in the parking lot area. They were reinterred in Pine Hill Cemetery. Information per Ellis Olson, local historian and Pine Hill sexton.

This is a very early photo of the swing bridge. The man with one leg is Robert Micheljohn, who was a bridge tender. Micheljohn had a foot amputated and got around with two crutches.

Photo by Johnson's Studios

After the log house on the river, my folks had a frame building in the block where the Eagles' Temple is. (West side of Main Street, between Pine and Locust) It was the only house in the block. My father died when I was 2 years old. My mother owned 40 acres opposite where Pinehill Cemetery is. We homesteaded there. I started working when I was 8 years old. I had to quit school and go to work steady when I was 12.

My school was where Ed Carrow's A and P store is now, at the corner of Main and Locust Street. [Where the Straits Area Federal Credit Union is located in 2011.] One day the Steamer *L.G. Mason* arrived with a circus. When the steamer blew, we kids streaked out of school and ran pell mell up town. The circus had a baby elephant. I crowded close to the stall and the elephant thrust out his trunk through a hole and grabbed my leg. I can remember one of my chums yelling "A snake's got Charley!"

I graduated from the second reader and worked on the farm. My mother died when I was 13. I left the farm when I was 14 and went to the lumber woods.

My first recollections of Cheboygan are of a town of about 100 people. Sidewalks were paths that used to get knee deep in mud. There was no church. There were two towns, Cheboygan and Duncan, with Cheboygan a little larger. The river was not over 3 ½ feet deep at the mouth, due to a sand bar. Near the Court House there was a rapids and the water was not over three feet deep there. There were really two towns here, one at Cheboygan and one at Duncan.

Cheboygan had no sidewalks. The only street in my childhood was Main Street. I remember when the street was a corduroy road from Division Street to State Street. It would be afloat in the spring. The first sidewalks were made of planks built on cedar ties. A single plank

View of the swing bridge from the water, looking north. The center pier or "artificial island" served as the pivot point on which the bridge rotated.
Collection of the Historical Society of Cheboygan County, Inc.

When a boat was too tall to pass under the swing bridge (State Street) the bridge tender and whoever he could get to help would turn this giant screw, which caused the middle section of the bridge to pivot until it was parallel with the river. After the boat passed, they turned it back and it was again passable by vehicles. The man on the far right is Pete Nichols who was a bridge tender in the 1930's.
Collection of the Historical Society of Cheboygan County, Michigan.

a foot wide provided walking space for one person, and across an interval of bare ground was another plank of the ties for another person to walk abreast or to pass.

Mickeljohn was the first tender for the State Street jackknife bridge, which was

wound with a windlass. [*Ed. Note: The first bridge was built in 1862 by J. F. Watson and F. M. Sammon and was tended by Peter Bellant. This first draw bridge was replaced by the Swing Bridge about 1877.*][12] The only bridge in the vicinity before that was a pier in front of the present gas plant, built of cribs filled with rock and covered with split cedar. Three floats were anchored to the pier, and in winter teams could be driven across. In summer the floats were taken out, and the pier used for dockage. Horses were used to pull lighters [barges] laden with cordwood upstream to the dock.

I began working in the lumbering camps when I was 14. I cooked in the camps in the winter and in the summer on the lake boats. I also cooked for spile driver outfits [They drove wood pilings along riverbank.] when the Inland Route was being developed. Wages used to be $1 a day and board, or $1.50 without board

Stores used to order all their supplies for delivery by boat before winter began. One fall, flour was ordered but did not come. We had wheat but no mill. The town faced a winter without bread. A meeting was called, and Dan Wheelock volunteered to go to Traverse City for help. He carried a gristmill in from Traverse. Another time winter set in early and flour had not arrived yet. On Thanksgiving night the steamer *Scott* ran aground on Lighthouse Point. The boat broke up. The public helped itself. I got seven barrels of wheat flour, two barrels of rye flour, and one barrel of dried apples.

12 Ware, p. 26.

I can remember when flour cost from $12 to $22 a barrel, and pork $60 a barrel, while sugar was a rarity, seen once or twice a year. Brown sugar cost 22 cents a pound. Tea was $1.50 a pound. We made a beverage from burned barley or peas that substituted for coffee, but we found carrots roasted and ground the best of all.

I moved my two sisters from the family burying ground to Pinehill Cemetery. When I was 21 I took up a homestead in Munro. I was one of the first settlers there. I built a cabin and farmed. I gave that up and returned to working on the boats in summer and sawmills in winter.

I have an engineer's boat papers, and also unlimited captain's papers. I was first mate on the White Shoals Lightship, No. 5. The captain sent me ashore in a 14 ft. sailboat. I was overtaken by a squall off McGulpin's point. My boat became caught in a pond net and filled with water. I was there all night in the storm. I vowed to God that if I ever got out I would never sail again. And I never have.

I have worked at many jobs. I was bookkeeper for McTiver & Hughes at Onaway several years. I was with that company 9 years. I bought timber, butchered, did the blacksmithing and ran the engines. I was foreman for McTiver two years at Prince Spur on the D. and M. Railroad. For 10 years I rode logs downstream in the spring.

Indians used to be numerous around Cheboygan. They would come in from Burt Lake and camp where the Sawdust Pile is, in their cedar wigwams. They were friendly though.

I have been married twice, the first time when I was 22. My wife was Elizabeth Cranson, and we were married by Thomas Bentley, justice of the peace. I have a suit of clothes that I have had about 60 years. I was married in it. I have worn it a few times since to funerals, but that is all. I keep it pressed to be buried in.

We had five children. One is dead. The others are Arthur, in Duluth; Mrs. Elsie Maxfield, Duluth; Mrs. Roy Freeman of Detroit and M.S. Sammons of Dedham, Mass. My wife died after we had been married 25 years. I was married again to Mrs. Angeline Eno, at Sand Lake Center.

I bought a farm of 32 acres across from the County Farm but sold it and bought 45 acres at another place. While farming in Munroe and Benton I was elected Munroe highway commissioner and Benton School Treasurer and member of the Board of Review. My legs finally failed me, and I sold my farm and came to Cheboygan to live. Now I don't do as much, but I fish a lot. Biggest fish I ever caught was a 48 pound muskie I speared at Beebe's (Hack-Ma-Tack).

MOSES WIGGINS HORNE[13]

Moses Wiggins Horne   *Sarah Tuttle Horne*

13 1939 Golden Jubilee Edition of the *Cheboygan Daily Tribune*.

CITY PARK CHEBOYGAN, MICH.
#4

Apple Tree in Washington Park.   Courtesy of the Patricia Wight Geyer collection

Millie Wilson Brazel, a grand-daughter of M.W. Horne, wrote this biography of her grandfather.

He raised fowl for his own use. Chickens, ducks, geese and turkeys. He also raised cows, pigs, and sheep. Then too, there were always a few young colts. There was an abundance of fish and wild game. He had two large barns, a cooper shop and a blacksmith shop.

In those early days there were no wells. They drank the spring water which was very clear and pure. Later they sank a well. Lotus trees and sugar pear trees were on the river bank by the boat house. My grandfather did a great deal to preserve them, however at night the beaver worked around the traps and cut down the trees one by one.

At that time there were no electric lights, nor even kerosene lamps. The tallow candles were made at home and used in brass candle sticks. Wood was used for fuel.

There were no railroads, no telegraph, telephone, or radio. No paved streets of sidewalks or sewers. No modern conveniences in the home. There were no grocery stores or bake shops, Even the soap was homemade and everyone was clean and happy.

Would it interest you if I told you that I have one of my grandmother's linen sheets and other pieces of linen? My great grandmother Bunker raised the flax, spun thread and wove the linen. It is stamped with my grandmother's maiden name. I have the pewter stamp which she used. In the center of the stamp there is a dove and the name of Sarah T. Bunker.

Their carpets were woven from rags and straw was used under them. The furniture was mostly walnut and cherry. I am taking the best of care of some of the pieces as I prize them very highly. In a few years the village of Cheboygan was incorporated.

My grandfather gave the streets to the village. Although both were Baptists, he gave the property where the Methodist parsonage now stands to the Methodists, as there were more Methodists there than Baptists. He gave a park near Horne Street.

Cheboygan, on the beautiful blue water in the Straits of Mackinac! I remember when a little girl of going to Mackinac Island in a sailboat to visit the Astors. (relative of John Jacob Astor) Such lovely water—just next to heaven. The Astors and my grandparents always exchanged gifts when visiting each other, and I'll never forget the little pats of butter stamped with a sheaf of wheat, which my grandmother made for them. The Astor House was owned by heirs of the late John Jacob Astor.

M.W. Horne was a very active man. About 5 feet, 8 inches tall and probably weighed about 150 lbs. He was elected president of the village and appointed marshal at different times, also appointed postmaster. This was before postage stamps were cancelled by machine as I have some which he marked in ink with his initials (M.W.H.).

Some winters he carried the mail to Detroit over the ice in Lake Huron by dog team, taking over three weeks to make the trip. In the good old summer time the mail came up by boat, as did all provisions, to last through the winter.

My grandfather was active in politics and was for the betterment of government

Sarah Horne Wilson, 14, daughter of Moses and Sarah Horne.

and civilization. He was very strict with regard to law and order. He was also much consulted by private persons about their affairs. He was a splendid man to his family and a good provider. Always cheerful and generous, looking on the bright side of life. At his table he liked to have some sensible friends or neighbors to converse with and always took care to start some useful topic for discourse. By this means he turned attention to what was good and just and prudent in the

14 *Cheboygan Daily Tribune* 1939 Golden Jubilee edition.

conduct of life. His library consisted not of how many books but how good the books were. I still have the old family Bible and other valuable volumes.

There were four children born in Cheboygan. My mother, Sarah, was one of six in all. On February 14, 1870, she married George Wilson, who was the first to build a set of lumber camps for lumbering the pine of Northern Michigan. He was born in Hull, England, November 12, 1845, and died November 12, 1928. He lived in Cheboygan 64 years. His old home is still standing on the corner of Huron and Elm Streets. He lumbered the timber for the home, sent the logs to Alpena to be sawed into lumber, which was the very best of white pine. My father and grandfather built several houses and sold them.

In 1864, the year my father came to Cheboygan, he was accompanied by several other young men. Among them were Dr. Perrin and his brother Charlie, Watts S. Humphrey, Bill Strohn, Bill Devine, and Dr. Gerow. Later came Ephraim Nelson, who built the lumber mill on the east side of the river across from the docks. And so Cheboygan grew and flourished and became a city fifty years ago. M.W. Horne died December 27, 1883 and was buried with Masonic honors in the family lot in Pine Hill Cemetery. His wife followed him January 14, 1889, fifty years ago.

LOUIS ADOLPHUS PAQUIN[15]

This oral history of Adolphus Paquin, one of Cheboygan's earliest residents, was recorded in the local newspaper in 1897.

Adolphus Paquin was one of the pioneers of Cheboygan. He was born at West Astoria, Canada, on November 20, 1824. In the spring of 1847 he started for the Soo, but without intending to stay. He stopped at Mackinac Island and found sufficient attraction there to induce him to go no further. He remained on the Island until the fall of 1848, when he came to Cheboygan and went to work for Sandy and Roland McLeod, who ran the water mill, having built the dam and the mill in 1847. When this mill was built there was joy in all the surrounding country, as it was the first mill in this section. The soldiers at the fort at Mackinac fired salutes all day long in honor of the great event. The first saw was an upright one, and Mr. Paquin ran this saw for years. He was on Mackinac Island when the smallpox affected the whole of this part of the country.

To return to the mill-Roland McLeod afterward sold his share in the mill to Richard Duncan[16], who built the Duncan Mill in 1868, which burned 15 years later. Mr. Paquin worked in this mill three days and then took an important step in life, for September 19th he went over to Mackinac Island with Miss Zoe LeGault and they were married on the Island by Father Pierre, he being the only priest in this part of the country at the time. Fr.

---

15 *Cheboygan Democrat*, June 19, 1897
16 Note: Richard Duncan was the son of Jeremiah Duncan, who owned the mill.

Pierre was known at the time as the only priest who wore a beard. Miss LeGault was born in Quebec the first year of the Cholera scourge. She lived in Cheboygan two years before she was married, having come over from Mackinac Island. Mr. Paquin says he will never forget the great time there was at the wedding. Their first baby was born February 8, 1855, and named Adolphus. Of the eight children born to the Paquins, six are now alive.

Mr. Paquin remembers vividly many of the incidents and happenings of the old times. It is interesting to hear him recall the names of the old pioneers and what they did to build up Cheboygan. He thinks Cheeseman[17] was the name of the millwright who framed the first water mill. Peter Label was the village blacksmith and was located at the water mill. Frank Sawyer and Joseph Agan came from Chicago and they built the Duncan Mill in 1852, which commenced to run in 1853. Tenice (Stanislaus) LeGault kept the first store in Cheboygan and sold everything. The second mill in the place was built in 1850 where McArthur's dock is now, by Mr. Sammons, who was a very tall man, big and strong, and proud of his strength.

McLeod and Duncan did not get along very well together and Mr. Duncan tried to shake McLeod. They began a law suit which lasted 10 years. The death of both men occurred before the suit was decided. John Duncan, a brother of Richard, took all the property and sold to Mears & Baker of Chicago. Mr. Baker was Harry Baker's father. Another part

he sold to Mr. McArthur and the Duncan property was sold to Thompson Smith.

The first flour mill was run by water power. The miller named Myers was a good miller and made excellent flour which made much better bread than can be made now, said Mr. Paquin. The miller was an odd man and if asked how much toll he wanted would reply, "I'll take enough to pay my time."

Jacob Sammons lived across the river where the bridge is now, and John Vincent lived in a log shanty where P.X. Moloney's bottling works stands. [NW corner of Main and Nelson]

When McLeod and Duncan failed, sometime in 1857, Mr. Paquin ran the mill successfully for 5 years. While running this mill in 1859 he bought a farm of Cyril LeGault, consisting of 120 acres and afterwards bought another 120 acres. He has the farm now and lives on the 240 acres, having a nice comfortable house of ten rooms, with a pantry, buttery and cellar, and all the farm buildings are in good condition. The farm, like all the French farms, faces the river, as the wise old pioneers wanted to be neighborly, and also wanted a convenient way of getting their goods to and from market, all the hauling being done on the river as they had no wagons or roads.

When asked if he ever had any trouble with the Indians Mr. Paquin said they never locked their doors, and one morning, when he arose, he found half a dozen Indians in his kitchen. It startled him, but fortunately for him that was

---

17 This was Alonzo Cheeseman, who was a Morman from Beaver Island. He later moved to St. Ignace where descendants still remain today

all the harm done, except perhaps to the food. The writer was a little disappointed at this as he would like to have slated an exciting experience with the red men.

Mr. Paquin did, however, have an exciting time at the breaking out of the Civil War. He was drafted in 1864. Up to this time he would purchase release from service by providing a subscription but a bill was then passed to prevent this. As it did not have immediate effect, Mr. Paquin was just in time to escape.

Peter McDonald built on his own land, the first church, a little less than a mile above the dam. Father Murray, an Irish priest from Mackinac Island, officiated. There were 30 Catholic families at that time. The first protestant church built was the Methodist Church.

Mr. and Mrs. Paquin both speak in rather regretful tones of the pleasant times they enjoyed in the long ago. Then there was Democracy and the rich and poor were equal. No one, because they happened to have, or had made more money than his neighbor, placed himself and family on a pedestal of superiority and said by his manner, "Touch me not.

I'm not common clay." Everyone was ready to enjoy what they had and the company of his neighbors. All were happy and enjoyed suppers, dances, picnics and fun to their heart's content.

Prices of furniture in those days were about three times as high as the present

Palace Grocery Store was a typical neighborhood grocery store—523 Mackinac Avenue— owned by Hugh Church in 1914 --They advertised Staple and Fancy Groceries, Meats, Provisions, Flour, Feed, Grain, Etc., Confectionery and Cigars.
Collection of the Historical Society of Cheboygan County, Inc.

prices. This would include carpet and kitchen utensils. Clothing was higher in proportion. A common suit of clothes would cost, during and after the war, $40, a flannel shirt $4, whole suit of underwear $8, cotton stockings .50 pair, black calico 60¢, stocking yarn $1.50 per pound. Mr. Paquin had two pairs of ladies shoes sent from Chicago, which cost $10, and this was cheap compared with Cheboygan prices. A common hat cost $10. Woolen dress goods cost $1 per yard and it took 12 yards to make a dress.

McArthur lumber Mill, with a steamboat coming through the lock. The bridge over the lock was used to haul sawdust over to the east side, where the big sawdust pile was formed. Note the men on the right side of the photo. They are piling cut lumber, getting it ready to transport to the river mouth for shipping out. Collection of the Historical Society of Cheboygan County, Inc.

There were no electric lights in those days, not even gas or kerosene lamps. Candles furnished the illumination for the most festive occasion and they cost from 25¢ per pound upward. Tea cost $2.50 per pound, coffee 40¢ to 75¢, starch 25¢, butter 30¢, sugar 18¢. Maple sugar was used, the Indians bringing the sugar to Mackinac Island in enormous quantities, and this sold from 8¢ to 12¢ per pound. Maple syrup was 75¢ to $1 per gallon. Little or no fruit was on the market. Pork was $40 per barrel. Rutabagas were so large that six would make a bushel which sold one year for 75¢ per bushel. Cabbage was scarce at $10 per 100 head. A plow cost $18 to $20.

These prices seem high but they were offset by wages and prices on farm produce. Men's wages were $2 and $2.50, cradlers [hay harvesters] got $3 per day. Mr. Paquin, during harvest time, paid workers for one day's work as much as $100. He tells of coming to town one day and meeting a man who owed him some money. "Come in," said the man, "and I'll give you a little bit of money on that account. Mr. Paquin went in and was paid $1,100. Imagine if you can anyone doing that nowadays. We cannot with the wildest stretch of imagination conceive of such a thing in our times. About twenty years ago and for five years before he sold hay at $40 per ton and on one occasion sold a ton for $35 and was paid $15 extra to deliver it at Black River.

The lock was built 20 years ago. Mr. Hyde with his tug was the first to be locked through and great was the excitement in town, everybody being there.

Mr. Paquin said he worked in 1847 four months for $10 per month, that being the smallest amount he ever worked for. When asked if he had experienced any hard times in the past he replied, "No." During the early eighteen seventies money was rather scarce, but he had money ahead and did not suffer.

Peter McDonald[18]

This story of Peter McDonald comes from his obituary.

The remains of the late Peter McDonald, who died at the home of his son, Patrick H. McDonald, at Louisville, Kentucky, last week Tuesday, at the age of 83, were brought to this city Friday night and on Saturday morning were buried from St. Mary's Church, the church he loved so much, in Calvary Cemetery, adjoining his old farm where he settled in 1849, and where he lived almost ever since until a few years ago. On the old homestead was a Catholic church, where Father Zorn used to hold occasional services, and where the people went from this side of the river in canoes to services.

Peter McDonald was born in Ireland, about 83 years ago, where he spent his young manhood, and was married to Miss Hughes, coming direct to Cheboygan in 1847. His location here, however, was an accident, he being on his way to Chicago,

in the fall, but his young bride was ill, and they got off at Duncan, and in the spring they decided to remain here, and it is well for Cheboygan that they did so for all the intervening years have been filled with pioneer services, and a life under the Golden Rule.

Everyone who knew him, remembers him with pleasure and all will hear of his demise with regret. Mrs. McDonald survives her husband and at the age of 80, and is in much better health than when she left here. The old pioneers of Cheboygan are rapidly passing away. The oldest, Philip O'Brien, is now nearly 90, but does not look over 70. Adolph Paquin comes next, nearly as old, and then Charles Bellant, over 80, but still able to drive a trotter and loan or borrow money anywhere.

Peter and Mary had seven children: Patrick, Mary, James, Francis, Alice, Catherine and Johanna. In her "History of the Catholic Church St. Mary's, Cheboygan, Michigan", Carol Stempky tells more about the McDonalds.

The first attempt at building a house of worship resulted in the erection of a frame which, after a struggle with the elements, was finally blown down; it was removed across the river to a lot on Peter McDonald's farm, where the effort to provide a house of worship was successful. Mr. McDonald gave 2 acres of land to Bishop Baraga for the purpose of building the chapel and the Catholic Cemetery. This deed is dated September 12, 1859. Peter McDonald's farm was on the east side of Cheboygan River—perhaps opposite the old tannery chimney, probably near present day Snow Apple court. In 1859 St Mary's became a mission, numbering about 35 families. Father Murry was frequently conveyed

---

18 *Cheboygan Democrat*, Dec 23, 1904

here from Mackinaw Island by Medard Metivier.[19]

MR. AND MRS. JOSEPH ALLAIRE[20]

This description from the Allaire family gave us the title for this book. They came when Main Street was a path among the stumps!

Mr. and Mrs. Allaire were married in Cheboygan and went to housekeeping with Mr. Allaires's parents in the Allaire home on a place near where is now located the Gas Office. Main Street then was just a path of trodden road around and through the stumps extending from the water mill, a saw mill located on the river bank at the present dam site, to another saw mill on the riverbank north of the present gas plant on the river bank. This latter mill was owned and operated by Mr. Sammons who had a residence on a plot of dry ground where is now located the gas plant.

There were only a few houses in the village then and they were all on the river bank as the river and lakes were the only highways at that time. There was no road in and out of Cheboygan as there was no place to go. When one wished to cross the river to a neighbors as there were a few living over on that side of the river, and a few more at Duncan, it was necessary to take a canoe, and the canoe was also the means of travel up and down the river to the scattered settlers that had early cut themselves a home out of the wilderness that reared its huge pine trees everywhere about what is now our fair city.

The little home of the Allaires' at that time was the principal stopping place for travelers to and through the village and the family supported itself largely upon what was received in that way. At that time during the winter months after navigation was closed the mail was carried from Marquette to Detroit by dog team.

Joseph Allaire, Senior, had been an agent for the Astor Fur Company on Mackinac Island. He was also a butcher on Mackinac Island during the summers. Joseph Sr. came to Cheboygan and opened a livery stable. His son, Joseph Jr. later took over the livery which was on Main Street, where Linde Furniture is now located. Eventually Joseph Jr. sold the livery and purchased a farm, which he ran for 35 years. He sold the farm in 1918 and it was then developed into the Cheboygan Golf and Country Club. Joseph Sr. also had a daughter, Cornelia, who married Archibald P. Newton. More will be told about them in the commercial fishing chapter.

SANFORD BAKER[21]

This story of Sanford Baker, by his son Harry Baker, tells us about the man who had been a partner with Thompson Smith at Duncan and who later was responsible for much development in the village of Cheboygan.

My friends have asked me to tell the life of my father, Sanford Baker, as it pertained to Cheboygan. His father came from England and settled on a homestead at Sackets Harbor, Oneida County, New York State. My father was born in 1811. He had two brothers and one sister. One brother became a banker and the other a merchant.

---

19 "*The History of the Catholic Church, St. Mary's*" Cheboygan, Michigan, Carol Stempky, 1998, p. 11.
20 *Cheboygan Democrat* June 17, 1926
21 Story told by Harry Baker, son of Sanford Baker, *Cheboygan Daily Tribune*, Golden Jubilee Edition, 1939

Downtown Cheboygan 1876.   Photo by Johnson's Studio

After completing school, my father taught school. He then took contracts to build railroads and to furnish meat for the Army, arranging for purchase of livestock and herding it in to the army locations to be slaughtered. He became a great friend to General Grant and had a personal request from General Grant to meet him at Philadelphia.

After the Civil War, he built part of the Grand Trunk Railroad in Ontario and became a great friend of Sir John A. MacDonald. He engaged in lumbering on the Trent River in Ontario. He sold his interests and came to Michigan in 1867.

He came by way of Saginaw and Bay City to Alger, the end of the Saginaw-Lansing railroad. From Alger he took the Alger Smith logging road to Alpena then followed the Lake Huron shore to McLeod's Bay [Duncan City] where he had bought large holdings.

When he arrived there was nothing at Duncan but an old idle mill that had fallen into disrepair. My father developed a splendid town there. He built two sawmills and docks, besides camps, and a boarding house. A company store was established. Mill workers built homes and the government opened a post office. Miss Sarah Elliott was post mistress during part of the time.

My father sold out a half interest to Thompson Smith and Robert Patterson. In 1877, Thompson Smith and Sons, Robert Patterson and Sanford Baker divided their interests and dissolved partnership. Mr. Baker and Patterson took lands in what is now the First, Second and Third Wards in exchange for their interests in the Duncan Mills and my father moved his family to Cheboygan.

Thompson Smith continued development of Duncan. One of the mills

22 This photo is sometimes identified as 1872 but Ellis Olson, local historian, dates it to 1876 or 1877 by the presence of the *Northern Tribune*, which was in business those years.

MOUTH OF THE CHEBOYGAN

The Baker & Son Dock was on the west side of the river, near the mouth. 1884 Lithograph of the mouth of the Cheboygan River.
Collection of the Historical Society of Cheboygan County, Inc.

1884 Lithograph—St. Mary's Church

Collection of the Historical Society of
Cheboygan County, Inc.

burned and he replaced it with a larger one. I imagine the town of Duncan grew to have a population of 1,000. [*Ed. Note: Actual population was about 60 families, with 300-400 workers at the mill*]

A stage made regular trips between Duncan and Cheboygan, much as a busline might do, and rails were laid on which a horse car brought the mail from Cheboygan to Duncan, which was the official post office for Cheboygan. I remember one time a baby was born in the street car although the driver was making a desperate effort to get back to Cheboygan in time with the mother.

After leaving Duncan, my father and I started development of Cheboygan. We cleared and fenced, and put in 40 acres of fall wheat and 20 acres of oats on the east side of the river. The piece was bounded by State Street, F Street, Seventh Street, and the river. It was a rough slashing of cutover land.

The next winter they lumbered and got out 20,000 ties and square timbers and logs. The square timber was taken to Quebec by barge and then shipped to England. The ties were shipped to Chicago.

In the following winter they got out timber, spiles and lumber for the Baker and Son Dock and coal sheds. With hard work and expense we arranged with S. B. Grummond of Detroit for his passenger and freight line to stop at the Baker dock. The steamers *Flora*, *Atlantic* and *State of Michigan*, made stops at our dock.

The Grummond wrecking tugs, *Leviathan*, *Winslow* and *Manistique* also made Cheboygan their headquarters, besides the S. Grummond tugs which were engaged in towing logs and other work. They stopped at the Baker dock for their orders. I had charge of the dock and the responsibility of handling orders for the boats.

The wrecking tugs had wrecks to handle from time to time. The largest wreck of my experience was when the *Albany* ran ashore. When wrecks occurred, tugs towed them into Cheboygan for the ship carpenters and divers to put them in condition. Sometimes they had to be taken elsewhere for more thorough repairs after first being prepared here for the trip, because Cheboygan had no dry dock. I tried with help of S. B. Grummond and Captain Swan to get a branch of the Manitowoc Dry Dock Company located here.

My father gave the property where St. Mary's church is situated to Father DeCueninck. He gave three blocks to the parish.[23]

The firm of Sanford D. Baker & Son built a planning mill and dry kilns and shipped the material to Mackinac Island to build some of the first cottages on the island. The planning mill is now the Novelty Works. Our planning mill was torn down and transported to South Main street location and rebuilt into the turning factory.

We tried to get a pottery here. We sent barrels of clay to a pottery and received a report that out of 500 clays that were tested, Cheboygan's was one of the best. However, transportation costs prevented the plan from materializing. Some of the samples were placed in the Griswold Hotel and St. Paul's Cathedral in Detroit.

When the Jackson, Lansing & Saginaw railroad was built to Cheboygan and Mackinaw City we helped in it because we hired our teams to the railroad. We also assisted for the D & M.

The Baker dock business suffered from competition of the D & C (Detroit & Cleveland) line which gave more frequent service than the Grummond line. The Grummond boats stopped at all the small ports and delivered freight. The dock finally had to be discontinued.

My father died in 1890. From the time I got out of college in Ontario, I was in charge. The house in which I reside was the Baker home at Duncan. I moved it to the present site. [NW Corner of Duncan and McArthur Street].

JOHN LEREAUX[24]

A story about John Lereaux, based on memories of an unknown author, appeared in the *Cheboygan Observer* on August 6, 1931, taken from a 1897 *Cheboygan Democrat*. The parts of the article that pertain to Cheboygan are copied below.

Among the names of the first subscribers to the *Democrat* is the name of John Lereaux, and he was also one of the

23 Ware, p. 32. Rev. Chas. L. DeCueninck's residence, on Third Street, east side of the river, was built in 1872. It is a two story, frame structure, 40 x 40, back building 20 x 30, one story. It has a very tasty appearance, being built with verandas on the south, east and west sides to both the first and second stories. It cost $8,000. Grounds adjoining are neatly laid out, occupying one block, and adorned with a great variety of fruit trees, some five hundred in number; also hundreds of evergreen trees and beautiful flowers.
24 *Cheboygan Observer*, August 6, 1931.

pioneers of Cheboygan and first to sign a petition for incorporating the township of Inverness. Mr. Lereaux was born in Lower Canada, 35 miles east of Montreal, in the year 1823, and came from Mackinac Island to Mullet Lake in 1847. In 1847 while on Mackinaw Island he met Sandy McLeod who hired him to work in a camp. Sandy was the business man of the firm, Ronald McLeod being a great worker around the mills. Mr. Lereaux was in camp only one night when Sandy McLeod, who had the contract to build the Waugoshance lighthouse, sent for Lereaux to work on a scow. John Vincent was drafting the scow for use in building the lighthouse. Mr. Vincent's reputation as a ship builder was excellent.

Mr. Flynn came here to work on the lighthouse. He was a hewer (cut down trees with an ax). He had been a soldier and was a good fellow. He lived in a wigwam and to show their good feelings of his fellows toward him, the boys went out to Watsons and cut logs for a shanty, then put it up for him.

Although a long time past to the pioneer it seems but short time when all this happened. He remembers one day that a companion and himself were walking on the ice, when his companion broke through and got very wet. They were near where the coal dock is now. Jake Sammons and a man named McKinley were building a steam mill there. Jake had some whiskey—the wet man took a drink. The whiskey must have been good, for the man, when he went to bed, was expected to die. Instead of doing this, he was all right in the morning.

At this time there were no teams and no roads. Four or five of the men clubbed together and purchased a yoke of oxen from the company, and then worked for each other for a few days and then went

logging. Arthur Watson was the first man to own a horse aside from the company. There were no stores here when they came. The company had a van from which the supplies were given out.

All the shopping had to be done at Mackinac Island and no boats made regular calls. Goods were brought in small boats to the east side of the river and drawn in jumpers [small barge type boats] with oxen and those who lived on this side of the river had to go for it.

Mr. Lereaux worked for John Vincent at ship building for three years. Vincent had a log shanty where Moloney's Bottling Works are now [Main & Nelson Street], and it was the place where the people met, and where all the dances were held. Vincent furnished the room, Sammons the whiskey and Fiddler Lemmerond supplied the music. Lemmerond was a widower and an old soldier, very smart, a good fiddler and lots of fun. Old Jake Sammons was a jolly fellow at any time, but when he had taken a little whiskey he was a whole crowd; he was a great man at fishing, shooting and dancing, and the first to begin and the last to finish. He was a good democrat, and was instrumental in making John Lereaux a citizen and a democrat, for which he is grateful.

Those who signed the petition for incorporating Inverness were as follows; the names were given as they occurred to the narrator. Jake Sammons, (affectionately called Uncle Jake) Sandy McLeod, Ronald McLeod, Mr. Pease, clerk for the McLeods, John Vincent, Wm. Flynn, John Lereaux and Jeriquette, who cut and shipped poles to Chicago, are all the names that occurred to him. This was done about 1850 to the best of the pioneer's recollection; he fixes the date by having to attend as a witness at the trial of a case, in which John Vincent and George Stevenson were the principals and as there were no court here, they had to go to Mackinac Island.

In 1851 John married Caroline Abbot, whose father was in the American Fur Company of Detroit. The marriage was celebrated at Mackinac Island. Mr. Lereaux at this time could speak the Creek and Chippewa languages. He went to farming in 1852, clearing up 80 acres; about this time a baby girl came to cheer the young couple and all went well until 1860 when his wife died. In 1861 he again entered the married state, wedding a Miss Carter, whose given name is that familiar Puritan name Priscilla. Two girls and two boys were added to the family; in 1884 he sold his farm to Olin Vorce and moved to St. Ignace where he went into the dairy business. After a 10 years stay in St. Ignace he returned to Mullet Lake and bought the farm he now has, and the sales store which he keeps being also the postmaster. While in St. Ignace Mr. Cheeseman, who built the first water mill here, died, this happened five years ago. In 1895 a daughter died and his family is otherwise divided, one boy being in St. Ignace and one daughter is married.

Mr. Lereaux is exceeding pleased at the improvements made around the Mullett Lake Station. He advocated changes for some time but everyone was not of the same opinion, for one man said "What do I want with a road? I have a boat."

Andrew Jodwin[25]

Andrew Jodwin died at age 100 and is buried in Calvary Cemetery. He was married to Salome Beaugrand. This story was written about him and published in the *Cheboygan Democrat*.

Mr. Jodwin's reminiscences of his life would have been interesting reading if they could have been had, for he came to Cheboygan a good many years ago and roughed it with the other few pioneers who were here at that time and thus he was one of the spokes in the wheel which has turned on and on to carve out the beautiful place now from the primeval forest it was when he landed here.

He first saw the light of day in Lower Canada, near St. Paul, on April 23, 1824. His father was of French decent and was born near Montreal. Forty four years ago he made up his mind to strike out in the world for himself and consequently took passage down the river through the lakes for no place in particular but like others of that time pressed his face to the west, where they believed great riches awaited them. He first landed at Port Huron, where he did not remain long when the journey was taken up again and the boat he was on turned into Duncan Bay. This place looked good to him and he decided to remain here. At that time there was no Cheboygan. There was a mill at Duncan. Frank Simon had a store near where the old brewery property now stands and Stanislaw LeGault lived near where the Charles Hotel [NW corner of State & Water Street] is now located. A road ran from Duncan to near the paper mill, following the east side of the river all the way. There were some lumber operations started here at that time and Mr. Jodwin hired out to a man who was operating along the Maple River, where he remained for seven years. His employer's name was Tom Cromley, who many of the old timers will no doubt remember.

After quitting the lumber camps on the Maple he came to near Cheboygan, which had then begun to grow, and worked in the woods around here and

---

25 *Cheboygan Democrat*, May 1, 1914.

also purchased a team and did teaming up to not so many years ago. Mr. Jodwin was twice married, his first wife having died some years ago. He next married Salomi Beaugrand, daughter of Oliver Beaugrand. He was the father of thirteen children.

MEDARD METIVIER[26]

Medard Metivier

This story about Medard Metivier appeared in *"The Traverse Region"* which was a Who's Who type of book about prominent businessmen from northern Michigan.

Medard Metivier was born at Labadie, Canada, September 25, 1815, of French parentage. His father was an architect and builder, and Medard's early years were spent assisting his father and in attending school. In May, 1836, at twenty-one

years of age, he left home and came to the United States, locating at Rochester, New York. There he was employed in a soap and candle factory, and afterward in a fruit garden. He remained at Rochester until November, 1837, when he moved to Grand Rapids, Michigan, and remained until August, 1839. He then went to Mackinac Island, where he remained twelve years and carried on a cooper shop, and a portion of the time kept a hotel. During his residence there he held the offices of sheriff and coroner, each for two terms.

January 2, 1842, Medard married Rosalie Hamel, at Mackinac Island. They had eleven children, eight of whom, four sons and four daughters, live in Cheboygan. In the spring of 1851 they moved to Cheboygan County and settled upon land bordering on Mullett Lake where they remained about two years. In 1854 Mr. Metivier built a hotel, called the Cheboygan House, and kept it two years. This was the first hotel built in the village and is now a part of the Spencer House. At the first county election in 1855, he was elected sheriff and the following year register of deeds. In 1855 he succeeded Bela Chapman as postmaster and retained the office until 1861. In 1872 he was elected clerk and register of deeds of the county, and has held those offices continuously to the present time. As a public officer he is exceedingly popular. Mr. Metivier is a veritable pioneer of northern Michigan, having been a resident of this part of the state well toward half a century. He has had to do with all the onward movements of Cheboygan. He is a prominent member of the Catholic Church and has been during the history of St. Mary's Church at Cheboygan.

---

26 *"The Traverse Region"*, H. R. Page & Co., 1884, p. 96.

The Spencer House was located on the West Side of Main Street near Mackinac Avenue. Medard Metivier built the "Cheboygan House" which became part of this later hotel.   Collection of the Historical Society of Cheboygan County, Inc.

SEWELL FORD[27]

Sewell Ford was born in 1868 in South Levant, Maine and spent much of his youth in Cheboygan where his father was the local postmaster. The family later moved to Haverhill, Massachusetts. Sewell became a well- known author and was asked to contribute his memories of growing up in Cheboygan to the 1939 Tribune Golden Jubilee edition. This is what it was like to be a kid in the 1870's and 1880's in Cheboygan.

I got there in the summer of 1876, which was so doggoned long ago that I doubt if anyone in Cheboygan remembers me or would be much interested in what I did there between the ages of 8 and 14.

My folks moved out from Maine because they had friends and relatives who had gone on before them, and because lumbering was one of the things my Dad knew how to do. They were cutting off the big timber then and Cheboygan was definitely a lumber town, with the river running full of logs and the sawmills running night shifts. The Great Sawdust Pile across the river was being heaped up.

Why my Dad wanted to be Postmaster I don't know. Perhaps he thought the Government ought to hand out a soft job to him for his five years' service in the army and navy during the Civil War. Anyway, he was appointed and we went to live over the Post Office. I liked it. Once a day the mail came in by stage from Petoskey, and twice a week Indian Joe

Aerial photo of the great sawdust pile which was located on the west side of the Cheboygan River, across from the McArthur Mill (present day Great Lakes Tissue). It reached from the parking lot of today's hockey rink to the softball field.

Collection of the Historical Society of Cheboygan County, Inc.

brought it over from Mackinac Island in a sail boat. In winter Joe used a dog sled across the frozen Straits and drove his four dog team right into the front office. What a lovely cusser he was. Only the Second Mate of the side-wheeler *Marine City* could beat him. At least, this was the verdict of the town boys who hung around the Post Office every mail time and gathered on the dock to watch every steamer land.

In 1876 Cheboygan straggled from the lumber docks on the north, back towards MacArthur's mills, along an unpaved street garnished here and there with board sidewalks. All the stores had imposing false fronts, such as you see in Western movie scenes. There were no street lights. But we had a Town Hall, two churches, a weekly newspaper, and a yellow brick school house.

That September I was sent to school and learned that the principal's name was O. B. Weed—otherwise called Onions, Beets and Weeds. Not to his face. He was too handy with his fists. Perry MacKay sassed him once and found out. A big boy, Perry, and a fighter. But O.B. floored him in the front hall with a stiff right to the jaw.

I am afraid I cannot claim to have been a brilliant scholar, although it would sound well, wouldn't it? But my sketchy knowledge of early American history, for instance, I lay to the fact that there were not enough history books to go around and we had to copy the day's lesson as they were read by the teacher. Hence my scraggly penmanship. Then one page of my arithmetic book was missing—the one that had liquid measure on it. And to this day I am not sure how many quarts there are in a gallon.

This is the east side of Main Street, the block between Division and Elm Street, north of the present day post office.

Collection of the Historical Society of Cheboygan County, Inc.

At spelling, though, I was good, chiefly on account of Rosie Lyon. And here romance slips in. For John Van Arsdale and I were sweet on Rosie, in a mutual, cooperative way. John and I were chums, and when we lined up in spelling class our plan was always to have Rosie stand between us. Perhaps you know the old system. If you missed a word you went down one, towards the foot. And while Rosie had snappy black eyes and a sweet shy smile, she was a rotten speller. So, to keep her between us we had to know the spelling lessons so well that we could not only spell a word right, but spell it wrong at least two different ways. Nothing much ever came of that romance, however. When we grew up and moved away each

of us married a red headed girl.

Nearly all my memories of life in Cheboygan seem more or less tied up with John Van Arsdale. He was perhaps a few months older, taller and much better looking. He was my model, almost my hero. His father owned the hardware store and was a Deacon of the Congregational Church. John and I shared a seat together in school, spent most of the long vacations together. We organized the Young American Ramblers, a secret company of choice of the Congregational Church. We had a log hut hidden in the big woods south of town, a cave rendezvous in the Great Sawdust Pile, and we owned the only two sailboats on the river. We planned to take the pick of our crew and run away to become smugglers, perhaps pirates—the Scourge of the Lakes. It never came off. John almost achieved his ambition. He got to be one of the leading lawyers of Buffalo.

Probably I might have had a more eventful career if I hadn't started so early to hang around printing shops. There was one weekly paper when I came to Cheboygan and I must have been underfoot most of the time. To get rid of me they sent me out passing handbills, and the first thing I knew I was the official distributer of dodgers. Also, the town's first bill poster. I handled all the paper for the Wilder Dramatic Company, which played for a whole week in the town hall. And between the acts of every performance I peddled lemonade and peanuts under personal direction of the glamorous Rose Wilder herself. I may have looked honest, but Rose kept my cap every night until I had made full accounting.

At the ripe age of eleven I became the local news agent, delivering the Detroit and Chicago newspapers to daily subscribers along Main Street. I collected metal junk and sold it at the foundry. I scoured back yards for empty medicine bottles which the druggist would buy. My savings box in the Post Office safe grew heavy. A common saying among the Main street merchants was "Watch that Ford boy. Gonna be a rich man someday." Sorry. It just didn't turn out that way.

1884 Lithograph of the Cheboygan County Jail.

Collection of the Historical Society of Cheboygan County, Inc.

When ice floes jammed the Straits and steamers stopped running, Cheboygan dug in for the long winter. "To get outside" as we called it, one had to take a 20 mile stage ride to Petoskey. Nothing much happened for months, except one heavy snowfall after another. Sidewalks were mere tunnels through the drifts. Things began stirring when the first lumber crews came out of the woods along in April. Bar room fights, when husky lumberjacks got full of cheap whiskey and mauled each other on the sawdust floor. Once I slipped into the Burns hotel bar and watched until I was actively ill from the sight of blood and so scared I could hardly walk. But later when the river drivers came down, there were even wilder scenes. We missed few of them; bloody fights, big poker games in the saloons, the arrival of the Painted Women from Detroit.

Early photo of sailboat on Cheboygan River, circa 1880
Collection of the Historical Society of Cheboygan, Inc.

At last the ice went out, the *Marine City* docked with the first freight, lumber schooners nosed in and began loading. As many as 20 schooners would be tied up at the mile long docks. Their rigging became our playground. True, we were chased off by profane second mates with belaying pins, but what fresh water sailor could catch a boy who would grab a fore-stay and slide from crosstree to bowsprit end monkey fashion? Why none of us ever broke our necks or got drowned I don't know.

A few stirring events stick in my mind.

The night the broom handle mill burned and I helped pass pails of water up to my Dad who kept the Post Office roof from catching

Cheboygan Circa 1880—Near Division Street, looking north on Main.
Collection of the Historical Society of Cheboygan County, Inc.

fire.

The coming of the first circus when I worked all the forenoon carrying blue seat boards, and came home with a pass number chalked on my back, only to find that Dad, as owner of the circus lot, had been given more free tickets than he knew what to do with.

The time a man exhibited in Town Hall a machine which could talk back at you invented by a fellow named Edison. Admission 25 cents. And hanged if it wasn't so. He got someone to sing into a horn while he turned a cylinder covered with tin foil. Then he put the cylinder into the machine, turned a crank, and out came a lot of squeaks and some of the song. Kind of interesting, but nobody thought it would ever amount to much.

Another new fad that spring in Cheboygan was roller skating. For a week the town went crazy over it. Then the man who rented out the skates moved on and prominent citizens rubbed sore spots and barked shins.

One night I was roused by hurried footsteps and hoarse shouts. Slipping out the back way I found a crowd gathered in front of Sheriff Paquett's house, across the street. They wanted the keys to the jail, and got them. I was on the fringe of the crowd when they took a man from the jail and strung him up. For the rest of the night I slept poorly.[28]

Then there was the time when my Dad took his rifle and joined a posse

Circus Parade, Main Street, Cheboygan. Three Story Building on left is the Frost-Kessler Building, corner of Division and Main Street. Building on right is the J.J. Post Hardware Building.
Collection of Historical Society of Cheboygan County, Inc.

called to quell a riot at a grading camp several miles out of town. The railroad was being built through and trouble had broken out. A foreman's head had been split with a shovel. Some of the men had guns. But the rioters gave up when they saw those sturdy citizens with rifles.

A few months later the rails were laid clear into Cheboygan and one night the Iron Gang came into town, broke into saloons, smashed store windows, terrorized women, and were finally shooed away without bloodshed. There must have been some sort of celebration when the first train came in but I don't seem to remember it.

Nor do I vouch for the accuracy of all these memories. Looking back through more than fifty years makes quite a vista of time. But a boy's impressions are apt to be clear and many of those scenes were vivid. For in those days Cheboygan was a frontier town where life was rough and strenuous. You can guess that there were no sissies in that crowd of youngsters. Imitating our elders we cursed roundly

---

28 For a complete story regarding this lynching of Tillie Comstock Warner, accused of raping a 7-year old girl, see Matthew Friday's, *Among the Sturdy Pioneers*, 2006, pp. 47-50.

1884 Lithograph—Yellow brick school house, located near Nelson and Main Street, where the Straits Area Federal Credit Union is located today.
Collection of the Historical Society of Cheboygan County, Inc.

Railroad fracas when the D & M came to Cheboygan and the already established Michigan Central objected.
Photo by Johnson's Studio

Michigan Central Railroad office, Court Street.

Postcard courtesy Patricia Wight Geyer Collection

and picturesquely, fought valiantly and unskillfully, stole anything that was loose, boasted, lied fluently, and committed such mischief as we could think up. Yet a few of us grew up to be almost respectable. I doubt if we were as tough as we thought we were.

With the coming of the railroad Cheboygan enjoyed its first mild boom. My folks took advantage of it, sold out their holdings, loaded their belongings into a freight car, and started back east.

This collection of voices from the past tells us a little about the social life of early Cheboygan. It helps us understand what it was really like to live here. As you read the rest of this book you will find many more stories about the fishermen, lumbermen, Civil war soldiers, doctors, merchants and farmers who came to make Cheboygan their home. – Sally Humphery

Thawing snow formed this pool on Main St.
Collection of the Historical Society of Cheboygan County, Inc.

DUNCAN CITY
CHEBOYGAN'S GHOST TOWN

BY ELLIS N. OLSON

Birdeye view of Duncan City, 1880.

Collection of the Historical Society of Cheboygan County, Inc.

Two things in particular have spiked my interest in local history. The first was the opportunity to play among the ruins of Duncan City when I was 6 to 10 years old. The other was to listen to the interesting former residents who would often spend hours talking about what they remembered while living there. As a young man of 11 or 12 years old, I used to ride my bike from home to Duncan Bay, a distance of about one mile. I would frequently stop at Charlie Peterson's house, where there was a flowing well in the yard. Not only was the water refreshing on a hot summer day, but I

had an opportunity to listen to the interesting stories of Charlie's experiences in Duncan City and the lumbering days.

In 1967, I had the opportunity to audiotape several of these men. George Nimmo first came to Duncan City in 1886 on the side-wheeler "Flora" with his dad who had accepted a bookkeeper's job for the Thompson Smith Company. Joe Viau used to walk to Duncan every day to bring his dad lunch. The family lived on Abrahamson Road in "Swede Town." Sam Campbell was a sawyer for Thompson Smith and later for M. D. Olds. He was

---

1 Photo taken from the top of the Duncan City Foundry looking south down Genesee Avenue, the main street of Duncan City, 1880. The double two-story house on the left belonged to Ed and Tom James. The house in the middle belonged to Captain William Burnett, and the house on the right to Sanford Baker. Baker's house was later moved to the northwest corner of Duncan & McArthur Streets. Photo courtesy of Ellis Olson.

also known for being one of the best "saw bangers" in Michigan.[2] George Lindeman worked in the Duncan City Machine Shop and after the street railroad folded, he purchased their barn on the northeast corner of Main and Second Street for his own machine shop. Rose Landrie, Edmund Robichard, and Charlie Peterson toured Duncan City with me when I was about 10 years old. Each took great delight in reminiscing as we passed up and down the vacant streets, pointing out where different friends and families once lived. Frank Merritt's father was a coachman for Egbert Smith. His uncle was coachman for Ephraim Smith. Frank, as a child, used to carry his father's lunch to him each day, and then would enjoy playing around the horse barn and other buildings.

Our Duncan story begins with two brothers, Alexander and Ronald McLeod, who were born in Messina, New York. They were businessmen who had traveled to Mackinac Island looking for opportunity.

In the fall of 1844 Mr. Alexander McLeod, brother of R. McLeod Esq., now of the McLeod House, Mackinac, built the first shanty ever erected on the sacred soil of Cheboygan. This shanty was built of logs, roofed with bark, and stood just in front of where the old Glove House now stands. This shanty was occupied during the Winter of 1844-45 by Mr. McLeod , and others who were engaged in getting out cooper stuff to be manufactured in Mackinac.[3]

The McLeod brothers also built a boarding house, called the "Globe" for the men who came to work in the mill. The McLeod brothers formed a partnership including what became the Duncan Bay property and the Cheboygan Dam property. Alexander patented section 28 T. 38 N., R.1 W. (bay property) and

Ronald patented section 5, T. 37 N., R. 1 W. (dam and watermill property). The property known as Duncan Bay was then called McLeod's Bay.

"The first water-powered lumber mill in the county was built in the winter of 1845-6, by Alexander and Ronald McLeod, some ten rods above the present works of MacArthur, Smith & Co (where the dam is located). It had two old fashioned upright saws set in frames, and a lath mill attached to it. It cut, in its best days, from ten to fifteen thousand feet of lumber in twenty-four hours."[4] Another description of this mill was "A. & R. McLeod came from the State of New York, bringing with them a number of men, machinery, tools, & c., and commenced the erection of a water saw mill some forty rods above the works of MacArthur, Smith & Co, which they completed and ran that year. This party shipped the first lumber from the Cheboygan River in the fall of that year to parties in Chicago, consisting of 500,000 feet lumber."[5] After the lumber was cut it was loaded on scows and towed to the Straits where it was transferred to lumber hookers and taken to the Detroit and Chicago markets.

6

"Ronald McLeod, one of the original settlers of Cheboygan, arrived on the City of Alpena Saturday evening to visit his son, R. McLeod, Jr. Mr. McLeod first arrived in Cheboygan 40 years ago last May and he and party had to cut the under-

---

2 A saw banger shaped and cupped the large circular saws used in the big mills. This was a highly skilled job.

3 Manitawauba Chronicle, Vol. 1, No. 5.

4 Ware p. 17.

5 Geo. Robinson, History of Cheboygan and Mackinac Counties, Business and Manufacturing Statistics, Detroit, Union Job Printing Company, 1873, republished in Centennial History of Cheboygan County, 1996, p. 85-86.

6 This broken piece of an old saw blade, 12 inches wide, was found in the Cheboygan River, near the location of the first water mill, by Ellis Olson in 1970. It is the same type of blade as described. Olson speculates that perhaps some of the early sawmill equipment for the Cheboygan watermill came from the Michael Dousman Mill at Mill Creek which had closed six years before the Cheboygan Mill was built. Ronald McLeod later married Dousman's widow so they were known to each other.

brush along the river to reach the Rapids, where the dam now is. He built the old watermill that stood near the dam."[7]

In 1846 a post office was established with Ronald McLeod serving as the first postmaster. It was on the east bank of the Cheboygan River, near its entrance into Lake Huron and later known as the Duncan Post Office. It was on the Saginaw and Sault Ste. Marie mail route, route number 1722. The mail was carried by lake vessels in the summer and by dog sled in the winter, along the Lake Huron Shore Indian Trail.

In 1848 A. R. McLeod & Company contracted with John Vincent, another early Cheboygan resident, to build them a schooner scow, named the *D. R. Holt*. It had an eighty-four foot keel, twenty-two and one-half foot beam and six foot hold. Its first cargo was twenty-eight cords of stone from Les Cheneaux for Waugoshance lighthouse.[8] This scow was probably used to transfer the cut lumber to the mouth of the river where it could be loaded on lumber schooners.

In 1850 the McLeod brothers built the first docks at McLeod's Bay. Transporting sawn lumber from the water mill on the river to the river mouth for loading unto lumber schooners had proven difficult because of the sand bars that blocked the river entrance. Transporting by road to the bay, with a deeper harbor, proved to be better.

One year later, in 1851, Ronald McLeod sold his interest in the Watermill property to J. W. Duncan and Company. This company was a partnership of Jeremiah W. Duncan, Jeremiah Woolston and Alfred D. Woolston, all of Chicago. On March 20, 1852, J. W. Duncan & Company purchased the interest of Alexander McLeod, thus becoming the sole owners of the "watermill" and

The Robert Stuart residence was converted to the "McLeod House" run by Ronald McLeod, until he sold it to James Cable in 1870.
Mackinaw State Historic Parks Collections

"bay" properties. That summer Duncan began the construction of a large mill at the bay and converted the upright saws of the watermill to muley saws. They made improvements in both places, which included a second mill at the bay. This concluded their building program.

The McLeods went back to Mackinac Island where Ronald had bought the Stuart House (former American Fur Company warehouse and clerk's quarters) and opened a hotel there called the "McLeod House." Alexander died there October 30, 1852, and was buried on the Island. Ronald's wife, Emaline Gates, died in 1854 and Ronald remarried Elizabeth Grove in 1856. Elizabeth[9] had been married to Michael Dousman until he died. Dousman was the former owner and operator of the Mill Creek sawmill, located between Mackinaw City and Cheboygan. Ronald sold the McLeod

---

7 Cheboygan Daily Tribune, July 1886
8 Ware p. 16
9 Elizabeth had three spouses. She had a daughter, Laura Messenger, by her first husband, who married a younger McLeod brother, John Raymond McLeod, who lived in Epoufette, Michigan.

1884 Lithograph drawing showing the first bridge across the Cheboygan River, built in 1850. The first electric plant is the building with four windows on the upper floor. A boat is coming through the locks which were built in 1868. A lighter (barge) is being loaded with sawn logs to be taken down the river. The first Lincoln Avenue Bridge is in the far background.

Lithograph from Historical Society of Cheboygan County, Inc.

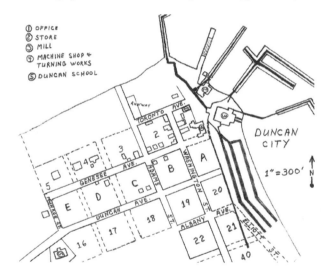

house about 1870 to James Cable from Beaver Island and moved to Attica, New York, with his family, where he spent the rest of his life.

A tramway was constructed in 1852 from the docks at Duncan to the watermill on the Cheboygan River. It was built by Swedish immigrants that J. W. Duncan brought in from Chicago. A bridge had been built, in 1850, across the river at the watermill, in anticipation of the tramway. This tramway followed the present Duncan Avenue, running in a straight line from the present Cheboygan River locks to Duncan. In 1858, this road was improved and renamed the "Bay Road." When the Duncan and Watermill areas prospered, a considerable number of homes were built along this road to accommodate the workers of J. W. Duncan & Company.

Town history recounts an amusing incident from those early days, crediting a steamboat named the *General Scott* for getting docks installed at the end of the town in 1850. It seems the *General Scott*

arrived at Duncan in 1847, intending to deliver a yoke of oxen. Finding no place to dock the boat, the crew threw the oxen overboard and they swam ashore. Docks were soon built and proved to be of major importance to the commerce of the town. The map shows the docks that were eventually built by the various owners of the mill.

Many lumber ships and schooners were required to move the sawn lumber to the city markets. In 1874 the lumber schooner *Duncan City* was owned by the Smiths and was used to deliver finished lumber. Their tug, *Crusader*, of 65 tons was burned in 1878. The schooner *Duncan City* was sold to Chicago parties in 1880, and in 1881 the bark *Parnana* was purchased for $13,000 from J. M. Long of Chicago. A new tug, called the *Duncan City*, was built for them in Manitowoc, Wisconsin, in 1883, and their old tug, *Decunick*, was discarded. The tug *Major Dana* was purchased in 1884 and both were operating in 1890. The Smith tugs, *Duncan City* and *Major Dana*, rafted booms of from 3 to 4 million feet of logs at a time to Smith's mills from their pineries in Canada. Each tug could make a round trip every 15 days by pulling the booms about one mile each hour. The Cheboygan Log Towing Association was formed in 1897, by the consolidation of the tugs and towing interests of John and Thomas Charleston of North Tonawanda, New York, and Thompson Smith's sons. The fleet consisted of the tugs of *Balize* and *Onapin* owned by the Charleston Brothers, and the tug "Duncan City" owned by Thompson Smith's sons. Each tug was espccially equipped and furnished with several strings of booms. [10]

Log boom being towed from Georgian Bay, Ontario.

Tug," Duncan City."

Photo courtesy Ellis Olson

10 Lloyd M. Atwood, *Cheboygan As a Nineteenth Century Lumber Area*, Master's Thesis, Detroit, 1947, p. 81.a

The Iroquois and Chippewa steamers of the Arnold Transit Company, at the Duncan Steamship Dock.
Photo ©Johnson Studio, From Collection of Historical Society of Cheboygan County, Inc.

In 1890 the five docks at Duncan totaled 5,420 feet with a double frontage of over two miles. They ranged from 40 to 60 feet in width, and the longest one was over 600 feet. As many as 15,000,000 board feet of lumber could be dried on the docks at one time. A 30 x 150 foot warehouse was located on the steamboat dock, which was 50 by 500 feet. The water depth at the dock was over 20 feet, more than adequate to float lumber hookers and schooners.

The steamboat dock was sometimes called the D & C dock because boats of the Detroit & Cleveland line made regular stops there. It was also used for docking the two tugs owned by the Smiths. The other docks, the Breakwater and "L," were used as a refueling point for steam-driven vessels and for storing lumber, lath and shingles.

By 1894 the docks had been increased to have a double frontage of over 3 miles, and 20,000,000 feet of lumber could be stored there.[11] Due to the extensive shipping carried on in both Duncan and Cheboygan, it was known as the "Port of Twin Harbors" by all the captains who sailed the Great Lakes. Many vessels made regular fueling stops at the dock, taking on slabs to "fire up" their boilers. To serve their own and the tugs of other companies of the area, the company built, in 1885, a very substantial marine railway. Often the ship repair business had more work than they could handle. Prior to 1900, a dry dock, the most important one in the Straits area, did a booming business in connection with the foundry, a machine shop, and ship carpentry shop located on the northern end of Duncan City.[12]

11 Atwood, p. 80.
12 Atwood, p. 81.

1884 Lithograph showing water view of Duncan City.

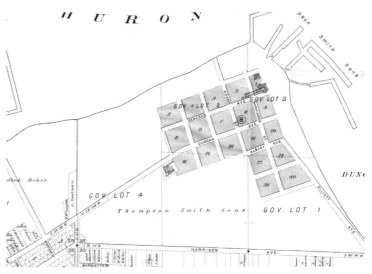

1902 Plat book, Duncan. Jeremiah Duncan owned the property for three years, until he died in 1854.

The dredging of the Cheboygan River about 1870 and the coming of the Jackson, Lansing and Saginaw Railroad in 1880 changed the commercial prospects of Cheboygan. Ships could now get far enough up the river to dock, and to load and unload passengers and freight. A railroad spur was built to the dock area which made it easier to transfer passengers from train to ferry. After the Duncan fire of 1898 the population shifted and there was little need to use the Duncan docks. Today only a few weather-beaten pilings and submerged slabs remain of the impressive docks at Duncan, which were in use from 1850 until the D & C boats stopped running in 1920.

Jeremiah Woolston Duncan was born in Baltimore, Maryland, on July 21, 1810. At a young age he became a clerk in a hardware store and then went into a hardware store partnership with his brother, John, in Wilmington, Delaware. By 1830 he went into the lumber business. In 1850 Jeremiah moved to Chicago to pursue the lumber business and soon owned large tracts of land in Michigan. He had just gotten started in developing Duncan City when he became ill and returned to Wilmington. He wrote out a will and died the following day, December 31, 1854. He left several partners and several children. His brother, John A. Duncan, became executor of his estate. John continued the operation of the mills at Duncan for a while and then filed suit to have the will probated so

Jeremiah Woolston Duncan

that the partners, the Woolstons, could get a return of their investment.[13]

J. A. Duncan, son of Jeremiah Woolston Duncan
Photo courtesy Ellis Olson

On May 31, 1859, John A. Duncan filed in the Circuit Court for the County of Cheboygan, asking that the property be sold to satisfy debts to the partners so Jeremiah's children could inherit their share. The property included some 12,000 acres of timber. Walter Crane, of Detroit, was appointed receiver and authorized to "sell lands, and to make, execute and deliver deeds, and thereby convey to the purchaser, his heirs and assigns, all the right title, interest and estate of the said complainant."[14]

On July 13, 1865, the property was sold to the firm of MacArthur, Southwick & Company for $20,000. This firm consisted of John Roofe MacArthur, Lucius Southwick, George W. Swan and John F. McDonald. After the purchase was completed, MacArthur and Swan returned to their hometown and left Southwick and McDonald in charge. Southwick and McDonald immediately repaired the dam and mills which had greatly deteriorated during the nine years they had

been idle. They also built a shingle mill near the watermill. When all the necessary alterations and repairs had been completed, they started operations of the mills at Duncan and Cheboygan. This was a welcome relief, since closing the mills has been a crippling blow to the economy of both Duncan and Cheboygan.

In July, 1866, William MacArthur, son of John R. MacArthur, purchased Southwick's interest in the watermill property and on September 28 he purchased Southwick's interest in the Duncan property. John R. MacArthur and John F. McDonald granted power of attorney to William MacArthur, September 17, 1866, for the purpose of selling their interest in the watermill and Duncan properties.

At this point, the economic bonds of the two communities were severed. The former J. W. Duncan & Company property had remained under the ownership of one company until October 6, 1866. At that time, John R. MacArthur, George W. Swan, William MacArthur, and John F. McDonald sold the Duncan property to Sanford Baker, Robert Patterson and Archibald C. Thompson, under the firm name of Baker, Thompson & Company. Their purchase included about 1200 acres of land, including some village property on the east side of the river at its mouth, and all of the Duncan Bay property west of Harrison Avenue and north of Eastern Avenue.

Sanford Baker had lumbered in Canada, and in 1866 sold that property and was "possessed of a fortune amply sufficient for the remainder of his life."[15] He traveled along Lake Huron in a Mackinaw boat, along with Robert Patterson and Archibald Thompson. While here they purchased the Bay property of MacArthur, Southwick & Company and also other lands in the county. The

13 Schaff, J. Thomas, *History of Delaware, Vol. II*, Richards & Company, 1888, p. 312.
14 Ibid., J. W. Duncan Will
15 Page, H. R. *Traverse Region, 1884.*

village of Cheboygan at that time consisted of a few scattered buildings and a population of about 250 persons. In 1868 Mears & Company of Chicago bought the interest of Archibald Thompson and Robert Patterson. Thompson Smith purchased the interest of Mears & Company on February 23, 1870, for $80,000.

Many improvements were made under the partnership of Sanford Baker and Thompson Smith, including the erection of another mill, several stores and additional docking facilities. But this partnership was doomed to a short existence, when on April 15, 1871, Thompson Smith and Sanford Baker divided the property and dissolved the partnership. Smith retained the Bay property and Baker took property in the village, part of which had been platted by him in 1869 as "West Duncan." The Bay property, 230 acres, including all buildings, later became known as "Duncan City."

Thompson Smith

Photo courtesy Ellis Olson

Thompson Smith was born in Toronto, Ontario, Canada on October 8, 1808. His parents were American—his father, Amos Smith, being a hero of the Revolutionary war. Thompson

began working early in life to help support his aged parents. He and a partner, James E. Craig, established an extensive lumberyard at Albany, New York. In 1870 he purchased the mills and land at Duncan, divided the property with Sanford Baker in 1871, and in 1876 Thompson moved his family to Duncan City and made it his home.[16]

Duncan City 1877 .

Photo from 1939 Cheboygan Daily Tribune Jubilee Edition

All those who knew old Thompson and his kin, warmly and affectionately referred to them as the "Smith People." They did everything they could to make life agreeable and pleasant for those who worked and lived in Duncan City. Thompson's thoughtfulness and generosity were appreciated by his employees, who even years later recalled the personal touch of the "Smith People." He not only gave them work year-round, but also provided extras, which enhanced their lives a little in that struggling workaday world. Because the "Smith People" always took a personal interest in Duncan City and its residents, high spirits prevailed and a good feeling was always present.

In the summer, the men were always home, but in the winter their work took them to the camps in the woods. To help their families while away the long winter months, the Smiths built a huge toboggan slide for everyone's entertainment, regardless of whether they came from Duncan or Cheboygan. It was so high that a plank was locked

16 *Cheboygan Democrat*, December 11, 1884.

STATE STREET EAST SIDE

CHEBOYGAN, MICH.

Collection of the Historical Society of Cheboygan County, Inc.

across the top to discourage small children from using the upper half, but they were permitted to use the lower section anytime they wished. It was possible to slide way out onto the ice of Duncan Bay when starting from the top of this 40 foot high toboggan run. Occasionally, church groups made tobogganing a Sunday afternoon's entertainment at Duncan City.

Other activities included skating parties on a rink maintained by the Smiths and ice boating on the bay. Frequently, these gala affairs were climaxed by refreshments donated by Thompson Smith and served by Mrs. Smith. Excursions to Mackinac Island were promoted and the funds raised were spent for the benefit of the reading room. The reading room gave an opportunity for the people to socialize, spiritually and intellectually. The Smiths also provided a billiard room for the men to entertain themselves. The Duncan School was used every Sunday for religious services, which included a Sunday school. During the week, the

ladies frequently held get-togethers, rotating from house to house.

Every spring, the Smiths held pre-Lenten parties, which resembled a Mardi Gras, inviting everyone from Cheboygan. These affairs lasted about one week, and were complete with costumes, music, and refreshments. They discontinued this custom during the 1890's.

One type of entertainment never permitted by Thompson Smith was the consumption or sale of liquor in Duncan City. Within the limits of his domain, he ruled with a mighty hand, making all decisions final, for his will was the law. There were never any recorded incidents of alcohol being sold in his camps. Because of the dangers that were always present in a sawmill town, it was not uncommon for mill owners to prohibit the sale of liquor where they had control.

If Duncan residents wanted to drink, they had to go to Cheboygan, which at one time

Duncan School Picnic Excursion, Mackinac Island, 1886.

Photo courtesy Ellis Olson

boasted of having over 42 saloons. Cheboygan was known as an "open town," because the municipal law, received its authority from the people, and on the question of saloons, they were wholeheartedly in favor. Many lumber towns, like Duncan, were "dry."

Duncan City, a company town in every respect, was owned entirely by Thompson Smith, giving him absolute authority. Every factory and house was company property. The houses were rented to the tenant-laborers for about $6 per month, and they were permitted to take, free of charge, all of the slab wood needed to heat their dwellings. If an employee wanted to build his own home on

This church was originally a Swedish church located at Duncan. It was located at 1609 Harrison Avenue, moved to the northeast corner of 4th and "C" Street, and then moved to the southwest corner of 6th and Garfield Avenue. It became the Pilgrim Holiness Church. It was eventually torn down.

Photo courtesy Ellis Olson

property acquired elsewhere, Smith allowed him to take any short or cull lumber from the mill. Cull lumber was that which had too many knots and was not valuable enough to be transported to a distant market. Short lumber was any board eight feet or less in length. Many homes in Cheboygan were built with short and cull lumber because Smith encouraged people to own their own homes and thus become relatively independent.

Duncan City house.
Collection of the Historical Society of Cheboygan County, Inc

Home of Sarah Durham Elliott, Duncan City.
Collection of Historical Society of Cheboygan County, Inc.

consisted of small, one-story dwellings. The larger more impressive homes of the "big row" consisted of two and three-story dwellings. The most prominent home in Duncan City was the "White House," a large mansion, where Thompson Smith resided. At one time, Smith maintained beautiful flower gardens around the company houses and employed a gardener, Fred Meggit, to care for the grounds about their mansion.

Duncan City house.
Collection of the Historical Society of Cheboygan County, Inc.

Genesee Avenue, the main street of Duncan City, was lined on both sides by rows of houses. The northwest side of the street were commonly known as the "Big Row" and the southeast side was called the "Little Row." The little row

Home of Thompson Smith which is still standing as of 2011. This home was later occupied by Egbert Smith, after his first house burned down. Ephraim Smith's home is on the right.
Collection of Historical Society of Cheboygan County, Inc.

Ephraim Smith's home, which still exists in 2011.

Thompson Smith's health began to fail about 1883. His sons, Ephraim and Egbert, took control of the company, renaming it Thompson Smith's Sons. Thompson died December 9, 1884, and his body was sent by train to Toronto, Ontario, Canada, for burial. In 1888 the business was reorganized as a stock company. The officers of the company in 1890 were: President, Ephraim Smith, Vice President, Egbert Smith, Secretary and Treasurer, Thompson Smith, Jr. (Egbert's son). In 1894 the same officers were managing the company which incorporated under the state law, with a capital stock of $500,000.

Left, Interior of the Big Store at Duncan. Jenny Burnett is the customer in the white dress. Notice the gas lights used to light the store.
Photo courtesy Ellis Olson

Right, Duncan Store (Standing left to right): M. Peterson, Frank Klingensmith, Arthur Gerow, E. R. Degereaux, Miss J. Burnette, Ed. Shawl, Grant Denison, Ed. James, Tom James, John Phelp, Walter Bell, Richard Thompson, E. Wright. Seated: Thompson Smith, Jr, Ephraim Smith, Egbert Smith.

Photo courtesy Ellis Olson

The accommodations at Duncan City were as complete as those in Cheboygan during its existence. Cheboygan depended on Duncan City's big store, which did wholesale business to Cheboygan retail stores for nearly 30 years. The store at Duncan was a two story 70' x 100' wooden structure, employing as many as 11 people at one time. In the year 1889, $110,000 worth of merchandise was handled, keeping two wagons constantly on the go delivering goods to the small Cheboygan neighborhood stores. The Smiths may not have allowed drinking at Duncan but they did allow smoking and chewing tobacco. Their store inventory included 9,141 pounds of tobacco and there was an additional 2,000 pounds in their various camps![17]

A large warehouse, 40 x 200 feet, was built on the docks, close to the Duncan store. Before the railroad era, practically all the merchandise was shipped by boat. Thompson Smith would stock up in the open season of navigation with enough provisions to last through the winter. He did a tremendous wholesale and retail business in general merchandise, heavy and shelf hardware, and lumbermen's supplies. In the fall of the year, the boats came to the docks loaded with provisions. The boats landed at the steamboat dock, unloading such items as tobacco, socks, boots, clothing and yard goods, various tools, butter, black strap molasses, beef and salt pork by the barrel, beans, flour, potatoes, onions, pickles, sugar, tea, coffee, lard, prunes, dried fruit, salt and pepper, mustard, spices, sausage meat and some fresh meats. Other boats would bring the heavy and shelf hardware which could not be manufactured at the Duncan foundry. Many items such as hay, grain, eggs, cabbage, rutabaga, apples and other fresh fruits were purchased locally from farmers in the area. After the lumber hookers had unloaded their supplies at the end of the season, they would take on a load of lumber, making this their last trip until spring.[18]

The importance of Duncan City, as a merchandising outlet, can only be exemplified by the presence of its foundry, blacksmith shop, harness shop, machine shop, carpenter shop, barbershop, drug store, warehouse, and general store. Many public services found in Cheboygan were also present in Duncan City, and in some cases shared by both. The City of Cheboygan had extended a 12 inch water main to Duncan in 1893, and a corduroy road was replaced with a railroad track for a horse- drawn streetcar. The Cheboygan Street Railway Company, owned by D. J. Kennedy of Bay City, was in service until it ran into financial difficulty about 1896. It started again the summer of 1898 but was forced to close after the big mill in Duncan burned. Suddenly there were not enough passengers to keep it profitable. The streetcar ran about four miles in the summer and six miles in the winter. The main route in the summer included the entire length of Duncan Avenue from the big mill to State Street, State Street from Duncan Avenue to Main Street, Main Street to the MacArthur store at the dam. In the winter, when the car was put on runners, it extended its route to the Tannery on the south end of Cheboygan. It scheduled regular trips in the summer and ran irregularly in the winter, depending on weather conditions.

Notice the track in the foreground. This is the track for the horse-drawn streetcar. The turntable allows for changing direction of the streetcar on the rails. The Duncan City LaFrance Fire Pumper is attached to the horses.
Collections of the Historical Society of Cheboygan County, Inc.

---

17 Atwood, p. 79.
18. Ibid

Horse drawn street car.   Photo courtesy of Ellis Olson

Mr. and Mrs. Egbert Smith

Collection of the Historical Society of Cheboygan County, Inc.

For the convenience of the residents of Duncan and as testimony of his civic mindedness, Thompson Smith constructed board sidewalks on every street of Duncan City. The streets were covered with sawdust and lined on both sides with 3 inch thick planks on 4 x 6 inch stringers, forming a wide board sidewalk. The longest sidewalk began at Eastern Avenue and ran on the west side of Duncan Avenue.

A sidewalk was built from the Cheboygan River to Duncan in August of 1876. Rev. Ware, in a Centennial speech prepared in 1876, stated that "Cheboygan thus made about seven and one half miles of sidewalk in the village. This for a population of fifteen hundred or two thousand inhabitants is worthy of note, and perhaps is not equaled by a village of this size in the state."[19]

The Beaver Saloon was owned by James Doyle and his wife, Matilda McGulpin. This building was on the corner of State and "B" Streets, looking east. Notice the wide, tree-lined sidewalks, which lead to Duncan Avenue.

Photo ©Johnson's Studio, from the postcard collection of Patricia Wight Geyer.

In approximately 35 years, the Duncan mills sawed over 800 million board feet of lumber plus an undetermined amount of lath, timbers, ties and shingles. The big mill had a capacity of over 350,000 board feet of lumber in an 11 hour shift. In 1883, it cut 26 million board feet of lumber, more than any mill in the Cheboygan area had ever cut in one season. In 1889, the company employed 325 men with a payroll of $132,000. During that same year the Duncan mills cut 15,000,000 feet of lath and 240,000 feet of square timbers. This scale of operations required the purchase of large areas of timber and extensive contracts for sawing. In 1881 Thompson Smith purchased 170,000 acres of pine lands on the Ocqueoc River. Merritt Chandler sold him 8,000 acres of Cheboygan county lands covered with pines and cedar in 1881 for $33,000. In 1886 the company purchased a tract of land near Grand Marais. In 1892 they purchased land in the Georgian Bay region of Canada. The logging operations of this company were the most extensive of any operations in the county. As many as 16 camps were operated during certain seasons and in 1884 they owned 180 horses. The number of employees in the various camps was between 300 and 400. [20]

The small mill was 70 x 150 feet and the dimensions of the big mill were a massive 150 x 100 feet. Each of the five mills that had been built at Duncan subsequently burned down. The last and biggest mill was destroyed by fire on September 26, 1898. It had been designed to chew up logs at an enormous rate. The logs that entered the mill were first run through the band saw and circular

Logmarks from the Thompson Smith Mills & Lumber Camps from Wood Butchers of the North, by Ellis Olson, 1971

Duncan Saw Mill.   Collection of Historical Society of Cheboygan County, Inc.

Atwood, pp. 74-75.
Note: Lath are thin wooden strips, which were nailed to wall studs. Plaster was then applied over the lath and then it was either painted or wallpapered. Lath was the precursor to drywall.

Interior of the Big Mill at Duncan.

Photo courtesy Ellis Olson

saws which cut the logs into square timbers. Then as many as four timbers were pushed through the gang saw, containing 42 blades. The 52 inch circular saw, band saw, and gang saw were all powered by steam. The carriage of the gang saw conveyed timber averaging 1200 board feet to be cut at one time. Under the roof of the same building were edging and trimming saws which created the rough pine boards. The boards were then sent to the planing mill to be finished and made ready for shipping.[21]

Six large boilers supplied steam to run the engine for the big mill built in 1880. That mill was designed for two circular and gang of saws, with all necessary edgers, trimmers and other machinery necessary for processing the lumber. In 1890 the mills reached a record when they produced 320,000 feet of lumber and 90,000 lath in one day. In 1892 they installed a band saw in the big mill, and changed the rig in the small mill to enable it to saw long timber. In that year they also installed an electric light plant to furnish light for the mills, store and machine shop. From 1892 on they often operated day and night.[22]

21 Atwood, p. 77.
22 Atwood, p. 77.

Duncan City Boiler Works.　　　　Collection of Historical Society of Cheboygan County, Inc.

Machine Shop, Duncan City.　　　　Collection of Historical Society of Cheboygan County, Inc.(2)

The lumber produced by the Smith Company reached a very large total. From 1872 to 1881 the yearly totals were from fifteen to twenty million feet of lumber and from one to eight million feet of lath. In the later period, to 1899, they annually reached twenty-six to forty million feet of lumber. In the last eighteen years of production they totaled 476,000,000 feet of lumber, and during the last ten years produced 9,000,000 feet of lath. No other company in the Cheboygan area came near those numbers.[23]

This company also operated a foundry and a machine shop which helped to avoid expensive delays in lumber production. There was always work required around any large mill but the facilities of this company allowed doing a considerable amount of outside work as well. The foundry was built in 1872 and was operated in connection with the already existing machine shop. The foundry building was 60 by 180 feet. The foundry was well known on the Great Lakes for doing custom work for the repair of heavy machinery for sawmills. They also had a dry dock on the northwest side of the company office.

The Brazel snowplows were first made in the Duncan foundry in 1883, and $20,000 worth of them were produced that year. The foundry manufactured and exported over 800 Brazel snowplows, invented by Peter Brazel. They were considered superior to any other type of plow in use at that time. The manufacture of those plows was an activity of the shops year after year through 1897. In that year they were rushed to fill orders for the Brazel plows, and they also built a set of live rollers for Mattoon and Robinson's mill, and two sets of hand blocks,

Brazel Snow plow, which was later made by Swartz Boiler Works.

two log carriages, one edger, two log loaders, and one log jacker for W. S. Smith's new mill. In 1886 they built a complete mill for Clay and Company of Detour, Michigan.

Before the huge refuse burners were built at Duncan, sawdust and slabs had to be disposed of

Below, this drawing of Duncan City was done by Charles Peterson in 1952, as he remembered it, circa 1895. He labeled buildings and homes with names. Notice the tramway that led to the burning pit along the shore.

Collection of Historical Society of Cheboygan County, Inc.

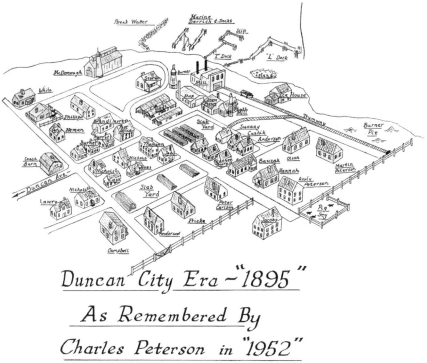

Duncan City Era ~ "1895"
As Remembered By
Charles Peterson in "1952"

23 Atwood, p. 78.

in a somewhat unorthodox manner. The Smiths hauled the slabs and sawdust in a cart, pulled by one horse, to huge trenches for burning. The trenches were about 6 feet deep and 400 feet long. The dump carts were pulled on tracks which lined both sides of the trenches. A perpetual cloud of smoke rolled from these trenches day and night. Alex Raville had the job of following the refuse to the burning pits. One day when he was dumping carts, he, along with the horse and cart, toppled into the flames. The horse died in the fire and Alex was seriously injured. He received extensive burns on his entire body and the right side of his face was badly scarred, but he survived the ordeal. Later on, when steamboats became coal burners, and the refuse burner had been built, the slabs were sold for home heating and cooking. The excess was sent to the burner.

The Smith stables at Duncan were large enough to accommodate 80 pairs of horses.
Collection of Historical Society of Cheboygan County, Inc.

In the 1870s and 1880s, many innovations appeared on the lumbering scene which made the hard-to-get-at pine more profitable. To boost production, the Katie-did or big wheels and the use of oxen and horses on the iced roads made it possible for the lumberjacks to haul great distances, winter and summer. The lumberman was always at the mercy of the weather for sledding conditions in

the winter, and if the snow cover did not hold, the logger often lost his entire winter investment. The winter of 1877-78 was virtually an open winter in Michigan. Many lumber barons and small operators lost entire fortunes then because they could not transport their logs to mills after they were cut. If the timber was close to a lake or river, they could raft at least part of their winter harvest to the mills. If the logs were deep in the woods, they rotted on the ground.

Big Wheel at Duncan —the logs were suspended by chain under the axle and could be pulled through the woods.
Collection of the Historical Society of Cheboygan County, Inc.

It was during the 1877-78 winter that Thompson Smith employed a new method for transporting out the logs from his extensive holdings east of town. Smith went to Chicago and had wagons built with wide low wheels for hauling the logs from his lumber camps. The wheels were approximately 12 inches wide and 18 inches in diameter with a steel band encompassing the center of the solid wooden wheels. These wheels would resemble an automobile rim today. Two rows of lumber were laid side by side like a railroad track, from the mills out to the camps. This method of transportation was called a poll road. Thompson Smith succeeded in getting almost all of his logs out of the woods that winter. That was the first and last time lumber wagons were used to any great extent in the Cheboygan area. The lumber wagons, having served their purpose during the open wintcr, were not used again, and soon the wagons and roads fell into disrepair.

Poll road lumber wagons.[24]

In 1879 the mills had completely burned. A new mill was constructed in 1880, built by John B. MacArthur. Thompson Smith took out $40,000 insurance on that building. A fire on the dock in 1885 consumed a half million feet of lumber, several hundred thousand feet lath, and some hundreds of feet of tramway, entailing a loss of $7,000 to $8,000 which was covered by insurance. Shortly after this fire, the company purchased a steam fire engine of the LaFrance patent, procured 2,500 feet of hose, and built a lighter [barge] on which the steamer could be placed to take it to any part of their extensive docks. In 1886, the steamer proved its worth when the granary caught fire, and it and its contents were damaged only to the extent of $1,000. The steamer proved to be just what was needed in the emergency and the Duncan Fire Department proved equal to the occasion.[25]

Duncan City Fire Department 1890.

Collection of Historical Society of Cheboygan County, Inc

24 Roy B. Clarkson, *Tumult on the Mountains, Lumbering in West Virginia 1770-1920*, McClain Printing Company, 1964, fig. 106.
25 Atwood, p. 84

Egbert A. Smith home which was destroyed by fire in 1887.   Collection of Historical Society of Cheboygan County, Inc.

.Hardly three months had passed when the fine residence of Egbert A. Smith was engulfed in flame at two o'clock in the morning on January 6, 1887, and was totally destroyed. Below zero weather and inability to get water, prevented saving any part of the property, estimated as being worth $25,000.

By 1890 the Smiths had found it necessary to raft logs from Canada and from the Upper Peninsula. They had exhausted the profitable timber from their extensive holdings of nearly 14,000 acres in the Cheboygan area. At one time, they owned most of the valuable pinelands from Cheboygan to Rogers City and south as far as Onaway, as well as large tracts of timber on the west side of Mullett Lake. The McKinley Tariff and the Dingle Tariff[26] made it less profitable to operate the Duncan mills in the early 1890's, and the company started failing. The "Panic of 1893" created havoc with the lumbering industry in Michigan. At this point in history, the Smiths began making preparations for liquidating their interest by platting Duncan City, making it possible to sell the land in small tracts or lots. This plat was never recorded. If it had been recorded, the Smith's would have had to relinquish their rights over the street right-of-ways, turning their jurisdiction over to the City of Cheboygan. They did not want to do that, and after the mill burned, there was little need for recording the plat. By 1898 the United States was suffering from a mild recession, the timber holdings in Michigan were exhausted, an embargo had been placed on importation of logs from Canada, and the insurance on the mill was more than the mill was worth, if it could be sold at all.

The value of property, especially in Duncan, was drastically reduced, making it impossible to sell without a substantial loss. The Duncan property

26 The McKinley and Dingle Tariffs were taxes on imports. They increased the cost of logs from Canada making it unprofitable to bring Canadian wood to the Cheboygan mills. The Canadian government, unhappy over the Dingley Tariff of 1897, forbid the exportation of any logs from Canada. This embargo was the death blow to lumbering in Michigan, which, for nearly seven years, had relied almost entirely on Canadian logs to keep its mills running.

Duncan Hose Company No. 3, 1904, in front of City Hall. Some names listed: Rock Featherstone, Frank Merrit, Mitchell Diebo, Cliff Dawson, Henry Miller, Sam Campbell, Louie Miller, Joe Esch, Joe Payer, Frank Miller, Jim Graham

Collection of Historical Society of Cheboygan County, Inc.

had been valued at nearly a quarter of a million dollars in 1889. Four years later, in 1893, it was only worth $78,250. By the time the mill burned in 1898, the value had fallen to about $55,000. Fire struck again on September 26, 1898, when the mills were entirely consumed at a loss estimated at $150,000, of which about $60,000 was covered by insurance. Since the fires started at one o'clock Monday morning and there had been no fire in the mill boilers on Sunday, the origin of the fire was a mystery.[27]

Alex Raville was the night watchman the night the mill burned. He stated "three fires started simultaneously in different parts of the mill. It went up like tinder. The whole place seemed to be ablaze at one." Frank Merritt, a member of the Duncan City Fire Department, related what he saw the night of the fire. "When the Duncan mill burned, it went up like a holocaust. We couldn't do anything with it. The whole place seemed to be totally engulfed. We had plenty of hose, plenty of men, and a pump that could do the job, but all we could do was to keep it from spreading to the company store."[28]

Duncan City had always maintained its own fire department when the mills were operating, but after the mill burned, the activities diminished. It ceased to function as a private enterprise. It was

27 Attwood, p. 84.
28 Taped interview with Frank Merritt, January 24, 1967.

equipped with a LaFrance Steam fire engine, whose capacity was 1,000 gallons per minute. It was possible to flood the entire yard on short notice. The fire department owned 4,000 feet of hose which they stored in their own hose house. 1904 was the last year the Duncan Fire Department operated; it was well organized and had 15 members. Joseph Esch, one of the volunteer members, served 50 years which was more than any other man in Cheboygan, as a volunteer firefighter. The Duncan City Fire Department continued to be used as Hose Company No. 3 of the volunteer fire department for the City of Cheboygan. The building for Hose Company No. 3 was located at the northeast corner of Duncan and Eastern Avenue.

Soon the trolley line folded up, schools and stores closed, and the tenant laborers moved out, leaving empty houses behind. Plundering took its toll and whatever was left was swept away by wind, fire and weather —except the two remaining Smith houses. As the years went on, nearby Cheboygan grew and enveloped what had been Duncan City within its own city limits. Duncan City became a ghost town.

Sam Martin moved many of the houses, purchased from the Smith property, to locations on the east side of the river in the City of Cheboygan. The Bank of Canada sold most of the buildings to local residents for a fraction of their cost. Part of the big horse barn was hauled to 309 Duncan and rebuilt. It was operated as the Cheboygan General Hospital by Ruth Nordman. Several houses on Duncan Avenue, Lafayette Street and Union Street, were sold and moved from Duncan City. In 1903, the original Duncan School was moved to the east side of the alley behind the residence of Gus Liebner, who lived at the northwest corner of Duncan Avenue and Third Street. Liebner used the school as a boatbuilding shop for many years before it was torn down in the mid -1950s.

Original Duncan School which was moved in 1903 and used as Gus Liebner's boat shop.   Photo courtesy Ellis Olson

Duncan School which became the Eastern Avenue School. The teacher was Mrs. Markle. She learned to speak Swedish so she could communicate better with her students.
Photo courtesy of Ellis Olson

The city moved the large two room school to Eastern Avenue, which residents began calling the Duncan School. Its proper name was Eastern Avenue School. It was torn down in 1958 by Morris Carlson.

Charles McCallum was hired by the Bank of Canada as caretaker of the Duncan property until it was eventually sold for unpaid taxes. By the end of the First World War, only Egbert and Ephraim [the former Thompson Smith home] Smith's homes remained. Dr. Martin J. Cain purchased the Bay property for back taxes and developed a Boy Scout camp there.

In 1934 the American Music Camp was formed. Dr. Martin Cain donated the land. The Civil Works Administration built various buildings with wood obtained from state lands. They hired Joseph Esch to construct a band shell on the premises. He had a small portable saw mill on his property on Harrison Avenue, which he used to prepare the logs for the rustic-style band shell building. This large music shell, named the Damrosch Bowl, was built for concerts. They also built individual studios for the faculty, a rustic recreation building, and a boy's dormitory. The large Thompson Smith home was used as a girl's dormitory. Michigan Governor William A. Comstock even came for the dedication concert. Several outstanding music instructors were hired, and they also developed a choral society composed of many Cheboygan members from area church choirs.[29] Music Camp founder, Frederick Lewis, had counted on paying audiences to supplement the

29 *Cheboygan Daily Tribune*, 1939 Golden Jubilee Edition

Damrosch Bowl Music Camp Auditorium,1935   Photo courtesy of Patricia Wight Geyer Collection

tuition paid by the music students. Many people took advantage of the opportunity to hear these programs, but the Music Camp was a financial failure and closed after two seasons.

There was fresh hope for a while when the Methodist Children's Home Society secured the property for summer use and operated a children's camp there while the buildings still remained. This camp at Duncan was named "Camp Knight of the Pines."[30] But after two or three years, the Methodist Children's Home, which had its headquarters in Detroit, bought property on Douglas Lake and abandoned Duncan Bay to build there.

By 1937 the Cheboygan National Youth Administration had located at the former American Band Camp. This was part of the WPA and their purpose was to give young men between the ages of eighteen and twenty one, who were unemployed and out of school, work habits and work experience

Bandshell fire of June 16, 1996.
Photo from Cheboygan Fire Department, Tom Bancroft

in a field of interest. They had two dormitories accommodating thirty two men in each, a library, study hall, dining hall, craft shop with a wood working department, a metal-working department, and auto mechanics departments. Four cabins were provided for staff. The youth worked 70 hours per month and then took classes for high school completion.[31] Several students left to accept

---

30 Gordon Turner, *Ghost Town Once Thrived Nearby, Cheboygan Daily Tribune,* June 8, 1981.
31 *Cheboygan Daily Tribune,* 1939.

The first airplane known to have landed in Cheboygan was this Curtiss Flying Boat. It landed in Duncan Bay on July 15, 1913, for a three-hour stopover. The plane was making the 1913 Aero and Hydro Great Lakes Reliability Cruise. It traveled 886 miles of the Great Lakes shoreline from Chicago to Detroit. This was the only plane to complete the cruise. The pilot was Beckwith Havens and he had one passenger, J. B. R. Verplanck, the owner. The plane was built by the Curtiss Aeroplane Company of Hammondsport, New York, in 1912. It looks like the whole town turned out to see this flying machine.

private employment and many others completed the course. This program ended in 1939.

The band shell remained vacant many years. The Marx family used it as an airplane hangar during the late 1940's. Part of it had caved in and on the night of June 16, 1996 the remains of the 60 year old structure burned to the ground. The firefighters were called in at 2:15 a.m. and finished up about 5 a.m. Two fire trucks and a dozen firefighters responded, keeping the fire from spreading to nearby woods and homes.

One day, in 1939, Erwin Marx, a pilot from World War I days, flew over Cheboygan on a cross-country trip from Detroit, took another look and landed in one of the fields of the old Duncan City. Standing on top of the ruins of a former mill hand's cottage, Marx visualized the runways, one north-south, the other east-west, both with approaches from the water so that a pilot could come in low and set a plane down almost at the water's edge—and still have a half-mile of strip ahead of him. Marx promptly bought Duncan City—now reduced to 230 acres and two fine mansions on a hill.[32]

32 Richnak, Barbara, *Cheboygan's Ghost Town Airport*, AOPA Pilot, July 1961

First airplane to land on Duncan City property.   Photo courtesy Doug Dailey

Marx had always dreamed of owning his own private airport. He also hoped to develop the property and make a pilot's "fly-in" resort hotel. He graded the runways and built a grass strip. The airport opened officially in 1947. He operated a flying school at the airport as well as a small shop to make aircraft parts. Erwin died before he could build the resort, and the property was inherited by his son, Edward Marx. Edward Marx sold a large portion of this property in 1980. Another portion was sold January 1, 1986, to a developer. On November 29, 1988, a large portion of property was sold and Duncan Bay Marina was constructed in the area where the burning pits used to be. The entrance into the marina is at the exact site of the large mill that burned in 1898. In 1989 the Duncan Bay Boat Club began selling individual docks in the marina. They also built a clubhouse and did a tremendous amount of landscaping.

Today, "Duncan City" is once more growing and coming to life with an active marina, the construction of many houses, and several condominiums. The Marx Airport has been replaced by the City County Airport on the Levering Road. The marina covers the sawdust dumping area and the burning pit of the Duncan mills. The large Thompson and Ephraim Smith homes have been renovated. The 230-acre Duncan parcel was subdivided for the construction of many new homes. Duncan Avenue and other streets from "Duncan City" have been dedicated and turned over to the City of Cheboygan, making them public roads. Sadly, the exciting lumber era has passed.

DUNCAN AND CHEBOYGAN LEGAL ORIGINS

BY ELLIS OLSON

A great amount of confusion regarding the name and location of Duncan, Inverness, and Cheboygan was created by the legislature in the early days. The close proximity of the settlements, the lack of accurate information, and the enormous distance separating them from the State Capitol caused most of this confusion. There was no legally established local government in 1840 when Sheboygan[33] and Wyandotte counties were set off from Michilimackinac County. Cheboygan was attached to Mackinac County for judicial purposes.

Settlements, villages, and townships were often referred to in vague terms. The original Sheboygan County had only one township named "Sheboygan Township," which included the entire county in 1849. The Cheboygan Settlement had been deemed a post village in 1846 for the establishment of a post office. It was soon called the "Duncan Post Office" and was on the east side of the Cheboygan River. When the state legislature established the county seat at "Duncan" it was not at the Duncan Bay Settlement but on the west side of Duncan Avenue, across from Sutherland Street. In 1850 Sheboygan Township was divided from the mouth of the river northward—the west side becoming Inverness Township and the East side becoming Duncan Township. To add to the confusion, a tract of land on the east side of the river was platted in 1869 and named "West Duncan."

A decision was made to remove the county seat from the settlement of Duncan to the Sammons Settlement in Inverness Township, on the west side of the Cheboygan River. This was after the death of Duncan, when the mills were shut down and Cheboygan showed more promise. They decided to hold a special election and let the qualified voters of the county decide the question on the last Saturday of September in 1856. The electorate voted to move the county seat from Duncan to Inverness. The vote from Duncan was 13 for and 4 against; Inverness 27 for and 0 against removal.

The first session of the circuit court was held in the United State Land office at Duncan, July 22, 1856, and was presided over by Judge Samuel Douglas. The back [of the land office buidling] also served as a jail until the county seat was moved to Inverness. The next Cheboygan jail was on the second floor of Bela Chapman's (the sheriff) house where court was held after its removal from Duncan. In 1858 a log jail was built by H. N. Stevenson. Its dimensions were 20 x 24 feet and it stood on Huron Street. The brick jail, which is now part of the museum, was built in 1880.

The fact remains that at no time did Duncan, Duncan City, or West Duncan ever gain official recognition as a legally defined,

---

33 Sheboygan was one of the early spellings on some historical maps and documents.

Duncan Land Office, Court House and Jail located at the end of Sutherland St. c 1855. The Land Office in front served here until 1869, along with the Cheboygan County Courthouse. The jail in back was located here until 1882.

Photo Courtesy of Ellis Olson

self- regulating governmental structure. Cheboygan was incorporated as a village in 1871. It made the transition from a village to a city in 1889.

The first United States Land Office for this region prior to the organization of Cheboygan County was the Genesee District Land Office, located in Flint. In 1855 it was transferred to Duncan. The Flint Land Office was originally moved to Duncan to make it more accessible for the "Soo Canal Company." The locks at Sault St. Marie were opened in June of 1855 and the company was granted thousands of acres of public land to help finance the cost of the canal. The entries of the Canal Company were entered as "Canal Lands" in the General Land Office books. The agent at Duncan was Hiram R. Rood. In the winter of 1857-58, the office, comprising the books, papers, and fire proof safe, were conveyed on a sleigh to Mackinac Island by Medard Metivier. From there the office was moved to Traverse City where it had the name "Grand Traverse District Land Office."[34]

Paul and Thura Nelson, who owned the property on Duncan Avenue where the first courthouse, jail, and federal land office was located, are descendants of the Swedes who built the Duncan Tramway in 1852. Their parents both worked at Duncan City. Paul Nelson, my brother, Ray, and I used to fish among the ruins of the old docks. When the fish weren't biting, Paul used to point here and there, while telling us where the mills, the store, a foundry, and other things were in Duncan City. Paul understood the importance of history and the significance of the relics of the past. He gave me this original photograph of the 1855 courthouse, jail and Duncan land office.

34   Ware, p. 23

CHEBOYGAN—
THE LEADING FRESH WATER FISH
SHIPPING PORT IN THE UNITED STATES

By Sally Eustice Humphrey

> *My dad (Dick Brownson) kept his first boat, the "Susie B" at Eddy's Fishery and his second boat, the "Linda B," at the end of 6th street off B St. . . . We lived on C Street at the time and he could walk to the boat. . . He also fished with Clarence and Louis Brooks. . . This was in the 1940's. . . Eddy fishery—I would play around there while my dad worked on his boat. . . I remember the sawdust and the room where the ice was stored. . . the boxes were packed with the whitefish as soon as the boat came in. . . rough sawed boxes that gave you splinters. . . I remember boxes of ice on the boat. . . the fish were packed in the ice when he came back to Eddy's. . . we always had fresh fish for dinner.*
>
> Memories of her father's fishing days shared by Gail Davison

Early pictures of Cheboygan's riverfront show a mixture of fishing boats, tugs, passenger steamships and lumber schooners. As late as 1960, it was common to go grocery shopping for fish down at the dock area. The Eddy Fishery was located on the riverbank, just north of Northwood Oil Company and you could see them unload the fish and watch them clean and wrap your selection. Today, fishing is mostly considered a sport and we don't realize the importance of commercial fishing to the beginning economy of Cheboygan. Perhaps a little study of the history of fishing in the area will help us understand more about Cheboygan's "fishing heritage."

Fishing in the Straits region has taken place for centuries. Pre-contact evidence of Indian fishing in the upper Great Lakes was discovered on Bois Blanc Island at the Juntunen Site and at many other archaeology digs in the Mackinaw and St. Ignace area. Charles Cleland, Michigan State University anthropologist, tells about the seasonal migration of the Anishnabeg natives.[2] During the summer they would travel the Great Lakes shores and form small villages of fifty to seventy people. Men would spear and harpoon large fish species and both men and women would use gill nets and hook and line for smaller fish. The men would take their canoes to offshore reef areas and use gill nets to harvest whitefish and lake trout when they were spawning. The fish was preserved by smoking and drying. They would also fish through the ice with gill nets and spears and preserve this harvest by freezing. This fish was for their own use as food.

---

1 *The Cheboygan Daily Tribune* of April 6, 1931, republished an article called "Cheboygan Called Leading Lake Fish Port in World." The Article had appeared in the Detroit Motor News. It was written by Harvey Kiemmer, a Cheboygan area summer resorter and a nationally known reporter.

2 Cleland, Charles E., *Rites of Conquest*, University of Michigan Press, 1992, p44-45.

Cheboygan Swing Bridge, Circa 1930. Collection of the Historical Society of Cheboygan County, Inc.

Even after the explorers, traders, missionaries, and soldiers came to the Mackinac region, this fishing pattern continued. Antoine Cadillac, a French commandant of Michilimackinac (which was then at St. Ignace) said, "the great abundance of fish and the convenience of the place for fishing have caused the Indians to make a fixed settlement in those parts. It is a daily manna, which never fails."[3] The Indians developed a commercial fishery by trading fish with the French traders and soldiers at Michilimackinac. Those trappers, who went out into the wilderness, adopted the Indian methods of fishing, and fish became a dependable staple of their diet. Many of the white men intermarried with the Indians and their Métis children sought their livelihood by fishing. Henry Jotel, a French explorer with the 1687 LaSalle expedition, wrote this description as he passed through the Straits of Mackinac.

They are very skillful at fishing and the fishing is very good in those parts. There are fish of various kinds which they catch with nets, made with a very good mesh; and although they only make them of ordinary sewing thread, they will nevertheless stop fish weighing over ten pounds. They go as far as a league [3 miles] out into the lake to spread their nets, and to enable them to find them again, they leave marks, namely, certain pieces of cedar wood which they call "aquantiquants," which serve the same purpose as buoys or anchors. They have

3 Kinietz, The Indians of the Western Great Lakes, 1615-1760, Ann Arbor, U of M Press,1965, p 239.

nets as long as 200 fathoms and about 2 feet deep. At the lower part of those nets they fasten stones to make them go to the bottom, and on the upper pan they put pieces of cedar wood which the French people who were then at this place called floats. Such nets are spread in the water, like snares among crops, the fish being caught as they pass, like partridge and quails in snares. The nets are sometime spread in a depth of more than 30 fathoms, and when bad weather comes, they are in danger of being lost.[4]

In the 1820's the fur trade in the region peaked and traders began to go further west and north to gather their furs. Those who remained in the Mackinac region looked for another source of income and subsistence. Dr. John Bailey, Fort Mackinac Surgeon, in his book, "*Old and New Mackinac*" explained:

As early as 1824 whitefish and trout, in small quantities, salted and packed in barrels, were caught and sent to the Buffalo market. All the fishing grounds for one hundred and fifty miles, or more, around sent their catch to Mackinac Island, where the fish were sorted, resalted, repacked in barrels ready for shipment. From 1854 to 1860 the trade in salted fish increased to over two hundred and fifty thousand packages, valued at over one million dollars. Whitefish were frequently taken in gill nets that weighed from twenty to twenty-five pounds, and lake trout were caught that weighed eighty-five pounds.[5]

Indian canoes were gradually replaced by flat bottom wooden boats known as "Mackinaw" boats.

Mackinaw boats were like a big canoe with a sail and centerboard. They had a shallow draft, and yet were stable enough to hold the weight of the fish or other freight. They were usually about twenty four feet long and seven feet wide and manned by two men. "A St. Ignace resident, Hyacinth Chenier, began to design these boats with two masts and sails, a centerboard and a round bottom that was pointed at both ends. These boats were able to handle nets and large catches of fish in deep and rough waters." [6] Joseph Derusha, Sr., also a St. Ignace boat builder, helped the Cheniers in their business in the 1840's. These wind- powered boats were built until 1915.

"Wabisi" Mackinaw boat, built by Chenier family about 1845.[7]

The first nets used by the Indians were woven of cord made from nettles and hemp fibers. The women would spin and twist the fiber into cord, and the men wove the gill nets.[8] After trade brought East Coast and European goods into the Great Lakes area, the nets were made of cotton or linen. These nets had to be cleaned and dried occasionally or they would rot. This involved removing them from the water and placing them on drying racks or reels. They were mended at this stage, placed back in net boxes, and could be returned to the water when needed.

4 Kinietz, p. 29.
5 Bailey, Dr., Mackinac, Formerly Michilimackinac, 1894.
6 Before the Bridge, A History and Directory of St. Ignace, Kiwanis Club of St. Ignace, 1957, p. 3.

By the 1890's fishermen had learned to treat their nets with coal tar, lime and salt, tanning liquid or lye. Treated nets could be left in the water for up to two months.

The seine was one of the first styles of nets used. It was a fine mesh and up to 1,000 feet in length. It had floats attached to the top and weights to the bottom. "One end is fastened to the shore, and the fishermen, awaiting an opportune time to enclose a school of fish, row out into the lake with the other end, and , making a wide sweep, bring it to shore, enclosing whatever fish may be with its sweep." [9]   Either men or horses hauled it in and then the men removed the fish from the nets on the beach. This was the safest way of fishing but the fish had to come close to shore at the right time, when the men were there and ready with the nets.

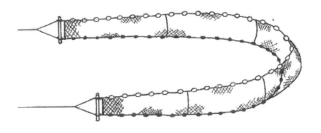

Seine Net.

Pound (pond) nets were also used to catch fish in waters up to 30 feet deep. The cost of a pound net was about $500 in 1879. A series of posts were driven into the lake bottom and nets were strung between them. They were laid out so that fish were funneled into smaller sections and trapped. The fishermen gathered the net to corral the fish into a small area, and then scooped them into their boat.

Fishermen generally used gill nets when fishing in deeper water. These were long nets,

Pond (Pound) Net.

with floats on the top and weights on the bottom. They were spread out in a long line, with buoys at each end. As fish tried to swim through them they were caught by the gills in the mesh. These 1,000 foot nets were packed in net boxes, and from 4 to 6 boxes of nets would be tied together and set out. They were left in place up to one week before lifting. The cold water from the lake bottom would keep the fish fresh and the fishermen would return home quickly, salt or ice them down and ship them out. A gill net cost about $225 and a Mackinaw boat about $100, so a man could get into the fishing business rather reasonably.

The following memories of gill net fishing were recorded by Gail Davison. Her father, Dick Brownson was a Cheboygan fisherman in the 1940's.

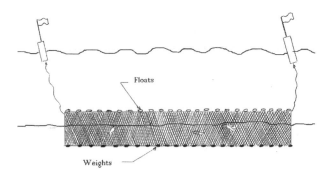

Floats

Weights

Gill Net.

7 Before the Bridge, p 4.
8 Margaret Beattie Bogue, Fishing the Great Lakes, An Environmental History 1783-1933, University of Wisconsin Press, 200, p.7.
9 Bogue, p. 38.

The nets were emptied and then put back in . . . I remember how the net came across the boat and you had to move or get swept overboard. . . so it was dangerous work . . . I think each fisherman had markings on the buoys that were his and no one else bothered the others nets . . . He always went out on Sunday mornings to pick the nets up and my mother and I would wait for him to come home so we could all go out to my grandparent's farm for the rest of the day . . . He would put big poles in the yard and hang the nets up to work on them . . . I had some of the netting needles that he used to repair the nets . . . I can remember the smell of the tar as they used that on all the nets. . . [10]

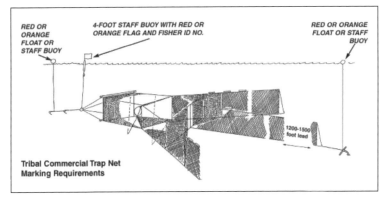

Tribal Commercial Trap Net Marking Requirements

In March, 1907, Will Syers, son of Joseph Syers, a fisherman, was rowing in from attending some gill nets at the mouth of the Cheboygan River when he discovered a body floating in the river opposite the gas plant. This turned out to be a local salesman who had been last seen on January 17." [11] This notice tells us that there was gill netting taking place in late winter at the mouth of the river, and the fisherman was just using a rowboat to gather the fish!

Another kind of net is the trap net which, since the bans on gill netting in the 1960's, is the most common commercial trap now used in the Great Lakes. They are shaped similar to the pound nets but the "pot" or collection area is covered on all sides. They are anchored in water up to 150 feet deep and the nets themselves are as much as 45 feet in height. The fish trapped in the pot remain alive and when the fishermen harvest the fish, they raise just the pot part of the net. The legal-sized whitefish are netted out and the rest are returned to the water.

There were three major activities of the fish industry. The first, harvesting, was the actual catching of the fish. This was usually done by the local inhabitants, often Indian or Métis, who went out in boats and gathered the fish in nets. The next step, processing, involved packing the fish for shipping. This included cleaning, salting or icing, placing in barrels or boxes to ship, and sending them away on steamers or railcars and later by truck. This was sometimes done by the person who caught the fish, but more often a local dealer would buy from several fishermen, process the fish in a local plant like Cheboygan or St. Ignace and then send it out by ship or train. The third step was marketing the fish in places like Chicago, Detroit, Buffalo, Toledo, and Cleveland. This was handled by the merchants who generally lived in the large cities.

Ketch-rigged Mackinaw style fishing boat.

10 Memories shared by Gail Davison of her father, Dick Brownson, a Cheboygan fisherman in the 1940's, recorded February 11, 2010.
11 *Cheboygan Democrat*, Mar 29, 1907

Don Bell holding a beautiful (brown/lake trout taken in Lake Huron's fresh waters.
Photo courtesy Stuart Ross Bell

Right, the White Swan hauled a variety of cargo in the Great Lakes including frozen fish.

Fish shed and docks on west side of river, just south of the State Street Bridge.

Collection of the Historical Society of Cheboygan County, Inc.(2)

1850 Mackinaw Census—which included Cheboygan and Duncan—finds these names listed as fishermen & living in the Straits area.

Charles Gallagher
Myron Greer
Amable Goodreau
Charles Gregg
Peter Groudan
James Hamlin
Peter Hance
John Kelly
Charles LaCroix
Joseph LaLonde
Narcise LeCuyler
Louis LeDuc
Michael LeVigne
Charles Louisigneau
Joseph Love
Alexander Lozon
Terence Mahoney
Leander Marshall
William Martin
Samuel Martin
Felix Martineau
Anthony McGill
Frederick McGulpin
William McGulpin
Andre Moran
Donald Morrison
Archibald Newton
Obadiah Newton
Ashlon Perry
Michael Plante
Peter Pond
Henry Ross
Louis St. John
Louis St. Onge
John Sullivan
John Trudo
Benjamin Winchell

The first step of gathering the fish was done by the local residents—mostly Indian, Métis, and French Canadians. The following list from the Mackinac Agency Letters, dated May 20, 1933, include these Mackinac Island and St. Ignace area fishermen who were requesting help from Henry Schoolcraft during the time the government was negotiating the treaty of 1835 which ceded much Indian land to Michigan. It is interesting to see how many names are still in the Straits area today. Not much is known about these individuals. The newspapers in their lifetime were few, and not much is recorded about their lives. (Modern spelling and handwriting would be much different today.)

ARDIN REARSOO	CHRIS MARTIN
LOUIS BELLANJAY	ALEXIS LABUTE
ROBERT CHANDLAIR	CHRLS ST. ANDRAY
DANIEL PALLADO	HENRY VIANCOUR
PETER GRONDIN	FRANCIS TROUTIER
PETER DUVERNAY	LOUIS TEBO
EMABLE CAYANE	G. CHARBONOE
FRANCIS LOUISGNAN	JOHN BT. TASROULT
JOSEPH LOSON	ANTOINE PAUKIN
CHS. DOBAIN	WILLIAM McGULPIN
T. LAPERE	I.W. ROBINSON
JOSEPH RECCOLLAY	LOUIS LaCROIX
ANTOINE FONTAINE	PETER POND
GEORGE GORMAN	FRANCIS DUVERNAY
JOSEPH RANVILLE	CHRLS MACAYE
T. FONTAIN	FRANCIS DOSSENY
LOUIS GRONDIN	GEO CHINIA
PETER ASHAY	MICHAEL LANTRY
WILLIAM LANCOUR	PETER PLANT
JOHN TAYLOR	T. I. TAYREIN
JOHN BT. CORBAIN	THOMASS A BOYD
CHLS CLOUTIER	PAUL BALLANJAY
ALEXIS CORBAIN	A. WENDELL
JOSEPH ROBSON	SAMUEL C. LASLEY
DANIEL BILAIR	MICHAEL DOUSMAN
ISAAC BLANCHARD	ABE BOUCHARIN
JEREMIAH LADUKE	FRANCIS ARCHAMBO
LOUIS MARTIN	ALEXIS PELOTT
LOUIS CHARBONOT	SIMON SHOMPINE
ANTOINE MARTIN	A.B. DAVENPORT
CHS MATTAY	HENRY DAVENPORT

In the St. Ignace history book, *"Before the Bridge,"* it was stated that by 1850 thousands of barrels of fish, at ten dollars each, were sent to Chicago, Buffalo and other eastern ports. This fishing industry gave employment to many men who spent their whole lives in gathering fish from the lakes. It also supported the side industries of boat building, coopering, ice storage and trade to supply the fishermen with food and equipment. Some men who cut lumber in winter fished in the summer. There was now enough boat traffic in the area to build a lighthouse on the point off Duncan Bay State Park, in 1851. Soon the various reefs and harbors were marked—including Cheboygan with the Range Light.

As steamships began to travel through the Straits during spring, summer and early fall, they would stop at various ports to load wood, freight, and passengers. They first stopped only at Mackinac Island. Later, when the Cheboygan River was dredged and docks were built at Duncan and the Cheboygan River mouth, steamships also pulled into these ports. Other stops were made at St. Helena, Beaver Island, Grand Traverse, Saginaw, Alpena, and Sault Ste. Marie. A researcher from the University of Michigan Biological Station recorded that there were 32 fishing companies in the Mackinac region by 1860.[12] These companies were putting their fish barrels on the steamships. These boats could transport fresh fish quickly to major ports in Detroit and Chicago. The fishermen began to supply vast quantities of fish, packed in salt brine or ice in wooden barrels. This fishing industry necessitated the founding of another industry–coopering–the making of barrels.

It was partially to fulfill this need for fish barrels that Cheboygan's first residents, Jacob Sammons and Alexander McLeod, moved to Cheboygan. Barrels required a lot of wood, and the saw mill at Mill Creek had gone out of business about 1839. In 1844 Sammons came from Mackinac Island and built a small home on the riverbank in Cheboygan. He soon built a steam saw mill near the mouth of the river to cut lumber and make barrel staves. A blacksmith, Peter LaBelle, came and built a blacksmith shop nearby. Sammons also built a wharf, for Medard Metivier, so boats could load the barrels and lumber and take them to Mackinac Island. Alexander McLeod and his brother Ronald built a water-powered sawmill near the paper mill site [today's location of Great Lakes Tissue]. These men and their saw mills were able to provide the wood needed to make the large number of barrels for shipping fish. Moses

CHEBOYGAN COOPERS

MATHEW GEARY	HENRY GUILMETTE	NATHAN HALL	RICHARD HALL
OLIVER HAMBLEN	WILLIAM HENDERSON	MOSES HORNE	WILLIAM HUNTER
JOSEPH JENKINS	JAMES KENNY	MATHEW KILLDAY	JAMES KINNEY
WILLIAM LAWLER	ISIDORE LOZON	JACOB MADIS	JOHN MAHONY
WILLIAM McGILL	WILLIAM McGUIRE	CHARLES McGUIRE	PATRICK McKINNEY
ROBERT McMILLON	MEDARD METIVIER	FRANCIS METIVIER	JOHN METTEZ
JOSEPH MILO	FRANCIS MORIN	BYRON ODEL	PATRICK PANETTE
ANDRE RAPIN	SAMUEL SHERWIN	RICHARD SMITH	WILLIAM SMITH
JAMES STEWART	CHARLES SULLIVAN	PATRICK SULLIVAN	ZADA WAITE
SAMUEL WILLIAMS	HENRY WRIGHT	CHARLES WRIGHT	

12 Wendy O'Neil, This Land and Man; An Historical Look at the Use of land and Natural Resources in the Inland Water Route Region of Northern Lower Michigan, U of M Biological Station, December 1977.

These biographies of Cheboygan coopers were written in 1884.

Philip Bries, one of the pioneers of Cheboygan, was born in Belgium in the year 1817. He served in the army from 1838 to 1844. October 21, 1847, he married Marie Struyf. In the spring of 1856 they immigrated to this country, reaching Mackinac Island in July of that year. The following autumn they removed to Cheboygan, where they still reside. Mr. Bries was a cooper by trade and has pursued that avocation to the present time. In 1858 he built, a house, still standing on Main Street, which was their home for twelve years. This worthy couple struggled with the hardships and privations of pioneer life, but by industry and frugality acquired a competency for old age.[14]

William H. Maultby,[15] one of the pioneers of Cheboygan County, was born in the city of Cork, Ireland, October 25, 1809. In the summer of 1828 he immigrated to America and settled in Vermont. May 4, 1831, he married Cynthia A. Breakneck, at Fairhaven, Vermont, and in 1833 they removed to the state of New York. He was a cooper by trade and followed it for several years. In 1851 he settled in Cheboygan County, living first on the east side of the river on land purchased of J. W. Duncan. He then purchased a place in the town of Inverness, where he still resides. They have had three children, two sons and one daughter, all of whom are now living. His wife died May 7, 1873. Mr. Maultby has had more or less to do with county affairs since its organization, having been Probate Judge, County Treasurer and is now Deputy Treasurer. He is well known and highly respected in the county.

Charles Brannock is the largest manufacturer of barrels in the county. He furnished several hundred half barrels to the fishermen of this region and is making preparations this winter to do a heavy business in that line next summer.[16]

Wiggins Horne, a cooper from Mackinac Island, came to Cheboygan in 1846 and made the first fish barrels in the county.

The art of coopering requires a good supply of wood—white pine or ash. Barrel staves were cut to length, planned smooth, and curved inward. The boards were tapered to be wide in the middle and narrower at each end. The barrel ends were prepared, and either wood or iron hoops were made. The staves were then soaked in water so they would bend. They were fit into the lid; the hoops applied, and then they were either fired or sealed with glue or pitch. Layers of fresh fish and salt would be placed in the barrel and the lid sealed. These barrels were the packing crates of the era. They could be rolled up a gang plank, stacked on end and they held large quantities of fish.

The population of the Cheboygan area remained rather stagnant during the 1860's, about 500 people during the Civil War. The local fishermen were kept busy supplying fish both to the Union Army as well as to eastern markets and the Chicago area. Those first residents continued to clear land, build mills, farms, and houses. After the end of the Civil War, there was a sudden increase in northern Michigan population. Men returning from war were ready to settle down and get on with their life and many came to northern Michigan to participate in the lumber boom. Wood was needed to build homes and businesses destroyed in the war. The Great Chicago Fire of 1871 created a huge demand for wood. The railroads were now spreading across the country and wood was needed for rail ties and for home in the "near treeless central states." By 1870 the population of Cheboygan County grew to 2,198, and by 1880 it was 6,624, tripling in ten years.[17]

Cheboygan was ready to supply the nation's need. They had the docks, the mills, the

13 Perry Powers, 113.

14 The Traverse Region, Historical and Descriptive, with Illustrations of Scenery and Portraits and Biographical Sketches of Some of Its Prominent Men and Pioneers", Chicago: HR Page & Co., 1884

15 Ibid.

men and the trees. The Duncan Mills, which had closed after the death of Jeremiah Duncan, were back in operation as the Thompson Smith Mills. Many other mills and lumber camps were located along the inland route. The river was widened, locks were built, and a real town had started to develop with boarding houses, businesses, a school, churches and a local government. The village of Cheboygan was officially organized in 1871. With all this growth the river mouth became congested but the fishermen managed to keep their space. Most of their dockage was near the State Street Bridge (called Third Street back then). The fishing business continued to increase in volume as more and more steamers came to transport their fish to city markets.

> *"F.M. Sammons shipped on Monday by stage to Grand Rapids the nicest lot of mackinaw trout we have ever seen. There were several hundred pounds and the average was 7 and a half pounds each. Three of the lot weighed 76 pounds and one of these weighed 31 pounds. These were caught by Peter Pond of St. Ignace with a snatch hook through a hole in the ice."* [18]

1860 CHEBOYGAN COUNTY CENSUS

FISHERMEN

FRANK JOHNSTON	FRANK LALONDE
ALEXIS LALONDE	SAMUEL LALONDE
OLIVER SPOONER	JOSEPH JESU
ANSON DODGE	WILLIAM DAVENPORT
LOUIS RECALLY	JEFFERY LAFAVER
NOEL LAFAVER	HARRISON AVERIL
LEVI AVERIL	HORATIO STEVENSON
CHARLES BENNETT	EDWARD LASLEY
CHRISTIAN BENNET	LOUIS MASTAN

COOPERS

JACOB SAMMONS	JOHN FERRELL
PHILLIP BRIES	MOSES HORNE
WILLIAM BARTHOLEMY	PETER FREDERICK
JOHN BICKER	SYLVESTER SAMMONS
HOLLIES KNIFFIN	JACOB NELSON
AUGUSTUS GRIM	WILLIAM MAULTBY
WILLIAM DOTY	JAMES BRANICK
CHARLES BRANECK	JOHN PENNMAN
STEPHEN WILLIAMS	FRANK WATERSIDE
PETER NELSON	

The ease of shipping fish by steamboat along with the increased market demand caused an increase in the number of steamboats passing through the Straits. It was now easier to ship the fish to Chicago and Detroit. Fishing stations on Beaver Island and St. Helena Island were forming at the same time Cheboygan was being settled. Peter McKinley came from Beaver Island where he was "chased out" by the Mormon residents. Alonzo Cheeseman and Lorenzo Wheelock also left Beaver Island and moved to Cheboygan, before the Mormons were driven off. Jacob Sammons owned the ship "Bunker Hill," with William Beloit, who owned St. Helena Island before selling it to Archibald Newton. When studying the fishermen and the fish industry of Cheboygan one needs to look at the whole region of the Straits— Cheboygan, Mackinaw City, Mackinac Island, St Helena Island and St. Ignace.

16 *Cheboygan Free Press*, January 27, 1876 reprinted in Cheboygan Observer January 28, 1932.
17 Powers, p 27.
18 *Cheboygan Free Press*, February 24, 1876, reprinted in the Cheboygan Observer 1932.

Fountain House Hotel with various boats along riverbank. This was on Water Street. Division Street is at left side of photo.
Photo ©Johnson Studio, from Historical Society of Cheboygan County, Inc.

Fishing was a dangerous business. The Cheboygan Democrat of December 1, 1884 reprinted an article from the *St. Ignace Republican*:

The fishing season of 1884 is closed, and the uniform report of the fishers is that there was much of trouble and hardship, but no money in their ventures. Following this avocation, five men were drowned at Drummond's Island, this season, four bodies lashed to a boat, drifted ashore on south Manitou; Joseph Marley was drowned at Detour; Joseph Lapine and his son were drowned at Scott's Point; two men were drowned at Manistique, and a man named McLean perished near Waugoshance. Add to this the four lives lost July 5th; the drowning of Rev.

Puddefoot's father at the Railroad dock; of Captain Caseaden on lower Huron; two deaths at Cheboygan in the aqueous element, and we have the frightful total of 23 deaths by drowning in this vicinity. Seven of the unfortunate men were residents of this city.[19]

The fishermen took awful chances with weather. If they didn't go out and pick up their nets a storm could destroy them. The *Cheboygan Democrat* reported:

During the gale last Friday Captain Mattheson, of the fishing tug *Messenger*, decided to make the trip to the Island as usual, notwithstanding the fact that all crafts were seeking shelter not already in

19 *Cheboygan Democrat*, December 1, 1884

some safe place. His engineer got frightened and would not go, but the fireman stood by the "old Man," and together they made the trip, and it was about as exciting an experience as one has in a life time. The boat behaved splendidly and proved herself a staunch and reliable sea boat, if she is small. The captain is as great a dare devil as sails fresh water, and it's a pretty stormy day when he would not go sailing. His fireman is a fit companion to such a master.[20]

Cheboygan Democrat October 31, 1888

When J. N. Uptam's fish tug went out last Saturday, after the severe storm, to lift, they found that a portion of the nets amounting to several hundred dollars were gone. And those remaining were full of seaweed.

Cheboygan Daily Tribune, May 21, 1934

John King , well known commercial fisherman, died here on Saturday at 209 North B Street from a stroke at the age of 84. He was known as one of the oldest fishermen on the Great Lakes. He and his fish boat, the Dora, were well known among local commercial fishermen. He was born May 16, 1850, in Kenosha, Wisconsin. Most of his life was spent in the marine activities. He was in the Coast Guard at a Wisconsin station for three years. He spent two years in the fishing business on the Atlantic Ocean. He lived for over 20 years on Beaver Island. He came to Cheboygan about 19 years ago.

The 1884 City Directory
INCLUDED THE FOLLOWING
FISHERMEN

John Corlett	George Cortes
Ross McCarty	Malcolm Matheson
Louie N Plant	John Riggs
Paul Simons	Frank Smith
Edward Tolsma	Stephen F Tolsma
Ed Carrow	Andrew Trombley

The location where these fishermen placed their nets was given in an 1887 U. S. Commission of Fish and Fisheries Report. A survey was made along the entire coastline of the Great Lakes, as well as along the ocean coastline. Excerpts from this report, which pertain to fishing in the Straits region, are given below.

The first important gill-net ground west of Detour Passage extends from Strong's Island, about sixteen miles in a southeasterly direction, to and about Spectacle Reef. The water is very deep in the southern part of this ground, in some places approaching three hundred fathoms, but about Spectacle Reef and near shore it is of course comparatively shallow, although in some spots, in very close proximity to the former, from forty to sixty fathoms may be found. The nature of the bottom differs very much from different parts of the ground, but mud, sand, and rock predominate. This ground has the reputation of being exhausted at the present time, and very little fishing is prosecuted on it.

20 *Cheboygan Democrat*, September 13, 1883
21 *Cheboygan Daily Tribune*, May 21, 1934

Some little gill-net fishing is carried on between Mackinac and Round Islands and to the westward of the latter, and also for a short distance along the shore north of Point Saint Ignace. These grounds are frequented, however, only by fishermen using but ten or twenty nets, who sell their fish to the steamers and hotels.

The whole northern shore of Lake Michigan, from the Straits to Seul Choix Point, is one vast gill net ground. It is considered one of the best on the lake. Fishing is carried on at a distance of ten, fifteen, or even twenty miles from land. The favorite grounds are southeast of Point Patterson, between Simmons's Reef and Point Epoufette, westward of Saint Helena Shoal, and southwest of Point aux Chenes. On the first-mentioned ground the bottom is chiefly sandy, but on the others the sand is largely mingled with rock and clay. The depth of water does not exceed sixteen or eighteen fathoms at any point, the average depth being considerably less. The boats fishing on these shoals belong at different points along the north shore and at Mackinac. Many Beaver Island boats also fish here, especially on the southern borders of the grounds.

Between Detour Passage and the Straits of Mackinac there are but two permanent fisheries. One is located at Strong's Island, the most easterly of the Les Cheneaux islands. Seven pounds were employed here in 1879. It is a very important and productive fishery. The second is situated at the head of Saint Martin's Bay, where, in 1879, six shoal water pounds were established.

On the north shore of Lake Michigan, west of the Straits of Mackinac, we find the most extensive and profitable fishing-grounds of the lake, as regards both pound-net and gill-net fishing. The first pound-nets to the eastward are those established at Gross Cap Point, eight and one-half miles west of Point Saint Ignace. The "six-mile sand-beach," further to the west, at Point aux Chenes, is a noted and productive ground. From this point westward we find pound-nets scattered along the shoals at Point Epoufette, Biddle Point, Mille Coquins Point, Point Patterson, and Scott's Point. Between Point Saint Ignace and Scott's Point, a distance of less than fifty miles, there were located in 1879 more than sixty pound-nets, and about seventy-five gill net boats also fished there.

Along this coast the pound-nets are all set quite close inshore, and generally each man's nets in a line. Prominent exceptions, however, are furnished in the case of two firms, each of which sets two nets on a shoal about seven miles south of Mille Coquins Point. Another firm has nets set in deep water about nine miles south-southwest of Point Epoufette, and two more are set a short distance west of Simmons's Reef, and about the same distance directly south of Point Epoufette. The latter two are among the most profitable pound-nets on this shore.

The shores of the Beaver Islands present very favorable conditions for the establishment of pound-nets, and they have therefore become the center of an extensive fishery. In 1879 thirty-two pound nets were in use at the islands, sixteen of which were located on the east side of the large island which gives its name to the group, and constituted the Sand Bay fishery. Of the remaining nets, two were located at the north shore of Hog Island, two at High Island, and the others at the north, east, and south shores of Beaver Island.

At Beaver Harbor, near Saint James post office, in the northeastern portion of Beaver Island, there is an extensive seining-reach, where, in 1879, two seines were employed. Off Gull Island, the most westerly of the Beaver group, is a noted gill-net ground. The island is owned by three persons, each of whom employs two boats in the fishery.

Important gill-net grounds extend from Charlevoix to Cross Village. The outer limit of the ground is about 4 miles from shore. Fishing is carried on at all seasons. The maximum depth of water is about 45 fathoms. The bottom is rocky and clayey. Off the east shore of North Manitou Island there is a small gill-net ground, which is visited by three fishermen. The water varies from thirty to sixty fathoms in depth. The bottom is clay. Due east of South Manitou Island, a distance of about three miles, there is one pound net station. Gill-net grounds extend from about South Fox Island to the outer limit of the great sandy shoal which exists there. The fishermen fish on the north and east shores of Fox Island in summer, but in winter usually fish most extensively on the west shore. Between the two islands two pound-nets are located.

Cross Village to Lake Huron

Between Cross Village and Point Waugoshance [today part of Wilderness State Park] there are a few pound-net stations, but in 1879 the fishery proved almost a failure. The shore is too rocky and exposed for successful fisheries of this sort. Two pound nets are set to the northward of Waugoshance, a few miles west of old Fort Mackinac.

Straits of Mackinac to Alpena

Very little fishing is done on the section of coast between Point Waugoshance and Thunder Bay Point. In Hammond's Bay, near the eastern entrance of the Straits of Mackinac, there are eleven pound nets.[22]

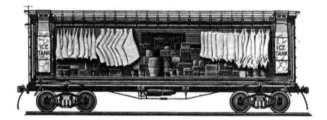

Illustration of an early refrigerated car. Ice was dropped through the roof into the chambers at each end of the car. Roof vents caused the air to circulate and keep the contents cooled. Locally, the fish was packed in ice in wooden fish boxes. These boxes were stacked in the box cars and shipped overnight to markets in Chicago and the east.

Fish Box.

22 *1887 U. S. Commission of Fish and Fisheries*, Report available, google.com/books

A dramatic change occurred in the 1880's when the railroads came to Cheboygan. Fish could now be shipped out of Cheboygan by rail, to Chicago or Detroit, and arrive fresh the next morning. One to five refrigerated railroad cars of fish were shipped from Mackinaw City daily.[23] Mackinac Island and St. Helena Island began losing business to Cheboygan and Mackinaw City, as fishermen chose to ship by rail rather than waiting for the next steamship. Large quantities of ice were placed in the box cars to make them refrigerated. This need for ice gave further employment to the fishermen. When the lakes froze over, the fishermen had another job. They went out and cut blocks of ice, which were hauled to shore and stored in sawdust, which was abundant in Cheboygan. A description of this ice gathering was found on the internet, written by Bob Baird in 1993.[24] He was friends with Don Bell, son of Ross Bell, of Bell's Fishery.

Ice was harvested in the wintertime from Joe Mel's Bay, a large bay carved by nature into the east bank of the Cheboygan River two miles above the Lincoln Avenue Bridge. It was a bay in which we teenage boys swam during the summer believing it to be above any of the sewer outlets we could see sticking out of the banks of the river below the bridge. At the east end of the bay, about 20 feet from the water's edge (in the summer time) stood a three-story unpainted wood shed, without windows or roof, but with a single 3 foot slit top to bottom in the wall facing the bay. It was an ice house.

In the winter, after the ice reached 12 inches thick, a workman using a long, two man, lumberman's crosscut saw with one handle removed, cut a 3 foot wide channel into the ice. The channel commenced as close to the ice house as possible then extended out into the bay. One end of a wooden trough was placed in the channel near the shore, the other end of the trough was raised and placed in the slit in the wall.

Eight foot long "logs" of ice were sawn from the ice alongside the channel, then floated into the channel. They were moved by logger's pike poles and were eased into the trough. A motorized conveyor belt built into the trough caught the bottom edge of the log of ice and raised it into the ice house where men slid it across the floor to build a layer of ice. When one layer was complete, the trough was raised to build the next. The incoming blocks of ice were positioned to leave an empty perimeter around the room. This perimeter was later filled with sawdust of which there was plenty in Cheboygan since the city's lumbering days produced a 12 acre sawdust pile lying not far from the bay and was free for the taking. Layer by layer the ice logs were stored inside the ice house, the perimeter filled with sawdust. A topping of sawdust was added. In summer the "logs" were dug out of the sawdust and slid down into delivery wagons where they were scored and cut into 25, 50 or 100 lb. blocks

23 Wendy O'Neil, *This Land and Man, An Historical Look at the Use of Land and Natural Resources in the Inland Water Route Region of Northern Lower Michigan,* U of M Biological Station, December 1977.
24 *"Life Before TV"* by Bob Baird, http/homepage.ma.com//phyzman//LBTV

Ice cutting at Joemel's Bay in Mackinaw City. The ice was sawn into ribbons and then cut into blocks 2 feet square and about 12 inches thick. The ice was hand sawed to free each length of block. Each row of ice was removed with an adz and then floated to the conveyer. They used a pike pole to move the blocks of ice. In the early days the ice blocks were hauled to shore by horse and sleigh. In later days electric conveyor belts and trucks made the work easier, but still dangerous.

Photos courtesy Stuart Ross Bell, grandson of Ross Bell

Cheboygan residents enjoyed many activities on Lake Huron, including horse-drawn sled racing and ice boating.

Collection of the Historical Society of Cheboygan County, Inc.(3)

The development of the steam fish tugs and later gas- powered tugs made fishing easier. When fishermen had to rely on wind power, they had to be close to their fishing grounds. They would go out in the morning, raise their nets , place the fish in their boats, reset the nets, and return to shore before dark. They had to keep their eyes on the weather, watching for squalls and sudden storms. Even more frustrating was getting ready to return to shore with a boatload of fish and having the wind die down as evening approached. The fish had to be cleaned and iced or salted down before they could spoil or the catch would be ruined. Also, a fisherman didn't want to spend the night in the middle of Lake Michigan in a small Mackinaw boat!

When steam and gas-powered fish tugs were introduced, they allowed the fishermen to go further distances and gave them more leeway with the weather. They could fish a little longer and not have to spend a lot of time tacking a sailboat back and forth in order to return to shore. These boats were also able to hold heavier loads of fish. They were constructed with a small cabin enabling the crew to get out of the weather. Some tugs had a roof over the deck area. The tugs also allowed more space for a larger crew to pull and set the nets. Some had power winches that were used to lift nets.

The 1906 *Cheboygan Daily Tribune* noted this about Captain D. E. Dues.

Captain Dues had 700 nets in continuous service. Of these 300 are 1,000 feet long each, and 400 are 500 feet long each, making a total of 500,000 feet, or about 94 2/3 miles in nets for catching lake fish. These consist of white fish, trout and long jaws, and Lake Michigan as well as Lake Huron are fished to obtain the finny beauties that Captain Dues ships to the Detroit Market. Besides the catch from his own nets he buys from a number of catchers, taking their entire product, for which he pays the highest price. During a season Captain Dues ships 5,000 boxes of fish, each box containing from 150 to 200 pounds. The tug, Sea Fox, a first class craft, is a part of the outfit, the warehouses and landing embracing a frontage of 125 feet. Ice houses that supply all the needs of the business occupy a part of the warehouse. Captain Dues is one of the best known sea-faring men on Lake Huron. He has lived in Cheboygan for many years, where his business relations have contributed to advance the city's well-being in no insignificant measure.

1914 POLK DIRECTORY LISTINGS
Booth Fishery, David Trumpour, supt., 1st St WestFred Chapman, wholesale fish, waterfront between State & 6th

LEVI AMO (IRENE) 729 S. MAIN
OLIVER ARCHAMBEAU (LINDA) 203 N B
FRED BELLROSE (MAUDE) 117 N C.
CHARLES CHEVALIER (JULIA) 611 ANTOINE
WM COOLEY (FREDA) 224 E STATE
FRANK CARROW (SARAH) 411 ANTOINE
OLIVER CARROW (OLIVINE) 17 FIRST
MAX FROEHLICH 976 MACKINAC
CHRISTOPHER KELLY 508 MACKINAC
HENRY KELLEY (DORA) 508 MACKINAC
(FISHERMAN FOR CHAPMAN)
OLIVER KELLY L(ROSE) 508 MACKINAC
ERNEST LaBOHN (ANNA) 200 S B
LOUIS PEETS (ALICE) 729 N MAIN
HENRY ROOT (LENA) 825 DUNCAN
PETER SILVERTHORN 311 DIVISION
JOHN THOMAS (MATILDA) 305 CLEVELAND
HARRY McCASH (VIOLET) NETMAKER 110 N B
WALTER McCASH (NETMAKER) 110 N B
JAMES McCASH (ARVILLA) FISHERMAN 121 S C

25 *Cheboygan Tribune*, September 20, 1906 edition

THE BLUE BOOK OF AMERICAN SHIPPING, 1911
FISHING TUGS OPERATING OUT OF CHEBOYGAN

DAVID A TROMPOUR—GAS TUG	*CASTANET*	13 TON, BUILT IN 1909 35 FT X 11 X 4
A.D. SHAWL—GAS TUG—	*RED WING*	10 TON
KENNEDY BROS.—GAS TUG	*BERTHA M.*	14 TON
W.B. CHAPIN—GAS TUG	*MYRTLE*	
F.S. CHAPMAN—GAS TUG	*PUP*	14 TON
JACK R. HILBORN—	*CARRIE E*	BUILT 1907 39FT X 10

OTHER FISHING TUGS WERE THE FOLLOWING:

CAPTAIN D.E. DUES	*SEA FOX*	
WILLIAM LeBLANC	*LORRAINE*	
ROBBINS CO.	*AMERICAN GIRL*	
LANCEWICZ & McCASH	*MINNOW*	
JOSEPH SCHLEY	*BUM*	
OLI HOILAND	*BERTHA*	GAS, BUILT 1930,
ALBERT LANNOO	*CLEO M.*	BUILT 1932
DICK BROWNSON	*SUSIE B.*	
DICK BROWNSON	*LINDA B.*	
OLMSTEAD & BACKUS fishboat	*TRITONIA*	OPERATED BY FRANK BLAY
MIKE WHITE	*KEEGO*	
REUBEN CORROW	*MARY C.*	

The "Sea Fox" belonging to D.E. Dues.   Collection of the Historical Society of Cheboygan County, Inc.

The "MYRTLE" belonging to W.B.Chapin.   Collection of the Historical Society of Cheboygan County, Inc.

Another prominent local fisherman was W.B. Chapin.

Mr. Chapin owns a staunch gasoline launch, in which he makes voyages to distant parts of Lake Michigan and Lake Huron, returning with the white fish and trout, that are so highly prized in cities throughout the eastern and central states. Mr. Chapin has been a fisherman upon the Great Lakes for many years. He owns a very complete outfit for the work, including extensive netting, besides his 5-ton launch. That makes his business of no small importance in the trade he follows. In summer he takes on an average of six boxes a day from his nets. Mr. Chapin resides in Cheboygan with his family, owning a comfortable home in this city.[26]

Companies listed as operating in Cheboygan were R.J. Bell, A.D. Shawl, Robbins Corp. and E.W Eddy. The *Cheboygan Democrat* reported:

A HEAVY CATCH OF FISH
The Fishing Tugs Bring in Tons of Them Wednesday Night.

Wednesday evening, the local fish tugs, brought in one of the largest catches of the season and the fish were the largest run they have had this year. Monster whitefish, weighing eight, ten and twelve pounds were in the nets by the score and averaging it up, the catch was the biggest of the season. Ordinarily by the time the tugs reach the docks with their load, the crew aboard have the catch all cleaned, but Wednesday evening, it was midnight before they finished cleaning and packing the fish for shipment. The Hart line steamer took out a big load from the local fish warehouses Thursday. The fishermen are paid 14 cents a pound for the big whitefish and the supply never equals the demand. The catch Wednesday unloaded by the local boats was nearly five tons.[27]

26 *Cheboygan Tribune*, September 20,1906 edition
27 *Cheboygan Democrat*, November 1, 1907

Above, the "American Girl" from 1939 Cheboygan Tribune. Below, before being rebuilt in 1931 to add 21 tons net cargo weight.
Collection of the Historical Society of Cheboygan County, Inc.(above)
Historical Collection of the Great Lakes Collection,
Bowling Green State University. (below)

The Robbins Fish Company of Chicago had a Cheboygan plant. They bought fish from the Purvis Brothers Fishery of Manitoulin Island, Canada. "They owned a beautiful boat, the 'American Girl', a fish dock, and a packing shed on the river by the Coast Guard station. This boat collects lots of fish across Lake Huron and it was shipped out of Cheboygan. When the price was right other Canadian fishermen brought their catch to Cheboygan to sell." The government assigned a customs officer, Lee Osgood, to Cheboygan full time to monitor this business.[28] The *American Girl* was owned by W. M. Walker, Inc. of Chicago, and the two firms used the boat and the Robbins Fishery in Cheboygan for packing. The vessel made three trips a week to Burnt Island, Cockburn Island, and the Manitoulin Islands. Captain Carl Comps averaged 12 tons per trip. Charles W. Linklater managed the fishery operations in Cheboygan. This boat made its first trip to Cheboygan in April, 1936, after almost being crushed by ice in the Straits. This tug replaced the "*Edna A.*"

The Booth Fishery was a major influence on commercial fishing in Cheboygan. Alfred Booth was born in Glastonbury, England, and immigrated to the United States in 1848. By 1850 he had opened a small fish store in Chicago. He was soon in the wholesale fish business, and by the end of the century he was buying fish from many locations on Lake Superior and Lake Michigan. He sent steamers to pick up fish from individuals; built a freezer plant in Escanaba; and had agents in many cities. He also employed several steam vessels on which he hired crews for fishing. By 1898 this giant "fish trust" corporation employed 5,000 men and combined 24 companies throughout the Great Lakes and Canada.[29] He did most of the wholesale business in Lake Michigan and Lake Superior. Although Booth lived in Chicago and did not personally do business in Cheboygan, he had a wholesale packing plant here, as well as at Mackinaw City and St. Ignace.

Over the years Booth had several local agents: Archibald Newton, Frank Campbell, David Trumpour, Ross Bell, and Ellsworth Eddy

The White Swan, owned by the Oriental Mills Trading Co. from 1925 to 1946, transported a variety of cargo. It was later stranded on Aux Galeta Reef, Lake Michigan, November 30, 1956, a total loss.
Historical Collection of the Great Lakes Collection,
Bowling Green State University.

28 Gearhart, Cliff, *The Fish Peddler*, Avery , 1987, p. 69.
29 *New York Times*, June 19, 1898

AGENT ARCHIBALD NEWTON

Archibald P. Newton was the first of Booth's agents about whom we know some details. Newton was born in Hamburg, New York, on July 8, 1814, and died at the age of 78 in Cheboygan. He moved to the St. Helena Island area when he was in his 20s. It was there that Archibald and his brothers, Wilson and Obadiah, built a dock, a supply store, a house, and established a business with the fishermen of lower Lake Michigan.[30] He purchased St Helena Island from William Belote in 1853, and the brothers developed a fuel and supply stop for passenger, cargo and fishing vessels. Various accounts of Beaver Island history list Newton as a leader in the group of fishermen who came to drive the Mormons off Beaver Island after Jesse Strang was murdered. Newton acquired the property of Seul Choix Point, and they fished between

Archibald and Cornelia Newton

there and St. Helena. His obituary states, "there was not an old settler from the Soo to Green Bay who did not know him and few who did not call him friend. Possessed of a rugged forceful nature he was always a leader. He was a shrewd businessman, and amassed considerable wealth in the fish business, merchandising, real estate, and many other affairs in which he was interested." [31] He

Temple Emery, left, at dock in Cheboygan River.

Collection of the Historical Society of Cheboygan County, Inc.

---

30 Elizabeth Whitney Williams, *Children of the Sea*, 1905, p. 12.
31 Obituary, *Cheboygan Democrat* 1892

was married twice and at his death left a widow, Cornelia Allaire (his second wife), and six children by his first wife. A nephew, Wilson Newton, was the namesake of Newton Township in Mackinac County. The 1939 Jubilee edition of the Cheboygan Tribune relates:

> A.P. Newton had one of the first docks on the west side of the river. It was located where Blake's Foundry now stands, and was built about 1866. . . A sand bar blocked entrance of deep water craft, and in fact only shallow draft boats could navigate in the river. Most of the boats to come here in the early days, landed at Duncan. The first steam boats were wood burning craft. Cheboygan was a fueling station for them. Piers were built in the Straits and wood was taken out in scows and piled on the piers for the vessels. . . A. P. Newton also had a pier opposite the mouth of the river, about a half mile off shore. Boats bound for Chicago and Buffalo stopped there to take on wood.[32]

Between 1872 and 1876 Archibald Newton was elected president of the village of Cheboygan four times. On December 26, 1871, at age 56, he married Cornelia Allaire who was 26.   By 1873 Archibald, his brother Carl, and other businessmen had established a factory on Mullett Lake to extract juice from the bark of hemlock trees to be used in tanning leather. It was known as the Newton, Ellis and Buckingham factory. Their fac-

Home of Archibald Newton and Cornelia Allaire, located at 337 Dresser Street, Cheboygan. This home is on the State Historic Register. In 1871 Newton built the two-story Italiante structure at a cost of $8,500.

Collection of the Historical Society of Cheboygan County, Inc.

tory burnt in 1875 and they rebuilt it a year later.[33] They were soon producing 900 tons of extract per year. Their office was at Main and Second Street (Mackinaw Ave). Senator Prentiss Brown wrote that "The Newtons, dominant merchants and fishermen, were by far the most prominent family in this part of the country." [34] By the time of his death in 1892 Newton even had his own wharf on the west bank of the Cheboygan River.

There was a humorous story in the *Cheboygan Democrat* about A.P. Newton, when he was 77, a year before his death.

A drummer [salesman] went into A P. Newton's store Monday and as business was dull, it was not long before he was engaged in a hot debate with the old gentleman on politics. One thing brought on another until the drummer thought he would clinch the argument with a bluff and offered to bet $5,000 Harrison would carry New York. Then he hurriedly got out of the store. Newton pondered a

32 *Cheboygan Daily Tribune* 50th anniversary Jubilee edition, 1939.
33 Guth, Fred and Eleanore, *A Bit About Mullett Lake Village*, 1975, p 2-16.
34 *Michigan Assessor*, April 1984, p. 3.

minute on the situation, and the more he pondered the madder he got, and in less than five minutes he locked up the store and made a bee line for the bank. Mr. Newton's personal appearance may lead callow drummers to infer that his head was full of hay seed, but drummers don't always size up a country merchant correctly and he didn't this time, for the bank account was solid, and the hay seed was only sand.

After getting a wad of greenbacks as big as a man's leg, he started out to find the rash drummer, and after a long search he did succeed in finding him at his hotel. Drawing the wad, he announced that he would make the landlord stakeholder, but the drummer crawfished at once. The old man was disgusted, and dropped his figures to $100 still the drummer would not bet. Then the old man got mad and talked to the drummer as he used to talk to the Mormon pirates after having a fish boat stolen in the old days, finally ending up with an emphatic assertion of his belief that the drummer was not worth $5 on earth. The clerk came to the rescue of the guest, and ordered the wrathy old man out, but he hotly replied that if the clerk did not shut up he'd foreclose a mortgage in the morning. But finally he quieted down and everything was lovely. The drumming fraternity should fight shy of A.P. Newton, when they have to back their arguments with bluff.

The next known manager of the Cheboygan Booth Fishery was Frank Campbell. Campbell came to Cheboygan from Charlevoix in the spring of 1907 to take over the operations of the Booth Fishery. He was soon followed by David Trumpour in 1909. Trumpour was born in Wellington, Ontario, on February 3, 1855, the third of ten children. He worked in his father's fishing business, starting on his own when he was twenty- three. David Trumpour married his wife, Hulda Esseltyn, at Cape Vincent, New York, in 1877. He moved to Bay City

in 1883 and then moved to Mackinaw City in 1895. Trumpour returned to Bay City where he became the manager for the Booth Company. In October of 1909 he came to Cheboygan, where he reorganized the operations of the local Booth Fishery and doubled its trade. They had a daughter who taught in the Cheboygan schools and a son Harold. He was a member of the Masons, Shriners, Odd Fellows and Elks. David Trumpour died in 1940.

In "*A History of Northern Michigan and Its People*" it was stated;[35]

He (Trumpour) has a large fleet of boats that go out into Lake Huron and up through the waters around the northern islands on regular fishing expeditions and bring in very considerable supplies for the work of the company and its dealings in the markets. During the year 1910 the company caught in these waters and shipped out of Cheboygan 1,250,000 pounds of fish.

Ross Bell was the next manager of the Cheboygan Booth Fishery until he opened his own fishery. Ross J. Bell[36] was born in Belmont County, Ohio, on August 3, 1875. He came to Michigan when he was 14, working on the railroads as a telegraph operator. He attended Ferris Institute. He came to Cheboygan and became interested in commercial fishing. He worked at the Lake Superior Fish Company, which was located where the Eddy Fishery was later located. About 1922 he started his own business, the R.J. Bell Fishery on Water Street. Ross Bell died February 20, and his son, Don Bell, continued the business, moving to Mackinaw City and operating Bell's Fishery there, near the City Marina. Donald Bell was born on July 19, 1922, and passed away on Tuesday, January 6, 2009.

---

35 Perry Powers, *A History of Northern Michigan and Its People*, Vol. III, 1912, p. 996
36 *Cheboygan Daily Tribune* February 20, 1947.

Bell's Fishery—notice the empty fish boxes billed on the dock.

Photo courtesy Stuart Ross Bell

The *Cheboygan Democrat* gave this report about local fishing.

In Ross Bell's talk to the Rotarians yesterday noon he stated that there were fourteen hundred tons of fish shipped from Cheboygan every year, and that the amount paid to the local express company for express alone would amount to over seventy thousand dollars per year from this city alone. One never realizes the enormity of our fishing industry until such figures are presented by one who knows, and with this amount of money being paid out and changing hands here one can readily realize what that business means to the community and how essential it is that we foster the same by every possible means at our command.[37]

Large sturgeon hoisted at Bell's Fishery.

Collection of Historical Society of Cheboygan County, Inc.

Ross Bell had a huge icehouse situated on a little bay off the Cheboygan River. They had a long, permanent conveyor that literally marched the huge cakes of blue ice right up into the icehouse. Men placed layer upon layer of ice there. During the shipping season, mornings were spent digging ice out of the icehouse, transporting it a

37 *Cheboygan Democrat*, May 18, 1922

Cygnet at Eddy Fishery.   Collection of Historical Society of Cheboygan County, Inc.

couple of miles to the packing shed, washing off the sawdust and then throwing the split up chunks into the crusher to fill the ice bin. This was a necessary routine before packing almost every day when the boats came in. This was the scene at the R.J. Bell Fishery for many years up until RJ's death on February 20, 1947."[38]

Ellsworth "Pudge" Eddy was the next manager of the Cheboygan Booth Fishery. Eddy came from St. Ignace in 1921 and ran the Booth Fishery which was located on the west bank of the Cheboygan river, at the foot of First Street. Ellsworth relocated the fishery further north, across from the turning basin of the coast Guard cutter, Mackinaw. He bought the business from Booth Fishery in 1936 and changed the name to E. W . Eddy Fishery.[39] Ellsworth Eddy[40] was born June 7, 1884, on St. Hel-

The Clayt and Cygnet laid up with a barge for the winter.
Collection of Historical Society of Cheboygan County, Inc.

ena Island. He was the son of William and Effie Chapman Eddy.[41] Ellsworth Eddy died August 23, 1967, at the University Hospital in Ann Arbor.

---

38 Gearhart, p. 143.
39 Gearhart, p. 69.
40 *Cheboygan Daily Tribune,* August 23, 1967
41 Ellsworth Eddy was married February 19, 1912, to Violet Jarvis. They lived at St. Ignace until 1921, when they moved to Cheboygan. He had two sons, Lyle and Postmaster Glenn Eddy, two daughters—Mrs. Charles Potter (Lorraine) and Mrs. Norman Beaudoin (Joyce). Lorraine was married to Charles Potter, a Representative and later Senator for Michigan. Cheboygan Catholic High students will remember Joyce as "Mrs. B" the school secretary.

The large, barnlike structure on the left is the Shawl Fishery building located on the Cheboygan River. It was later used by the Gearhart Fishery where fish was prepared and packed in ice for shipping by rail.

Photo ©Johnson Studio, from collection of Historical Society of Cheboygan County, Inc.

Arthur D. Shawl had a large fish business just north of State Street. He used the dock first built by Nelson and Bullen in 1876. Shawl fished for mullett in the Straits area to supply the Jewish market in the east. "He had as many as twelve trap net boats fishing for him. The price wasn't high except during Jewish holidays, but the tonnage was great."[42] The 1939 Polk Directory lists Arthur as living at 456 S. Huron (the large brick home corner of S. Huron and Taylor) with his wife Helene and sons, Philip and Wallace, who were also fishermen. Another son, Cecil, lived on "C" St. A 1937 Cheboygan Tribune article said this of Shawl:

> Arthur D. Shawl is one of the best known commercial fishermen of the Great Lakes region. His principal fishery is in Cheboygan, but he also has a branch fishery at Fairport, Wisconsin, over 150 miles away and another at Hammonds Bay, near Cheboygan. Shawl operates 19 boats and five trucks. His fishermen set nets in Lake Michigan, Lake Huron, Potagannissing Bay, and Green Bay. Tiny James Island, only 30 acres in size and dwarfed by nearby Drummond Island is one of his centers of operations. Shawl owns James Island. He also has an icing station at Drummond Island.
>
> Fish from his northern operations are taken to the mainland at Gould City and Detour. From there they are brought by truck to his fishery at Cheboygan. Shawl operates nine months a year, including one month spent in getting ready before the actual fishing commences. Shawl's transportation relay by which a trout caught in Potagannissing Bay, for example, would reach a hungry housewife in New York, includes by boat to Detour, from there by truck to Cheboygan, via St. Ignace and Mackinaw City where the trucks cross the Straits of Mackinac on a state ferry, and from Cheboygan to New York by railroad express refrigerated car.

42 Gearhart, p. 70.

A news item told of a conflict Shawl had with Michigan Conservation Officers.

A.D. Shawl, of Cheboygan, was arrested Thursday evening at the St. Ignace ferry dock when his truck was found by the officers to contain 826 pounds of undersized pike perch taken from the waters near Drummond Island. There were also a muskellunge, which are unlawful to take by nets. He pleaded guilty and paid a fine of $25 and costs of $6.85. The fish were being trucked from Drummond to Cheboygan for packing. Conservation officers pointed out that it is unlawful to take perch from the Great Lakes less than six inches in length by hook and line and not less than nine inches in nets by commercial fishermen. The legal length for pike perch taken by commercial fishermen is 16 and one–half inches.[44]

After 1945, Shawl's now-closed business location was rented to Gearhart Fisheries to use as a packing shed. Gearhart was bringing fish from the Paradise and Two Heart River area in Luce County, processing it in Cheboygan, and shipping it out by rail.

"In 1936 about 200 men were employed in the Cheboygan fisheries. These included those who set nets, operated boats, cleaned and worked at the packing plants, the owners, and truck drivers. The fisheries, land, boats, nets, trucks, and other equipment owned and used in Cheboygan's fishing industry were valued at about $400,000. They shipped about $450,000 worth of fish at 15 cents per pound. A.D. Shawl shipped 360 tons, Bell's Fishery 350 tons, Robbins Corporation 350 tons, E.W. Eddy 300 tons, and the others about

Transferring fish.
Collection of Historical Society of Cheboygan County, Inc.

100 tons. They had a fleet of forty boats fishing out of Cheboygan." [45]

Next we can look at some of the fishermen who went out in their boats to collect the fish from the nets. The 1939 Golden Jubilee edition of the Cheboygan Daily Tribune had this to say about the early days in Cheboygan.

The Corlette and Trombley families were among the first to conduct commercial fishing operations out of the Cheboygan harbor. John Corlett fished at Point Au Sable, aided by his sons, Maynard, Charles, Dan and Claude. Andrew Trombley was one of the fishing pioneers. William Robarge was another of the early fishermen. A.P. Newton conducted a fish wholesale business. Charles Brannock, Wm. Bartholomew, Ligente, Paquin, Jacob Sammons, Moses Horne, Jake Wilson, and Mickeljohn cooper shops engaged in manufacture of fish barrels.

John Corlett came from Ohio to Beaver Island where he fished off Cable's Dock. He then moved to Cheboygan with his son-in-law, Andrew Trombley.[46] Trombley's obituary[47] of April 26,

43 *Cheboygan Daily Tribune*, 1937
44 *Cheboygan Daily Tribune* July 12, 1934.
45 1939 Jubilee Edition of *Cheboygan Daily Tribune*.
46 Elizabeth Williams, *A Child of the Sea Among the Mormons*, 1905, p. 187.
47 *Cheboygan Democrat*, May 1, 1912.

Photo of Gustav Nordberg, born 1859 in Norway, died 1948 in Cheboygan. This is a typical fish station with a dock, fish shed and reels to dry nets.
Collection of the Historical Society of Cheboygan County, Inc.

his nephew John Hoiland and a boarder, Gustav Larsen who immigrated from Voss, Norway. Another Norwegian fisherman was Gustave Nordberg. Ernest Joseph Lannoo (1881-1954) was an immigrant from Belgium. The Schley family came from Schutterwalt, Germany. Most of the others came through Canada, including Last, Peets, Phillips, and Adams and Hilborn. The fishing industry was easily entered by recent immigrants. It was possible for them to get their own boat and nets and then sell to the wholesale companies.

1912, gives us some more details of his life. He was born at Bay City May 9, 1843, grew up and entered the fishing business. Through this business he met Margaret Corlett (born November 1849 in Concord, Ohio, died January 1927) and was married to her in 1868. They lived at St. James on Beaver Island for several years and left there in 1871 for Cheboygan. They were involved in the fishing business in Cheboygan and then turned to general work. He was city commissioner for many years. They had ten children: Mrs. E.E. Andrews of Fostoria, Ohio, Andrew of Erie, Pennsylvania, Mrs. Andrew Morrow, and Hazel, Laura, and Alice of Cheboygan. Alice became a teacher at Central School and married Howard Scott.[48]

Fishermen mentioned in Cliff Gearhart's book, "The Fish Peddler" included Bob Last, Jim Phillips, Louis Peets, Frank Peets, Charles "Babe" Adams, Henry LaPlaunt, Pete LaPlaunt, Jack Hilborn, Joe Schley, Louis Brooks, Oll Hoiland and Ernest Lannoo. Many of the fishermen were related by family ties and worked together, as in the case of Oll Hoiland, his brother Louis S. Hoiland,

Another business which benefited from the fish industry was the Cheboygan Novelty Turning Works. This business was established in 1882 and in 1906 G.A. Hugill was the proprietor. They employed 25 men and operated all year. The turning works made floats and buoys for fishermen. They also made handles, toys, druggist and grocers' boxes, life rafts, spindles, and other turned wooden goods and novelties. The company was located on South Main and had 300 feet on the street and their property extended to their docks on the Cheboygan River. They bought birch, basswood, cedar, and poplar which was brought in by tugs as well as horse teams. They had a saw mill, picket mills, and turning machines. They had a 50 horse power boiler and engine to furnish power.[50]

In the 1800's, sturgeon caused a lot of damage to gill nets and they were considered a nuisance fish. They were killed when caught so as to lessen future net damage. However, they were not considered a marketable fish until their roe became popular as caviar. Heavy fishing, particularly during spawning seasons began to affect the number

48 *Cheboygan Democrat* January 6, 1927
49 Gearhart, Cliff, *The Fish Peddler*, Avery , 1987
50 *Cheboygan Tribune* September 24, 1906.

Independent Fish Dealer.
Steamer Ogontz.

J. R. HILBORN

Producer and Wholesale
Dealer in

All kinds of
Fresh Water Fish

Fish House and Office Next South
McArthur Dock.
Telephone No. 110.
CHEBOYGAN, MICH.

Novelty Turning Works building.

of other fish. One fisherman in Wisconsin reported taking thirty-five 100 pound kegs of white-fish eggs to make caviar.[51] Many other fishermen on the Great Lakes were doing the same. As the white fish declined during this time, Michigan and Wisconsin began enacting "seasons" for fishing. By 1885 the states began to regulate the size of mesh in the fishermen's nets. A larger hole would allow small fish to escape and grow up.

The pound or trap nets introduced about 1865, in which fish are taken while on the shores and shoals spawning, and at all other times, have nearly ruined the business, and if it were not for the artificial hatching and annual planting of fry, there would be very few fish left in the lakes. Most of the catch now is packed in ice and shipped fresh to Chicago and other points; few are salted. The business can only be revived by national legislation of a protective character, as the states cannot control the "high seas." [52]

Senator Ming, from Cheboygan, introduced legislation in 1907 to help local fishermen. He proposed a local license for every steamboat, tug, or launch used for fishing at $10 a year‑‑$25 if they had a steam lifter. A non-resident fishermen license was $100 per year, $200 if they had a steam lifter for nets. This was in part to keep Canadian fishermen from coming into American waters, and also to keep the "trust" companies, such as Booth, from overfishing and running local fishermen out of business. This issue was finally resolved through a treaty between Canada and the United States government. The treaty was the beginning of limitations on pound nets, the location of nets, and use of trap nets.

51 *Cheboygan Democrat* Feb 17, 1911
52 www.michiganfoodways.org/cheboygan/foodways.html

Some local fishermen; Charles Corlette, J.R. Hilborn and J.E. Olmstead, three of Cheboygan's prominent fishermen in company with Attorney C.S. Reilley (of Cheboygan) were in Grand Rapids last week conferring with Senator William Alden Smith relative to proposed changes in fishing regulations . . . .the boys returned home very much encouraged since their talk with the senator, and feel that they will treat them fairly and that the waters they are used to fishing in will not be affected by any fool legislation that will injure the industry.[53]

In his book, "*The Fish Peddler,*" Cliff Gearhart reflected on the many causes in the decrease of commercial fishing. He noted that when fishing became unproductive the fishermen switched to other jobs. In 1912 the State of Michigan planted rainbow smelt in Crystal Lake. They planted 16,400,000 eggs and later planted 37,000,000 into the St. Mary's River. These were meant to feed game fish. The smelt soon flourished and the natural fish, especially herring, declined. In 1932 the lampreys reached the Great Lakes system where they attacked lake trout, whitefish, walleye, and mullett. Mercury, D.D.T., chlordane, and P.C.B. contaminants have caused the public to rethink how much Great Lakes fish they eat. Mining runoff from the taconite plant, dumped into Lake Superior, has covered spawning beds and destroyed the herring fishing in Lake Superior. A botulism scare in 1963 caused much of the public to shy away from smoked chubs. Warnings from the government suggest pregnant women and children limit their intake of Great Lakes fish. The introduction of sport fishing for steelhead, lake trout, and brown trout, have created predator fish that go after the fry of young whitefish and other commercial fish.

The DNR outlawing of gill net fishing to protect the sport fishing industry has meant no more non-Indian licenses are granted to new fishermen.

The Michigan Foodways Project stated that in 2005 more than one million pounds of whitefish were harvested in the Straits of Mackinac. In the area near St. Ignace, west of the Mackinac Bridge and stretching east to Marquette Island in the Les Cheneaux Islands and south to Cheboygan, 400,000 pounds of whitefish were harvested in 2005. The value of the local fishery was estimated at $2.2 million. When whitefish conditions were at their peak in the early 1990's the local fishery brought in an estimated $7.65 million into the community's economy.[54] The *St. Ignace News* told how researchers are concerned about new invasive species in this same area. Zebra and quagga mussels are entering the Great Lakes from ocean-going ships' ballast. They are reproducing at an enormous rate and they are taking food away from the whitefish population. The salmon population is dropping because their food source, the alewives, is down. The alewives are down because the mussels are consuming their food. The mussels are also causing problems with fishermen's nets. They are eating huge amounts of plankton which allow light to go deeper, which increases the amount of algae which is now clogging fishermen's nets. This same article also states:

All commercial fishing in the Straits area, and almost all in the state, is tribal based. Among all five tribes, the fishery supports hundreds of families through 133 licensed fishing operations, each of which may employ several people. In the Straits area, 28 operations are harvesting fish this year. Area fish markets, smokers, and restaurants are part of the network touched by the commercial fishery.[55]

---

53 *Cheboygan Democrat* Feb 17, 1911
54 www.michiganfoodways.org/cheboygan/foodways.html

Today, some of the locally caught whitefish is sold in local fish shops at Stone Bay and Bells in Mackinaw City and Mackinac Straits Fishery in St. Ignace. The rest is mostly sold to Bay Shippers which has a fleet of 14 trucks that pick up twice a week from 35 locations around the Great Lakes. This fish is taken to their terminal in Saginaw where they sort and reship to restaurants and larger markets in Detroit, Chicago, and New York.

Most of the area restaurants serve fish and many like to serve "local" white fish, walleye, trout, salmon, or perch. The chain restaurants usually serve frozen cod, tilapia, or fish sticks from elsewhere. In days past, older residents will remember all the church "Friday night" fish fries with local fish. Cheboygan had four Catholic churches and, during pre-Vatican II days, every Friday was a meatless day but fish was allowed. Many churches also had meatless days in Lent. This made a ready market for fish. This observance has declined through the years, which has lessened the market for fresh fish. Many of today's working moms don't even know how to fry fish. They prefer to heat up fish sticks and tater tots on a cookie sheet!

Today the Cheboygan River shows no sign of the early commercial fishing. The fish packing houses are gone. The small docks are replaced by steel pilings and modern marinas. Sport fishing is the best reminder we have of the former days. Many marina boats have an outrigger pole system and participate in tournament fishing. Wouldn't those fishermen of the past have loved to have the modern fish finders, GPS systems, and cell phones to communicate with those on shore? Local restaurants still serve fresh whitefish brought in from Stone Bay Fishery and Bell's. Gone are the days of going down to the dock, picking your fish as they unloaded the boats, watching them gut and wrap your fish in paper, and taking it home to fry, just hours after swimming in the Straits.

As a reminder of our town's fishing heritage you might like to try some of these recipes which were in community cookbooks of our past.

Fried Brook Trout

Recipe from Mrs. I. S. Cooper, 1896 St. James Church "Cheboygan Cook Book." Louise Cooper was the wife of druggist Isaac Cooper.

Clean, wash and dry the fish, roll lightly in very fine corn meal. Have a pan very hot, put in enough clarified dripping or butter to cover the bottom of the pan. Put in the fish when the fat is smoking hot, fry a delicate brown on one side, then turn fish and fry a delicate brown on the other side, fry until well done. A 3/4 lb. trout will take half an hour to cook. Lay for an instant upon a hot folded napkin to absorb whatever grease may adhere to the fish, range side by side in a heated dish, garnish and send to the table. Use no seasoning except salt. Always leave the head, tail, and fins on trout.

Codfish Balls

Recipe from Mrs. George P. Humphrey, 1896 "Cheboygan Cookbook", St. James Church Mrs. Humphrey's maiden name was Mary Redmond, her husband was a former Cheboygan Mayor and sold insurance and real estate.

One teacupful of codfish picked fine, 2 teacupful mashed potatoes, one egg, one small piece of butter and salt and pepper. Stir well together with a spoon, beating as light as possible. Shape into balls and roll into batter of beaten egg and bread or cracker crumbs and fry in hot lard until of a light brown.

---

55 *St. Ignace News*, Ellen Paquin,"Lake Invaders Stress EUP Commercial Fishery," March 23, 2006.
56 www.greatlakeswhitefish.com

Baked Whitefish

From Mrs. W. L. Martin, 1896 "Cheboygan Cookbook", St James Church. She was the wife of Bill Martin, part owner of Embury - Martin Mill in Cheboygan

Fill the fish with stuffing of fine bread crumbs and a little butter; sew up the fish, sprinkle with butter, pepper and salt. Dredge with flour and bake one hour, basting often, and serve with parsley or egg sauce.

R. J. Bell's Fish Recipe Book, circa 1940 Fish Chowder

2 lbs. lean fish
3 Cups sliced potatoes
2/3 cup sliced onions
2/3 cup salt pork, diced into small pieces
1 tsp. salt1/4 tsp. pepper
1 cup water

In a heavy kettle of Dutch oven, fry the salt pork to a golden brown color, add the onions and fry these to a light yellow color. Add the potatoes, sprinkle with the salt and pepper, add the cup of water and cook until the potatoes are about half done. Then add the fish (flesh side down) and cook until the potatoes are soft. Remove any skin from the fish, and break the flesh into coarse flakes.

– *Modern hint—used boned filets to lessen the possibility of bones in the soup!*

If you have a large group to feed try this wonderful recipe. It works well to cook outside, on a grill or over a campfire, if you have a big pot.

White Fish Boil Recipe

Need–large pot with a removable basket, steamer or colander. (A canning blancher works great)

Fill pot with 2 gallons water and set to boiling.
Meanwhile clean and prepare small redskin or new potatoes –about 12
Clean and peel 12 small onions.
Cut 12 white fish steaks into slices about 2 inches thick.
Put potatoes into boiling water with one cup salt (That's right—one cup!)
Boil potatoes about 20 minutes.
Add onions and boil 4 more minutes.
Add one more cup salt. (That's 2 cups total—you don't eat the juice!)
Add fish–placing in basket, colander or steamer and boil 7 to 10 minutes, until fish is firm but flakes from bone.
Remove fish, potatoes and onions from water with slotted spoon, and place in bowl to serve.
Serve with melted butter and lemon.

This recipe is traditionally cooked with bones in—but boned fish is much easier to eat. It is often prepared and served outdoors—great for a beach picnic. Just add some rolls, coleslaw and a dessert for an easy company meal.

Cheboygan area residents erected a shanty village along the Cheboygan River each winter to catch a variety of fresh fish.
The Historical Society of Cheboygan County, Inc.

OF THE DAYS WHEN WE WERE A FISHING TOWN

57

By Gordon Turner. Originally printed in the *Cheboygan Daily Tribune* on October 12, 1981. Gordon died in 1995—It is his story that tells us most about the daily happenings in a Cheboygan fisherman's life.

For many years dozens of boats came in regularly with cargos of fish for big Cheboygan fisheries, in an era when Cheboygan was recognized as one of the leading fishing ports on the Great Lakes. The industry was going strong here as early as the 1920's. Commercial fishing still continues here on a small scale. But the big fish packing plants are gone. The Booth, Eddy, Shawl, Bell and Robbins plants are gone. So are smaller ones that operated simultaneously, like Deroshia Brothers, Fred Chapman's and others.

Glenn Eddy, retired postmaster, worked at the Eddy Fishery as a young fellow with his dad, the late E.W. "Pudge" Eddy. He recalls his father saying that 20 boats delivered fish regularly to the Eddy Fishery. Don Bell, who operates Bell Fishery at Mackinaw City, is a son of the late Ross Bell, who operated Bell Fishery in Cheboygan. He said that probably a similar number was delivered to the Cheboygan Bell Fishery. Don helped in the Bell Fishery in Cheboygan for years. He started in as a 7 year-old youngster nailing fish boxes together. He had to stand on one box to reach while hammering.

57 Captain Due's tug, *Sea Fox*. Collection of the Historical Society of Cheboygan County, Inc.

Cheboygan rail connections to the eastern market were so good that the Robbins Company operated a plant here for Canadian fish. It had its own boat, the "American Girl" which brought cargoes of fish caught in Canadian waters to be shipped out of Cheboygan. Other fishermen also brought fish from Canada to sell to Cheboygan fisheries, wherever the price was best. Fish importing from Canada was such a big business that the government assigned a customs officer here full time. Lee Osgood had this position.

The big market was in the east. Refrigerated cars of fish were shipped out on night train from Cheboygan to markets in Boston, New York and Philadelphia. Fish from Cheboygan was also shipped to Chicago. John Stempky remembers this well. He started working for the railroad express company when he was 18 years old. "Carloads of fish were shipped out of Cheboygan nearly every day," he recalled. "The heaviest shipment was on weekends. From ten to twelve cars would go a week. A car would hold 600 boxes, each containing 50 pounds of fish, packed in ice. Boxes would weigh up to around 150 pounds. One time six cars of fish were out in one night. That is the most I have seen." Asked when the big shipments of fish faded away he said he thought it would be around 1960 when the passenger night train was taken off. After that he said, fish shipment was by truck.

A Michigan Central Railroad locomotive arrives at the Cheboygan Depot on Main St. Refrigerated cars of fish were shipped out on the night train to markets in Chicago, Boston, New York and Philadelphia.

Collection of Historical Society of Cheboygan County, Inc.

Mrs. Metz, with the Bell brothers.   Photo courtesy Stuart Ross Bell II

Fishing at one time was the heart of the Cheboygan economy, in the opinion of Glenn Eddy. Around 1930 when the Paper Mill was closed and there was little industry, commercial fishing was a mainstay to the community. "It was all outside money coming into the town," he pointed out. A great many Cheboygan people worked in commercial fishing. Many are no longer here. Some who have died have widows or families remaining and some have retired or are still doing some fishing. Councilman Louis LeBlanc worked on a fishboat at one time. He fished with Frank Lancewicz and Harry McCash on the fish tug Minnow. George McCash operated with his own boat. The councilman's uncle William LeBlanc fished with his tug Lorraine. Mike (Alex) White was another fisherman. Captain Frank Davis, who has retired, ending out his career as engineer on the Chief Wawatam, operated a fish tug in the early years for the Lixey Company of Tawas which delivered fish to Cheboygan. He sold some to Bell and some to Shawl. Some of the other fishermen that he recalled were Fred Bellrose and sons; Reuben Corrow, with sons Charles, Bill, Walt, and Roy; and Louis, Herman, Jack and Alex White.

A Mrs. Mertz and daughters had a fish boat, captained by Frank Blay, Davis recalled. Mrs. Mertz took over the business after her husband drowned. Davis said the accident occurred when an anchor became caught in Mertz's overalls and jerked him overboard. Other fishermen recalled by Louis LeBlanc include Bob Last, Jim Phillips, Louis Peets, Charles Adams, Henry LaPlaunt, Pete LaPlaunt, Frank Peets, Jack Hilborn, Jim King, Joe Schley, and an Ernest Lannoo. Others are Dick Brownson, Roche Sikorski and Louie Brooks. The list is incomplete, and very likely there are many others whose names were not immediately recalled.

The big fisheries were all on the west bank of the river. The Booth Fishery was at the foot of First Street. Ellsworth Willis "Pudge" Eddy came in 1921 from St. Ignace to manage it. He was transferred here from the Booth Fishery at St. Ignace. The Cheboygan plant was relocated by Eddy further north to a site across from the present turning basin. He bought the business and changed the name in 1936 to E.W. Eddy Fishery. He operated there until finally going out of business around 1960. Though Eddy owned the building and equipment, the railroad owned the land. This worked out well, because the railroad ran a spur back of the plant to ship out fish. Before Pudge Eddy was sent here to operate the Booth Company, Ross Bell was manager of the Cheboygan Booth Fishery for a little while. Then Bell opened his own fishery, located across from the Mike Glenn store on Water Street.

A.D. Shawl had a big fish business at the same time just north of State Street, where Pat Maurice now has a marina, and where the federal ship Grayling ties up. These fisheries bought fish from the commercial fish boats at wholesale and sold them to metropolitan buyers at retail. Eddy did a commission business, and would charge fishermen a small amount, like a cent per pound, to ice and pack their fish. Bell besides buying from the boats operated several of his own boats. Babe Adams and Frank Davis were some of his captains.

Plaunt Dock area, with fire in building behind. Photo from collection of Historical Society of Cheboygan County, Inc.

Don Bell says that at Bell's Fishery in Mackinaw City, white fish is the most popular species. But back in Cheboygan's booming commercial fishing days, suckers were in special demand from the east, as Glenn Eddy recalls. That was especially true around the Jewish holidays. Glenn assumes that this species has a special ceremonial dish. Only they were not marketed as "suckers," the trade name was "mullett."

The fishing business depended on ice, and the fisheries would cut supplies in winter and store in ice houses for packing the fish. Some, including Eddy, cut in the Straits off the present Gordon Turner Park. Shawl cut in Joe Mel Bay. The ice would be kept insulated in ice houses with sawdust, which probably came from the big Cheboygan sawdust pile.

Fish boats would take out boxes of ice. When they pulled their nets in full of struggling fish, they would put them in ice to keep until they could deliver to the fisheries. Then the fish would be repacked in an orderly manner in shipping boxes that would be sealed and finally loaded into refrigerated cars. The melting ice provided some oxygen and helped keep the fish alive longer, Glenn Eddy believes." I have seen fishermen unload cargoes of fish from their boats at the fisheries, with fish still alive and flipping, and then seen them covered up with ice while still alive and encased in sealed boxes."

An offshoot of the fishing business was a box building industry. A lot of mills in the area cut to specifications for fish boxes. Donald Bell was only one of a lot of boys who got spare time jobs nailing boxes together. Don said that his father's plant bought from the Bishop Mill at Black River. The Carlson mill also was cited. Another part of the business was making bobbers for fish nets. The Cheboygan Novelty Works probably cashed in on them.

Glenn Eddy, working with his father, helped ice freight cars to haul the fish. "We ice'd hundreds of cars." His brother Lyle, he said, had no special interest in the fish business, being more interested in his band and in sign painting. The big shipping time was the weekends, mostly on Sundays. During other days business slacked off, and people worked to get ready for another big weekend. Lyle worked with his father from 1930 to 1941. "Pudge" Eddy is gone, but his widow, sons Lyle and Glenn, and daughters Lorraine (Mrs. Don Deinzer) and Joyce Bedouin remain here.

Don Bell worked with his father until he was 25 when R.J. Bell died on February 19, 1947. It was at a Masonic meeting. The father was stricken while in the act of presenting a

Ernie Rose and Earl York at Bell's Fishery in Cheboygan. Notice the pile of wood fish boxes piled behind them.

Photo courtesy of Stuart Ross Bell II.

ceremonial apron to his son Stuart. Stuart and Irwin Schally took over the business. They opened a bookkeeping operation there while also running the fish trade. They kept the fish business going for a year or two. Don, meanwhile, was working for Haut Grocer Company in Cheboygan. Stuart, now deceased and Schwalm finally sold the property to the City. The City of Cheboygan was buying up Water Street homes, giving the elderly residents lifetime occupancy, said Donald. Gradually the city took over and finally was able to develop the dock site and big parking area fronting Water Street in downtown Cheboygan. The fishery building and houses were torn down.

After leaving the Bell Fishery in Cheboygan, Don worked for a short time at the Paper Mill and then for Haut Grocer Company. But in 1949 he was back in the fish business, this time at Mackinaw City. His brothers Stuart and Bob went to other interests. Don bought the former Bob Robinson fishery at Mackinaw City from Clyde Cousineau. As time went on he expanded by enlarging the plant. The property runs from the highway to the lake. He believes his business has grown to equal the volume formerly handled by his father's Bell Fishery in Cheboygan. One reason is that there is less competition now. Donald Bell has one of the few fisheries left in this part of Northern Michigan. He is a wholesale and retail dealer. Some of the fishermen who sell to him are Indians, he said, operating out of rowboats. A by-product business is caviar. This is eggs from whitefish. He sells them to a company which exports to the European market. Don also makes and sells ice. He has special stove equipment for smoking fish and Bell's smoked fish is in big demand. During the peak of the summer season, he employs 15 people. Working with him is his son, Donald R. Bell, 36; daughter Meridith Cole helps sometimes. And there is a third generation Bell doing a little work in the fish business. He is a grandson Pat, 12 years old, who helps in summer. Bell Fishery at Mackinaw City ships to Detroit, New York, Philadelphia and Chicago. "We shipped 29 tons once on a Friday night," Don related. The Bells have their own refrigerated trucks. They have a big area business delivering fish to restaurants in Mackinaw City, Cross Village, Pellston, Harbor Springs, Petoskey, Indian River and Cheboygan. Some fish are shipped by Greyhound to Gaylord and Grayling. Bell trucks go to pick up fish from fishermen at Cedarville, Epoufette, Charlevoix, Rogers City, Alpena, Big Bay de Noc, and even at Batchawana Bay in Canada.

The fishing business was struck a hard blow when the lamprey eels took over in the Great Lakes. Commercial fishing was at a low level, but revived when control of the lampreys was gained by development of lampricides, and when the state resumed stocking of the lakes. Some local fishermen report another trouble. Jim Phillips said that at one time there was a big die off in the river. Many fish were floating dead in the stream. Phillips said fishermen blamed this on a discharge into the river by the Paper Mill. The trouble was corrected after a while. Cheboygan is no longer famous for commercial fishing, but it has become a popular place for sports fishermen to try for "big ones" like trout, muskies, sturgeon and salmon.

MEMORIES OF CHEBOYGAN PAST

BY STUART (ROSS) BELL II, GRANDSON OF ROSS BELL

Don, Robert, Stuart and Ross Bell.

Photo courtesy Stu Ross Bell II

R . J . Bell's Fishery:

Being born in 1945, I have few memories of my grandfather's fishery on Water Street. He died in 1947, at a Masonic ceremony while giving Dad his first degree belt. Grandpa had purchased this property, located along the Cheboygan River, from Miriam A. Crane, in 1910. I am not sure if the building existed or if Grandpa built it. Dad ran the family business another two years after grandpa died, then sold the property to the city. I am of a mind that the City of Cheboygan Fire Department used the building for fire practice-wood, sawdust, and all.

The first thing that comes to mind when you say fishery is playing on Grampa's old roofless jalopy, located at the pier on the north side of the fishery. The engine was still operable. Grandpa rigged it so it powered the belt-driven conveyor used to transport the blocks of ice to the fishery loft. Trucks would drop off the huge ice blocks. The men would rinse off the sawdust, then place the ice blocks on the conveyor, using large ice tongs. Once in the loft, they were broken down into smaller pieces by heavy duty ice picks before pushing them into the ice crusher. The crushed ice would fall into the ice bin on the fishery floor, where it was stored until needed to ice down the 100# boxes of fish to be shipped out on rail.

As I remember, the fishery contained a large warehouse, a retail store, and an office. The warehouse had large entrance doors on the East and West sides of the fishery. The

East side door, abutting the pier, was used for loading and unloading the boats. The West side door was the entry for trucks to pick up the processed fish to be delivered to the railroad station for shipping to markets in Detroit, Chicago, and out East.

The warehouse contained stainless steel cleaning tables for processing the fish prior to boxing and icing. The fish would be held in the warehouse until they could be shipped. The ice bin held the crushed ice used to ice down the boxes of fish before the lid was nailed shut. Sadly, I remember well the warehouse floor cluttered with discarded fish with lamprey eels attached to them. The fish could have several lampreys on their bodies. This predator played a significant role in the diminishing fish population in the Great Lakes during the 1940's, 50's, and early 60's.

The fish market was located in the Southeast section of the fishery. It had glass refrigerated counters to hold and display all kinds of fresh and smoked fish. There were shelves of fish accompaniments such as sauces, batter mixes, jars of pickled fish, tins of smoked clams and oysters, assorted crackers, and all kinds of goodies. Grandpa always got in 60 gallon wood barrels of New England lobsters during the Holidays. They were kept alive by packing them in salt water and seaweed. Once, I remembered Dad getting a call that a barrel of lobsters had been toppled over and there were lobsters everywhere! Although not funny at the time, it was hilarious to watch the crew running around trying to catch them without getting pinched before putting them back into the barrels. Could one of Dad's brothers been up to no good? The brothers worked well together. Once, Dad told me that, to break the monotony of processing fish, the boys would get into a fist fight using fish discarded on the floor. I can imagine the mess they made.

The fishery office was located in the Southwest side of the building. I remember that the fishery kept a daily journal on top of Grandpa's roll top desk. There were entries indicating dates, deliveries, and shipments of fish. Dad told me he remembered one weekend the fisheries in Cheboygan sent out 9 boxcar loads of fish with 600 fish boxes each. This equates to fifty- four hundred 100# boxes, or 270 tons of fish.

Bell's Fishery employees sort a catch.
Collection of the Historical Society of Cheboygan County, Inc.

Crushed ice and fish boxes were loaded onto the fishing boats prior to departure. Ice was dumped into the boat's hold and boxes were tied down on deck. After the fish were brought into the boat, the fishermen would place the live fish in the boxes, ice them down, then store them until the boat returned to the fishery. The crews assigned to the day boats would eviscerate some fish while the boats were returning after the day's catch. I knew this from seeing the swarm of sea gulls at the boat's stern, feeding off the fish guts thrown overboard while cleaning fish.

Due to the distances away from Cheboygan, the boats, working remote locations like Hammond Bay and the Les Cheneaux Islands, had overnight accommodations on location (I'll explain below). Grandpa sent out his trucks to locations along Lake Huron, like Bell's Landing at the mouth of the Ocqueoc River, and Albany Island, located in the Les Chaneaux. It was not practical for boats fishing these waters to trawl back and forth the 20 to 35 miles each way daily.

Ross Johnston Bell, The Man:

R.J. died between my second and third birthday so I never really got to know him. But, as I grew up in Cheboygan, it became apparent that he was respected, well liked, and admired. He was the kind of man who attained his 32 degree in the Masons, was a respected family man, leader in the First Congregational Church in many capacities, a devout Rotarian, and helped promote Cheboygan in many ways. He was active as a representative for the northern Michigan fishing industry on state issues. Once, R.J. was honored with the title of Whitefish King by a group of New York fish marketers. He developed his business into one of the biggest fisheries in Northern Michigan by purchasing a considerable amount of property along Lake Huron, employing up to 20 employees to man his boats, scows, nets, trucks, out buildings and other assets that supported his business.

As a boy growing up at 327 Sammons Street, brother Scott and I would walk the four blocks to Central School and go in the entrance to the boiler room. Usually we got there early enough to sit and listen to Ole Josh Phillips, the custodian, talk about the days he rode the fishing boats for Grandpa. From his stories, which may had been a bit exaggerated, it was evident he was taken by Grandpa's generosity and concern for his employees and their families.

Aunt Betty remembered how the Great Depression hit the Bell family and the community. As she reflected, R.J. had to either sell off or relinquish much of his property to the state due to tax issues. Although much of his wealth was gone, she was proud of the fact he took care of the fishermen and their families. The fishermen were too proud to get a hand-out, so Grandpa always kept the access to the root cellar at the back of the house open for all who needed help. Grandma was required to keep a large stock of potatoes, onions, cabbage, apples, and other seasonal fruits and vegetables. There were plenty of canned foods as well. R.J. lived the Golden Rule.

In the fifties, our monthly trip to Huff's Barber shop would commonly find some old timers reminiscing of days gone by. Knowing we were Ross's grandsons, quite often they would mention personal incidences where R.J. may have shown a bit of generosity or helped in some meaningful way. We never heard a bad opinion of him.

Riparian Rights:

During the 1920's and 1930,s Grandpa acquired a significant amount of property along Lake Huron. Deeds to lake front property included a provision for Riparian rights, whereby The State of Michigan gives the landowner the exclusive right to use the shoreline and lake beds for coastal fishing. One such pickup location was Albany Island, located in the Les Cheneaux Island chain. These islands, spanned from just East of St. Ignace to De Tour, in the Upper Peninsula. The island encompasses several hundred acres. A trout stream runs through the property. Back in the day, a rundown rustic two story lodge and several small cabins were located on the island. The rustic 1800's vacation lodge had a huge room with a fieldstone fireplace on the first floor and bedrooms on the top floor. The fishermen would use the lodge while fishing the area. There were the remnants of a pier located on the South side of the island. Originally, it was used for docking boats carrying vacationers from Chicago and Detroit, prior to railroad service to Northern Michigan. Water levels between the shore and north end of the island was very shallow, which enabled R.J. to construct a causeway for his trucks to access the boats docked on the island. From stories told by my Aunt Betty (Mary Elizabeth Bell), the Bells frequented the island lodge and cabins in the summer months. As a small child growing up in the early 1950's, my memory of Albany Island is vague since we only visited there on two or three occasions, when our cousins visited us from Southern Michigan and Iowa.

Albany Island, 1940.   Photo courtesy of Stuart Ross Bell II

58

Bell's Landing was another primary pickup spot located at the mouth of the Ocqueoc River located in Presque Isle County. This was an ideal place to unload a day's catch in the Hammond Bay area, onto trucks to deliver fish to the fishery. The pier was located just inside the river mouth a few hundred feet. The property was sold to William Spens in 1946. In March of 2011, I visited the site and found out that the Spens family still lived on location. I had the pleasure of meeting and talking at great length with William's son, Paul Spens. Paul was very familiar with Bell's Fishery. He remembers as a boy, helping his dad work a team of horses to pull the fish boats over the ever present sand bar at the river mouth and help them returned to Lake Huron for another trip to the fish beds in Hammond Bay. As Paul reflected on the past, he mentioned that the property had several storage buildings. They were used to repair and warehouse nets, maybe some used for boat maintenance and others for temporary shelter from inclement weather.

Hammond Bay was a popular fishing ground. Fish were plentiful and easily caught close to the shore, in 6 feet to 30 feet of water by using pound (pronounced pond) nets. Pound nets had fishing stakes (also known as spiels) which held a line of leaded netting, typically 1200 feet long. You can still see submerged lines of these fish stakes just off Bell's Landing and at other locations in Hammond Bay. Lead netting directed fish off shore and into deeper water where the pot nets were located. Pot nets are typically 30 to 40 feet square and run 25 to 30 feet deep. Once the pot nets were full, the fish were hoisted out of the water by wenches and pulled into the boat to be dumped into the hold for storage on ice for boxing. Pound fishing was the most popular type of commercial fishing during the era when fish were plentiful.

58 Gearhart, p. 5.7.

Joe Mel's Bay:

Grandpa's primary ice house was located at the Northeast end of Joe Mel's Bay, on the Cheboygan River, just south of the county fairgrounds. He owned all the property on the northern shore to the east end of the bay. During the winter months he would cut 100 lb. blocks of ice from the bay and fill the ice house. This ice would last from spring to the following winter. During the summers in the late 1950's, brother Scott, some of my buddies, and I would take a hike to the bay for a day of catching crayfish in the rocks just off shore and hunting chipmunks with BB guns. Mom would make me a bag lunch and I would walk up Sammons Street and we all met at the Lincoln Avenue Bridge.

Lincoln Avenue (John F.) Bridge.   Collection of the Historical society of Cheboygan County, Inc.

The old bridge was worn, rusty, and had a wooden deck. There was a long rope hanging off the side for kids to swing out over the water to drop 20 feet to the river. Anyway, the walk from there took us up the old Riverside Drive and through a grove of tall hardwoods and we eventually made it to the ice house ruins. There wasn't much left to the building. The sides had crumbled to the point where they only held the remnants of saw dust piled on the floor. The rusty conveyor remained. It ran from the ice house and parts were still seen 50' off shore. Uncle Don inherited this property and eventually sold it to Dad and Dr. Carl Rauch. They built homes on the first two lots at the entrance to the grove and eventually sold lots to Francis Lindsey and Dr. William Mead and other family friends.

The Shamrock:

On the Northwest side of the river above the State Street Bridge, where the condos are now located, was the remains of the tug boat Shamrock. Someone had taken off the top sections and relocated it on the pier. The housing of the main deck was situated directly on the pier. Add the wheelhouse and bridge sections and the structure rose approximately 30' over the river. There was a diving board located on the roof. The Chimner brothers, the LaHaies, Maltbys, Caswells, and Robsons, frequented the old tug. We fished from the large opening on the main deck towards the river. It is no fish story when I tell you that during the spring perch run we used 3-hook harnesses with worms on the end. We just dropped the line in the water and in seconds would get bites. There were three perch on the rig when you lifted the line out of the water. This was a yearly event until the mill dumped a huge amount of chemicals in the water and killed most of the perch that spring. The city also dumped truckloads of snow into the river. The salt content killed off a bunch of fish that spring.

Cheboygan Winters:

Winters were fun in Cheboygan. There were a lot of things to do when you weren't in school. The city rink was located on the old vacant football field behind St. Charles Church. West Side Elementary School is on this location now. It took up a full city block. There was an old quonset hut on location, used as a warming house. Wooden benches, used for changing into your skates, were lined up on the outside walls and down the middle of the large changing area. The attendant had several responsibilities. He stored your snow boots in numbered slots while you were out skating. You received a metal tag that had the slot number where your snow boots were located. You didn't lose the metal tag if you didn't want to go home without your boots. The attendant also tended to the music blaring over the loud speakers on the roof. Back in the day, he may load up a bunch of 45 rpm records made for skating- Christmas music, Gene Autry, Brenda Lee, Les Paul & Mary Ford, Teresa Brewer, to name a few. We usually played a pick-up game of hockey, using the snow banks as goals. The city did a great job of keeping up the ice. After closing time, they first used the rotary brush at the front end of a tractor to push the snow to the banks. Then came the water tanker that sprayed the water that added new layers of ice.

Records will show that we got much more snow back then. After heavy snow fall county road graders would push the snow to the center of Main Street. The snow in the center was so high that I couldn't see over it. Cars and trucks tied red flags on their aerials in order that they could be seen by cars stopped at the cross streets, waiting to turn onto Main Street. Next came the county truck backing a conveyor belt into the snow pile, forcing the snow into the back of a county truck. The trucks would haul it away. The trucks would dump the snow into the river until salt tainted snow killed many fish one year.

Collection of the Historical Society of Cheboygan County, Inc.(4)

Snow plows plowed snow to the curb of all side streets. As snow accumulated along the banks, neighborhood kids built igloos into the sides of the banks. It's a wonder we didn't have the top cave in on us. Constructing forts was another fun thing to do. Armed with some 100 snow balls, we held off the enemy for a long day. Sammons Street , running South to North, had a downhill slope. (Also called Piety Hill). When snow on Sammons became slippery from traffic, we got the sleds out. Starting up hill towards Court Street, we ran as fast as we could before dropping on our sleds. A good run took us past Nelson Street, a good distance. Go-carts were the vehicle of choice for summer racing. Life was good for a kid growing up in Cheboygan.

Mail by Dog Sled. Fred Roberts with his dog team in front of the Cheboygan Post Office which was north of the present day post office.

Logging sleds, Main St. Cheboygan.

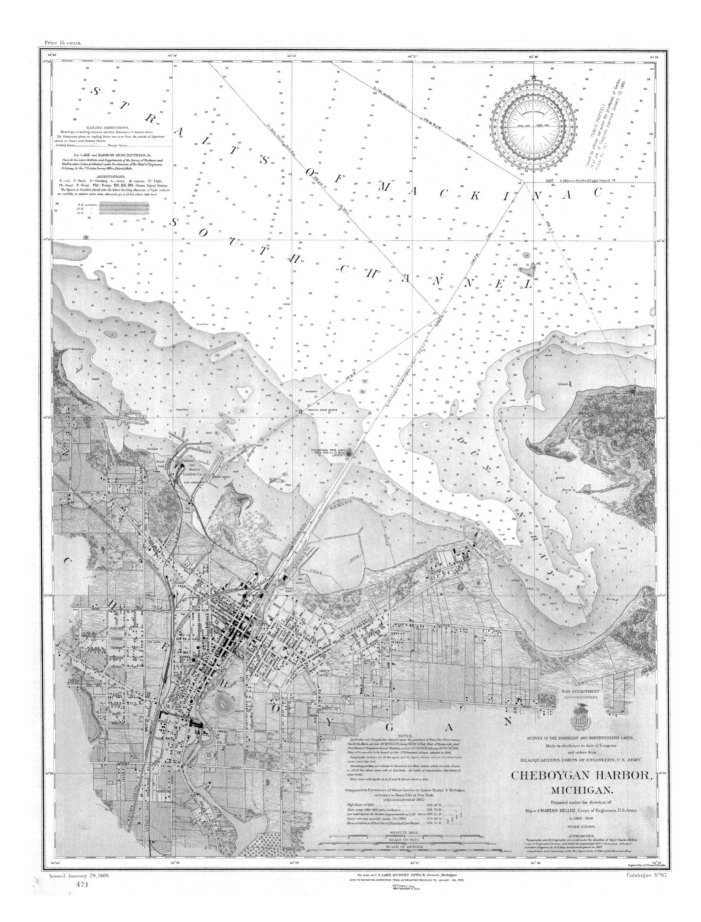

SEEING THE LIGHT
CHEBOYGAN AREA LIGHTHOUSES

By Terry Pepper

Executive Director of the Great Lakes Lighthouse Keepers Association, GLLKA

Spectacle Reef Light

Terry has researched many Great Lakes Lighthouses and is working on a book covering the Cheboygan Area Lighthouses. Enjoy the summary and look for Terry's website at www.terrypepper.com Above, Spectacle Light. Photo by Terry Pepper

LIGHTHOUSE POINT, CHEBOYGAN STATE PARK, MICHIGAN

In 1851, Duncan City was the only town of prominence near the mouth of the Cheboygan River. It was located at the western edge of McLeod's Bay, a little over a mile to the east of the river, where the McLeod brothers had established the area's first sawmill in 1846.

Duncan City was a "company town," and took its name from Jeremiah W. Duncan, whose lumbering operation eclipsed all others in the area. Duncan's docks along the bay established it as a fueling stop for the wood-burning steam vessels passing through the Straits. As Duncan City grew, it did not take long for the bay itself to take on the Duncan name.

Located directly across the three mile width of the Straits from the southernmost point of Bois Blanc Island, the eastern prominence of Duncan Bay marked a natural turning point for vessels entering the Straits, and the growing bounty of Lake Michigan beyond.

On December 21, 1850, Congress appropriated the sum of $4,000 for the purchase of a 41.13 acre reservation on what would become known as "Lighthouse Point" at the western end of Duncan Bay for the construction of the first Cheboygan light station. The construction contract was awarded to Rhodes and Warner, of Ohio, and under the superintendence of Captain Shook of the Army Corps of Engineers, construction of the station began in the spring of 1851. Consisting of a round 40-foot brick tower on a stone foundation, the lantern was outfitted with a Fifth Order Fresnel lens manufactured by L. Sautter of Paris, making it one of the first on the Great Lakes equipped with a lens of the Fresnel design. William Drew, the station's first keeper, took up residence in the detached keeper's quarters, and exhibited the light for the first time in September, 1851.

The tower was evidently poorly located, as high water was found to be undermining the stone foundation soon after construction. Fearing collapse was imminent, in 1859 the newly-formed Lighthouse Board decided to build a new station and demolish the original tower, only eight years after its construction.

The replacement station, was similar in design to that built at Port Washington the following year, consisting of a combined keeper's dwelling and tower, with the tower located at the north apex of the hipped roof. The tower stood thirty-one feet above the foundation, and was capped with an octagonal iron lantern into which the Fresnel from the old tower was carefully relocated. The lights' thirty-seven foot focal plane provided a twelve mile range of visibility, thereby providing coverage throughout the Straits.

The arrival of the lighthouse tender *Ruby* in the Fall of 1889 was a momentous, but not altogether enjoyable occasion for the Cheboygan keepers, when the apparatus for duplicate fog-signals were delivered to the station. The arrival of the fog signal equipment not only meant more work, but sleepless nights until they adjusted to the noise!

The *Ruby* returned the following spring with additional materials and a construction crew, who quickly set about construction of the new fog signal, close to the lakeshore approximately one hundred feet to the east of the station.

All was not bad news for the keepers, however, as the construction crew also improved the dwelling with the installation of running water pumped from a cistern installed in the cellar. The boat house was relocated from Duncan Bay to the shore in front of the fog signal building, and a circular iron oil house of 225-gallon capacity was constructed to allow the storage of a year's supply of oil a safe distance from the dwelling. Finally, with the construction of plank walkways connecting the new structures to the dwelling, work was completed on June 2, and the fog signal was placed into operation. Over the remainder of that year, the fog signals were operated for a total of 96 hours, their boilers consuming 4 tons of coal.

This was the time of peak production for Cheboygan's lumber industry, with the area's eight mills producing over 100 million board feet of lumber, of which the Duncan Mill produced 27.5 million feet alone. Thompson Smith took over as the owner of the Duncan Mill. A religious man, he forbade the construction of any saloons in his town. It would appear safe to assume that this may have contributed to the 42 saloons located in Cheboygan in 1895!

As was the case with most of Michigan's lumber towns, the boom days were short-lived. The area's forests were quickly clear-cut, and the lumberjacks began picking up stakes to work the virgin forests of the west.

A Brief History of the Cheboygan Range Light

In 1870 Cheboygan had a population of approximately 800 and a growing number of lumber mills along the shores of the Cheboygan River. The Army Corps of Engineers conducted their first survey of the Cheboygan River that year to evaluate the possibility of improving navigation within the river. Determining that the channel could be enlarged to a width of 200 feet and a depth of 14 feet, Congress responded to the Army Corps of Engineers recommendation with an appropriation of $160,000 to begin the improvement the following year. After dredging the river to the required depths, a free-standing "dummy" crib was placed to mark the outer end of the channel.

Anticipating an increase in vessel traffic entering the improved harbor, Congress responded to the Lighthouse Board's request for funds with an appropriation of $10,000 for the construction of a set of range lights in the river in July 1876. However, with the Corps of Engineers improvements still in progress, work on the range lights did not begin until 1880, four years later. The Front Range light was designed as a combination tower and keepers dwelling. The rectangular brown-painted, two-story wood frame building stood some twenty-four by twenty-seven and a half feet in plan. Its integral wooden tower, six feet two inches square, was located at the apex of the north end of the gabled roof. Since range lights are designed to be seen from within a narrow arc of visibility, a wooden lantern, rather than the normal cast-iron multi-sided lantern in general use at the time, was constructed on the tower gallery. The light was equipped with a fixed red Sixth Order Fresnel lens manufactured by Henry-Lepaute of Paris. It was displayed through a single rectangular window on the north side of the lantern where it would be visible to vessels in the Straits off the mouth of the river.

The Rear Range originally consisted of a spindly wooden structure with a vertical oval daymark consisting of horizontal wooden bars. It held a lens-lantern which was located at the top of the structure. The work was completed that same year, and the station was illuminated for the first time on the night of September 30, 1880. With the exhibition of the new range lights, mariners making their way through the Straits towards the dummy crib could bring the two lights into alignment in such a way that the rear light would be positioned immediately above the front light. By maintaining them in this alignment, the center of the channel could be followed right up the river.

The ranges were established just in time because Cheboygan was in its heyday in the early 1880s. The eight huge mills on the banks of the river shipped 127 million board feet of lumber, and the town's population had exploded to 6,956. The town was growing rapidly and the Front Range light, being located a mere block from downtown, was able to share in the conveniences of its location. In that year the station was hooked up to the city water supply; however, the small plot of land on which it was situated was found to be poorly drained. The station frequently was surrounded by fetid standing water and its cellar inundated. Reporting on the unsanitary conditions at the site, the Lighthouse Board requested the sum of $1,500 to purchase adjacent property in order to re-grade and improve the drainage. For some reason, Congress turned a deaf ear to the request. It was not until the Board had restated its case in each of its eight subsequent annual reports that Congress responded with an appropriation of $1,700 in July 1898 to fund the purchase of the much needed land. The process of obtaining title began immediately.

In 1894, with increasing maritime traffic entering the river, the decision was made to place a light on the dummy crib which marked the end of the dredged channel, and that light's management was added to the list of responsibilities of the range light station. Since the light was manually operated and a full-time keeper would be needed to ensure its continued operation, an assistant keeper was added at the Front Range light. With three lights to maintain, the oil storage room in the cellar of the Front Range light was clearly inadequate. In 1891 a circular iron oil house was built on the station property with the capacity to hold 72 of the Board's standard five-gallon kerosene butts (containers) which were delivered by the lighthouse tender *Marigold* during the District Inspector's annual inspection and re-supply visits.

Work on replacing the old wooden Rear Range light with a new skeletal iron tower began in 1900. Standing 75 feet high, the structure was equipped with an integrated ladder to reach the lamp and a small, wood frame cleaning room at its base. With completion of the new tower in December, the old tower was demolished. The Cheboygan River has a relatively strong and fast current and it seldom freezes, even in the harshest of winters. For this reason, the station dock was called into service as winter mooring for the light ships which had

The Cheboygan River Front Range light as it appeared in 1925. At this time the entire building was painted a dark red color with the exception of the white tower band black lantern. Light was built in 1880 and held a Sixth Order Fresnel lens originally lighted with a wooden lathern.   U.S. Coast Guard Historian's Office

been placed to mark shoals and reefs throughout the Straits. It was not uncommon to see up to six lightships tied-up in front of the lighthouse during the winter.

After eleven years of legal wrangling, title to the adjacent property was obtained in 1909, and the property was graded to its present condition. Sometime thereafter, the Fresnel lens was removed from the Front Range, and both front and rear range lights were replaced with locomotive style lanterns with 10,000 candlepower electric lamps which were visible from a distance of 14 miles.

With a major wave of offshore lighthouse construction underway in the Straits of Mackinac in the late 1920s, the Cheboygan River Front Range light took on a critical support role, making the diminutive station one of the busiest on the western lakes. Not only was the station now responsible for the two range lights and the light out on the Crib, it also began serving as the primary support base for the lights on Spectacle, Martin and Poe reefs. All supplies for the lights were delivered to the Front Range, and all inbound and outbound crews mustered at the station. In addition to providing support for these offshore stations, the Range light keepers were also responsible for 41 aids to navigation along the inland route between Cheboygan and Alanson, some 40 miles to the west. When the icebreaker *Mackinaw* was commissioned in 1945, Cheboygan was designated as her home port. The Front Range light served as shore support for the vessel for approximately 20 years, until proper storage facilities finally were established at her berth off the turning basin near the river mouth. With the dissolution of the Bureau of Lighthouses and transfer of responsibility for the nation's aids to navigation to the Coast Guard in 1939, civilian keepers were given the option of staying on in their civilian capacity, transferring into the Coast Guard at an equivalent rank, or resigning. While many of the old keepers resigned rather than enter into military-style service, a number stayed on as civilian keepers. Such was the case at the Cheboygan River Front Range light where Keeper Clarence Land, who had entered Lighthouse service as a Mechanic in the early 1920s, stayed on as a civilian keeper at the Front Range light until his death in 1964. Clarence was so well respected that he was posthumously awarded the Albert Galatin Award, the U.S. Treasury Department's highest career service award, which was presented to his wife Marie on the deck of the icebreaker *Mackinaw.*

The Front Range light served as the primary Coast Guard station for northern Lake Huron and the Straits of Mackinac until the mid-1980s when the decision was made to consolidate all area operations out of St. Ignace because more land for future expansion was available there. After the Coast Guard moved out, the lighthouse and riverside dock were taken over by the US Geological Survey and the Department of Fisheries to serve as their operations base in the western Great Lakes. The lighthouse thus began service as office space for the two federal agencies. A large pole barn-type structure was erected immediately behind the lighthouse to provide the necessary equipment storage and repair space.

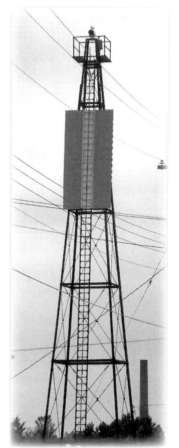

The original wooden rear range light was eventually replaced by this steel version. Sailors could safely navigate the Cheboygan River by lining up this light with the lower Front Range light.
Collection of the Historical Society of Cheboygan County, Inc.

In 2001, the Coast Guard decided to make the Cheboygan Front Range light available as part of the first group to be excessed through the National Historic Lighthouse Preservation Act. The Great Lakes Lighthouse Keepers Association successfully filed for ownership of the station, receiving the deed from then Secretary of the Interior Gale Norton at the National Lighthouse Conference held that June in Traverse City. After receiving ownership of the lighthouse, a Michigan Lighthouse Assistance Program grant to undertake an engineering study was successfully obtained. The study identified significant deterioration in the lantern box and gallery which was allowing water into the building and causing moisture damage to interior walls on the second floor. The rubble stone foundation also was found to be in deteriorating condition, requiring that the entire foundation be excavated and rebuilt and that perimeter drains be installed. A second MLAP grant, obtained in 2008, paid for 2/3 of the cost of rebuilding the lantern box and gallery and re-sheathing them in materials appropriate to the target historical period of significance, determined to be 1910 when commerce in the river was at its zenith. Once the lantern has been repaired, attention and fundraising efforts will focus on rebuilding the structure's foundation.

A wonderful group of dedicated GLLKA volunteers has been opening the lighthouse to the public on weekends and holidays from Memorial Day through Labor Day since 2005, affording visitors the unique opportunity of viewing the restoration effort in progress. The lighthouse still serves as an active aid to navigation, not only serving the large number of pleasure boaters and sport fishermen who frequent the area, but also providing safe passage to the new icebreaker *Mackinaw,* the Bois Blanc Island ferry boat and a large gasoline barge which enters the river to fill tanks on the shore a couple of times a week.

CHEBOYGAN CRIB LIGHT

The plan for the Cheboygan Crib Light as drawn-up by the District Engineer called for a round crib with an octagonal cast iron pierhead beacon centered upon it. While a contract for the fabrication and erection of the cast iron tower was awarded late in 1883, work on the crib itself did not begin until the opening of the 1884 season of navigation.

Work began with the construction of a wooden crib onshore in Cheboygan, which was then lowered into the water and towed out to the specified location at the entrance to the dredged river channel. Sunk in place with the addition of crushed rock, an upper level consisting of oak timber framework was then constructed atop the crib, with a basement oil storage room beneath the location in which the tower was to be installed. The deck of this superstructure was then leveled at a height of eleven feet above the water, planked with timber and fitted with a circular oak ring centered over the oil storage room to serve as an anchoring foundation for the cast iron tower itself.

On October 15, 1884, the cast iron tower was then assembled atop the oak ring and securely bolted in place. After a set of cast iron spiral stairs were installed to provide access to the lantern, the interior walls of the structure were lined with 2 1/2 inch wide beaded pine paneling to help provide insulation, and to prevent condensation. Glass prism grates were installed in the lantern floor to allow light to pass into the structure's interior, and a pot-bellied stove was installed in the lower level, and a

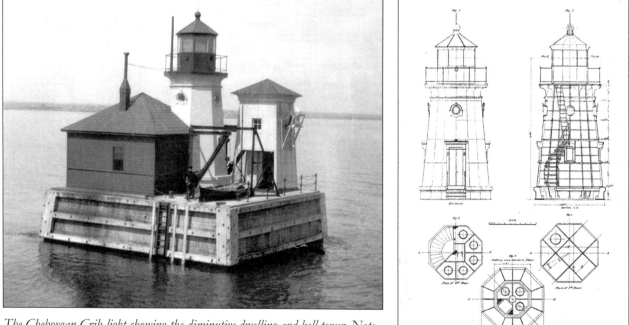

The Cheboygan Crib light showing the diminutive dwelling and bell tower. Note the davits which were used by the keeper to lift his boat onto the crib deck away from action of the waves below. Light was placed in service in 1884 and used a Fourth Order Fresnel Lens with a 159 candle-powered kerosene lamp to guide mariners. Above right, the Lighthouse Service "Iron Pier Head Beacon" plan used in building the Cheboygan Crib light. The cast iron tower featured beaded pine paneling inside for insulation and to prevent condensation.

Terry Pepper Collection, left; Nationals Archives, right

The tower became known as the "The Dummy" about the same time the last keeper left in August, 1929. By 1980, it had a visible "leaning tower of Pisa" list. It was donated to the city of Cheboygan and moved to the Gordon Turner Park break wall in 1984.

Photo by Terry Pepper

hole drilled in the gallery floor for its galvanized iron stovepipe. Atop the gallery, a prefabricated octagonal cast iron lantern was installed with a copper roof surmounted with an 18-inch copper ventilator ball. Atop this ventilator a lightning rod was installed and grounded to the water by way of a cable attached to the exterior of the structure.

The district Lampist arrived at the site to install the flashing red Fourth Order Fresnell Lens with a 159 candlepower kerosene-powered lamp. The occulting mechanism was carefully adjusted to ensure that the station's designated repeated 2 1/2 second cycle was attained, consisting of a single 1/2 second flash followed by a 2 second eclipse. By virtue of the tower's location atop the eleven foot high crib, the lens sat at a focal plane of 36 feet, with a resulting range of visibility of ten miles under clear conditions.

With construction complete, the entire structure was given a fresh coat of brown paint, and the Light was officially exhibited for the first time on the evening of November 1, 1884.

The station was built without a dwelling in the crib, and since there was insufficient room within the tower for living space, it would appear that it was District Inspector Commander Francis A. Cook's plan to have the keeper live on shore. Since the Lighthouse Board annual reports of the time make specific mention of the fact that an Assistant Keeper was assigned to this station, it would appear likely that he operated under the supervision of the Keeper of the Cheboygan Range Lights, and thus likely lived in the Front Range dwelling with the Head Keeper.

One can only imagine the drudgery involved for the keepers who manned this station. Every afternoon he would have to leave the safety of the dwelling in Cheboygan and row the 1/4 mile out to the light in whatever weather the lake was dishing-up that day. On arrival at the crib, he would carefully secure his boat at the foot of the crib, and then gingerly step from the heaving boat onto the eleven foot ladder, climbing up to the deck while simultaneously carrying any supplies needed for the night. The lamp would be illuminated at dusk, and the keeper would then sit in the solitude of the tower, huddled close to the stove to keep warm on cold nights during the late season, making frequent climbs to the lantern to adjust the light by trimming the wick, winding the occulting mechanism and adding fuel to the lamp. As dawn finally raised its head across the Straits of Mackinac, the lamp would be extinguished, and the illuminating apparatus, lens and lantern would be cleaned in preparation for illumination later that day. The keeper would then row the 1/4 mile back to shore to get some sleep, knowing that he would have to be back out on the crib to repeat the cycle a few short hours later.

To provide an extra measure of safety for the keeper, and to facilitate the transfer of supplies, a work crew from the Detroit depot arrived at the station in 1892 and installed a pair of iron boat davits on the crib. The keeper no doubt considered this addition to be a real improvement, since it would allow him to raise the boat to the crib deck, where it would be safe from being broken against the crib by the crashing waves, and allow for far safer unloading of supplies.

In 1897, it would appear that the difficult conditions on the Crib came to the attention of the District Inspector, since it was in this year that a small dwelling and a pile protection for the boat were constructed on the crib. At the same time three and a half cords of riprap were placed around the base of the crib to protect against the action of the seas. The following year the District Lampist delivered a new and improved Fourth Order lamp to the station, increasing the distance of visibility to twelve miles.

It is a particular property of wood that if it is either kept dry or wet at all times, it holds up for

Spiral stairs which lead from the first to second level within the Cheboygan Crib light. A new masonry foundation was installed in 1903 to replace the original wooden version that had suffered extensive rot damage. Photo by Terry Pepper

extremely long periods of time. However, wood that is subjected to alternating periods of wet and dry will begin to rot. With the crib and decking being constructed entirely of wood, it is not surprising that by 1899 the entire deck needed replacement, and an additional 28 cords of riprap were installed at the crib's base in an attempt to stave off the complete re-facing that was becoming clearly inevitable.

To increase the effectiveness of the structure as a day mark, the main body of the tower received a coat of white paint in 1901, with the lantern room roof being painted a contrasting bright red.

By 1903, the deteriorating condition of the crib had reached a point at which it was critical that major repairs be undertaken to prevent its total collapse along with the tower above. A contract was awarded for the replacement of the wooden structure with something of a more substantial and permanent nature. The contractor arrived in Cheboygan and began the rebuilding by removing the entire wooden superstructure to a level twelve inches below the water level, a point at which constant immersion had prevented rotting of the timbers. On this solid foundation, a new concrete pier, faced with masonry was constructed, incorporating a new oil storage room below the tower and a cellar beneath the dwelling formed within the mass of concrete. To enhance safety, an iron hand railing was installed around the perimeter of the deck level. This railing was subsequently replaced three years later when an unnamed schooner collided with the tower.

To help prevent a reoccurrence of the 1906 collision, an automated fog bell was established on the crib in 1911, sounding a characteristic single stroke every ten seconds. Automation came to the crib in the late 1920's when the kerosene lamp within the Fourth Order Fresnel was replaced with an acetylene system equipped with a Sun Valve. The Sun Valve was designed to automatically turn the gas on as the cold of night arrived and off with the arrival of the warmth of day. Equipped with a tank into which acetylene could be pumped from the lighthouse tender *Amaranth*, the light could be supplied with sufficient acetylene to stay lighted for the entire season. Any emergency troubleshooting could be done by the keepers of the Range Lights, and a full-time keeper was no longer needed on the Crib. Thus it was that the last keeper assigned to the Cheboygan Crib Light left the structure on August 6, 1929.

Photo by Terry Pepper

It was likely during this time that the Crib Light became fondly known to locals as "The Dummy." A name that was commonly used when referring to the Light into the early 1980's, by which time crib had taken on a noticeable "leaning tower of Pisa" list, and was believed to be in danger of collapsing into the water. By this time, the use of Radio beacons, RADAR and LORAN-C had become universal in Great Lakes navigation, and the value of the Cheboygan Crib Light as an aid to navigation had decreased considerably. After evaluating the condition of the structure, the Coast Guard determined that the cost of stabilization and restoration would outweigh any navigational benefit, and made the difficult decision to scrap the iron tower and dynamite the crib into oblivion.

Hearing of "the Dummy's" impending de-

struction, a number of Cheboygan citizens raised their voices to see if some arrangement could be made to save the century old landmark. An agreement was reached with the Coast Guard whereby the tower would be donated to the City of Cheboygan for display as a historical attraction, and a new home for the structure was identified on the west breakwall off Gordon Turner Park. A contract was entered into with Ryba Marine of Cheboygan to relocate the tower and remove the crib.

In the 1984, a Ryba barge with a boom arrived at the crib, and by means of a bar placed through the tower's round upper widows below the gallery, the tower was lifted from the crib and lowered onto the barge. From there it was transported to the breakwall and lowered into the position in which it sits to this day. After installation, the glass windows were replaced with Lexan for safety reasons, and the tower was given a new coat of white paint, with the windows and door frame receiving a historically inaccurate coat or bright red paint.

When Dick Moehl and Sandy Planisek of the Great Lakes Lighthouse Keepers Association visited Cheboygan early in 2001, they were dismayed to find that the tower had deteriorated, with the Lexan having crazed, and the station leaking as a result of the caulking having fallen out over the years. They approaching the City with the proposal that they would offer their labor to restore the structure if the City would cover the cost of materials. Receiving approval for the project from the city, Dick and Sandy set to work on August 2, 2001. After re-caulking all joints throughout the structure and replacing the Lexan windows, they painted the tower in its historically accurate white paint, gray gallery and red roof and ventilator.

MARTIN REEF

With less than a foot of water covering the rocky bottom of its shallowest point, Martin Reef lurked menacingly offshore to the east of Les Cheneaux Islands, approximately seven miles east southeast of Cedarville, and had long represented a significant hazard for maritime traffic threading its way between the Straits of Mackinac and the entrance to the DeTour Passage.

With maritime traffic through the area increasing dramatically toward the end of the nineteenth century as a result of the discovery of inexpensive ore along Superior's north shore and the resulting rapid proliferation of steel mills at Chicago, Milwaukee and Joliet, the Lighthouse Board evaluated various aids to navigation at the reef to increase the safety of mariners passing through the area. With the realization that the cost of a permanent station would be prohibitive, in its annual report for 1896 the Board recommended that $15,000 be appropriated for the construction of

a wooden lightship to be placed on Martin Reef. While Congress was unresponsive to the request, the Board remained convinced of the need to light the reef, and reiterated its request in its reports for the following three years. In fact, in its 1900 report the Board increased the amount of its request to $35,000 after realizing that the reef's exposed location at the northern end of Lake Huron would subject the vessel to the full fury of wave action building up along the entire length of the lake, and that a steel-hulled vessel would better suit such an exposed location. Congress continued to ignore the Board's repeated annual requests for the vessel until June 20, 1906 when an act was finally passed authorizing a contract for the construction of a vessel at a total cost not to exceed $45,000, with a partial appropriation of $25,000 for the work approved ten days later.

Plans drawn-up by the engineers at the Detroit depot for what was to be designated as LV89 called for a vessel of unique design, featuring a whaleback forecastle deck designed to easily shed water as she rode at anchor. After submitting the lowest bid, the Racine-Truscott-Shell Boat building Company of Muskegon was awarded the contract for the vessel's construction, and work on the hull began in the spring of 1907. She was to be 88' 3" in length, her hull 21' in beam and her draft 7'. While her single cylinder steam reciprocating engine with 17" bore and 16" stoke would not afford her great speed, it was more than sufficient to allow her to get on and off station under her own power. Her single mast, mounted forward allowed her cluster of three oil-powered lens-lanterns to be raised to a focal plane of 35 feet, and her six-inch steam whistle would allow her to announce her presence in thick weather. With her hull painted a bright red, and "89 MARTIN REEF 89" emblazoned in large white letters on each side, she was completed in the fall of 1908, and officially delivered to Eleventh District Inspector Commander James T. Smith in October of that year. As a result of her

Martin Reef light under construction.
Courtesy Terry Pepper, Great Lakes Lighthouse Keepers Association

delivery so late in the season she was docked in Cheboygan through the winter, and was not placed in her position one mile south of the reef until the opening of the 1909 season of navigation.

With the size and strength of commercial vessels increasing through the 1920's, the season of navigation was beginning earlier in the year as these larger vessels were able to make their way through some of the thicker ice impenetrable to smaller vessels under their own power. However, with pack ice around Martin Reef frequently remaining in place late into the year, and with her diminutive size and power, LV89 was frequently unable to make her way into position on the reef until a considerable number of vessels had already made their way through the area.

To this end, the engineers of the United States Lighthouse Service began working on a design for a permanent light for Martin Reef, to allow the station's keepers to gain access to the station earlier in the season using a smaller boat which could

by carried across the thicker ice.

With Congressional approval for the construction of the new station, the first order of business was the establishment of a land-based camp as close as possible to the reef. Here, the cribs and concrete forms could be constructed and the 18-man crew could be housed until work progressed sufficiently to allow the establishment of quarters on the reef itself. By the twin virtues of having deep water close to its shore and its proximity to the construction site, Scammon's Harbor on the north shore of Government Island in Les Cheneaux Islands was selected as the best location for the base camp. This was not the first time that Scammon's Harbor had been used for such an operation, as the base camp for the Spectacle Reef project had been located there some fifty years previous, and the island on which the harbor was located had received its name as a result of the Government's use of the island at that time.

With the establishment of the base camp, work began simultaneously at both Scammon's Harbor and Martin Reef. At camp, the massive 65' square wooden crib was constructed of 12" square oak timbers on a skid-way down which it would eventually slide into the water. On the reef, hard-hat divers worked with a scow equipped with a crane system to clear and level an area in ten feet of water at the southeast end of the reef where the crib would eventually be placed. With the site on the reef prepared, the crib was lowered down the greased skid-ways into the water, and the lighthouse tenders *Marigold* and *Aspen* attached lines and carefully guided the huge structure out of the harbor, through the 100-foot channel between the islands and into the open water of Lake Huron.

Arriving at Martin Reef, the crib was carefully centered on the cleared and leveled area, and ballast pockets built into the crib were filled with crushed limestone delivered by freighters and transferred into the crib with the assistance of the scow's conveyor. Eventually overcoming its natural buoyancy, the crib sank on the prepared bottom. Divers then descended to the bottom of the crib and filled all gaps between the surface of the reef and the lower edges of the crib with rope caulking and Portland cement to create a water-tight seal. With the pockets completely filled, the water was pumped from the open areas in the crib, prefabricated forms were attached, and the work of filling the crib with concrete from a mixer aboard the scow began. As the pour continued, forms for the four arch-roofed cellar areas for coal and water storage were installed and cast in place.

At this stage of the construction, the work crew continued to spend their nights at Scammon's Harbor, with the lighthouse tender *Aspen* transporting them to and from the reef twice each day. With the pouring of the curved wave apron, work on the crib was complete and the upper surface of the pier was carefully leveled in order to create a level foundation for the lighthouse structure itself, which was to be erected at the exact center of the pier. Completion of the pier structure also allowed the construction of a bunkhouse on the reef, and work on the tower progressed quickly since the twice daily trips transporting the crew between Scammon's Harbor and the reef were no longer necessary. A temporary light was also installed on the railing, and with this new light to mark the reef LV89 was no longer needed at the reef, and was reassigned to North Manitou Shoal in Lake Michigan.

The twenty-five foot square station structure was designed with three-stories, its exterior walls of reinforced concrete and iron over a skeletal steel frame. A stairway connected each floor and continued above the living quarters into the centrally located tower. With the lower floor designed as an engine room for the station's machinery, the second and third floors served as living areas for the station's keepers. The second floor featured an office in the northwest corner, a bathroom on the south side, and a kitchen on the southwest corner,

while the third floor was divided into bedrooms for the head keeper and his assistants. The four concrete rooms within the crib served as coal and food storage, and water cisterns contained drinking water that was fed by down spouts from the station's roof

Atop the center of the main structure, a ten-foot tall watch room, sixteen feet square was capped with an octagonal cast iron lantern with vertical astragals. The lantern contained a flashing white fourth Order Fresnel Lens manufactured by Sautter & Cie of Paris, and was powered by an 8,000 candlepower lamp with a characteristic of three flashes every ten seconds. The sixty-five foot focal plane of the lens created a visibility range of 14 miles during clear weather. For periods of thick weather, the station was also outfitted with a compressed air diaphone fog signal powered by an oil-powered air compressor located in the first floor equipment room.

With construction of the station completed in the summer of 1927, the work crew loaded the camp buildings and bunkhouse onto the scow and lighthouse tenders *Marigold* and *Aspen*, and relocated to the Cheboygan pier to begin construction of a duplicate of the structure at Martin Reef on Poe Reef, off Cheboygan Harbor.

With the transfer of responsibility for the nation's aids to navigation to the Coast Guard in 1939, electrical generators were installed at the station and an electric light was installed within the Fourth Order lens. Under the Coast Guard, the station was manned by four-man crews consisting of a Chief Engineman, Boatswain's Mate, a Fireman and a Seaman. The station would usually be opened for the season of navigation around the beginning of April, and the crew would assemble at the Cheboygan Coast Guard station where they would purchase their initial supplies at a local grocery store. A Coast Guard 180' foot boat would then push its way through the ice to deliver the men at the reef. On arrival at the station it was fre-

Located approximately seven miles east southeast of Cedarville, Martin Reef light stands proudly to guide merchant traffic between the Straits of Mackinac and the entrance to the DeTour Passage. Its 8,000 candlepower lamp lights three times each ten seconds, with a visibility range of 14 miles.
Courtesy of Terry Pepper, Great Lakes Lighthouse Keepers Association

quently caked in ice, sometimes reaching as high as the third floor, and the first order of business was to chip away around the door to gain entry. The station was heated by an oil-fired furnace in one of the "dungeons," as the four storage areas within the crib were irreverently called by the crews. This furnace fed the rooms through ducts which were located throughout the structure. Once the furnace was operating, the temperature warmed to a comfortable level, however the coldness of the structure itself caused the walls to sweat for the first three or four weeks every year. Electrical power was provided by a bank of DC batteries that were charged by a pair of duplicate GM 271 twin-cylinder generators. Living conditions at the station provided as much comfort as such cramped conditions could afford, and the men quickly set-

tled into the daily routine of cleaning, painting and equipment maintenance.

Cooking was done on a propane-powered stove, and meals usually consisted of a lunch of soup and sandwiches, with a large supper served in the evening which everybody who was considered capable would help prepare. While the station was outfitted with a television set in the 1950's, for some reason the location of the station only afforded a selection of a couple of French language stations! Jack Stiehl recalls some of the men building plastic ship models as a diversion, launching them in the lake, and then using them for target practice as they sailed away from the station. One particularly melancholy recollection of Jacks is looking out the kitchen window, watching a neon "BEER" sign flashing on the east side of Cheboygan on clear nights!

The station was outfitted with a 20' boat with a cabin that was raised onto the pier by one of the two deck-mounted cranes. This boat was used by the crew members to run "liberty parties" to Cheboygan, but the boat was removed in 1959, with transportation to and from shore subsequently provided by the Coast Guard station at Mackinaw Island. Since Huron's northern offshore lights were so remotely located, the crews of Poe, Martin and Spectacle Reef lights conducted a radio check every morning and evening. If any of the crews missed two consecutive checks, a boat was dispatched from Cheboygan to check up on them.

At the end of each season of navigation, antifreeze was poured into all drains, the window shutters were closed, and the generating and heating equipment was winterized. The rack of batteries was left fully charged to provide power for a 200 mm, 110 candlepower light that was left burning throughout the winter to provide direction for any late vessels making their way along the north shore. Every year care was taken to ensure that all the food was consumed by the time the station was closed for the year. However, in 1958 a small private aircraft crashed in north Lake Huron, and the pilot managed to make his way across the ice to Spectacle Reef Light station. Entering the station, and finding no food, he left a note and set out for land. The pilot was never heard from again, and it could only be assumed that he had perished on the ice. From that point on, the crew at Martin Reef always made sure that they left a supply of non-perishable food at the station before departing at the end of each year's navigation season.

On a date which we have as yet been unable to determine, Martin Reef was automated through the installation of a solar-powered 200 mm acrylic lens, and the Fourth Order Fresnel was carefully removed from the tower and shipped to Point Iroquois Light Station, where it is proudly displayed as part of that station's museum.

During a ceremony at the annual Coast Guard Festival on Thursday August 3, 2000, ownership of Martin Reef Light Station was transferred to the Bureau of Indian Affairs, who remain the current custodians of the station

POE REEF

Poe Reef lies just eight feet beneath the water's surface between Bois Blanc Island and the Lower Peninsula mainland, and as such has long represented a significant hazard to vessels making their way through the Straits between Lakes Michigan and Huron.

In the early 1890's the Lighthouse Board faced a vexing problem. Increasing vessel traffic created a need to install navigational aids at a number of offshore shoals and reefs. With Congressional funds increasingly difficult to obtain, and the costs of offshore lighthouse construction prohibitively high, the Board determined that the use of lightships to mark such hazards would be both significantly more expeditious and cost effective.

Unable to convince Congress to free up the funds for these lightships, the Board took the chance of redirecting an existing $60,000 congressional appropriation for a lighthouse off Peninsula Point to the purchase of four lightships.

In 1892 two contracts totaling $55,960 were awarded to the Craig Shipbuilding Company in Toledo for the construction of four lightships. Designated as Lightships LV59, LV60, LV61 and LV62, all four vessels were built to similar specifications. Framed and planked of white oak they measured 87' 2" inches in length, 21' 6" inches in the beam, with a draft of 8 feet. In a cost-cutting effort, the vessels were un-powered, outfitted with only a small riding sail carried on a short after mast. Equipped with a cluster of three oil-burning lens lanterns hoisted on their foremasts, each was also equipped with 6" steam whistles and hand-oper-

This modern "turtle-decked" lightship with a bright red hull, known as LV96 was the last of three lightships to be placed to mark Poe Reef on April 24, 1915. It served until the construction of Poe Reef light station, whereupon she was relocated to service in California. The 101.5' Lightship LV96 succeeded the LV 62 and served at Poe Reef from 1915 to 1920 before being replaced by a LV 99 until the permanent station was completed in the summer of 1929.   Terry Pepper Collection

ated bells for fog use. Work was completed on the four vessels the following year, and after sea trials, all four were commissioned by the Board and placed into service, LV59 being assigned to Bar Point, LV60 to Eleven Foot Shoal, LV61 to Corsica Shoal and LV62 to Poe Reef.

With the words POE REEF brightly painted in white on her fire engine red hull, LV62 was towed to Poe Reef by the lighthouse tender *Marigold*, and anchored on station to begin her vigil on September 29, 1893. For the next seventeen years LV62 spent every shipping season faithfully guarding the shoal. With the end of each shipping season, one of the lighthouse tenders would make the rounds of all lightship stations in the Straits area, and tow them into Cheboygan harbor for winter lay-up. While in Cheboygan, necessary repairs and improvements would be made in preparation for

the following season. At some time in March or April, the ice would break up sufficiently to allow the vessels to be towed back to their stations to stand guard for yet another season.

1910 would be LV62's last season on Poe Reef, since for reasons we have as yet been unable to determine the decision was made to trade assignments at Bar Point with LV59. LV59 was delivered to Poe Reef at the beginning of the 1911 shipping season, remained at the reef for the following three seasons. During a departmental survey of lightships in the fall of 1914, she was found to be unseaworthy and thus condemned at the end of the season. To replace her, LV96 was repainted with POE on her sides, and transferred from Buffalo to Poe Reef at the beginning of the 1915 navigation season.

Built by Racine-Truscott-Shell Lake Boat

Construction of the permanent station at Poe Reef began with the excavation of the reef to form a flat surface to construct the 64-foot square mansonry crib foundation using timber forms. Once work was complete on the main structure and the deck of the crib free of obstructions, the bunkhouse was moved from the pier at Cheboygan in September, 1928, and placed on the lighthouse deck so the construction crew could live at the lighthouse. When the poured concrete tower was finished, a decagonal cast iron lantern room was installed on the roof of the watch room and outfitted with a Third Order Fresnel Lens. US Coast Guard Historian's Office

Company in Muskegon in 1914 at a total cost of $71,292, LV96 had only seen one year of service at her Buffalo station before her transfer. 101' 6" in length, 23' 6" in beam and drawing 9' 5", she was constructed of steel in the whaleback design, with her pilot house forward. Equipped with electrical generators and batteries powered by two 3-cylinder kerosene engines, she displayed a large cylindrical lantern housing with a thousand-candlepower electric lamp. A revolving parabolic reflector provided her with a unique light signature. A six-inch air siren, submarine bell and a hand operated bell made her presence known whenever fog shrouded the reef.

In the spring of 1921, LV96 was reassigned to duty on Corsica Shoal in Lake Huron and the newly commissioned LV99 was delivered to Poe Reef in her place.

LV99 had her keel laid in June of 1919 at Rice Brothers in Boothbay Harbor, Maine, and work was well underway on July 10 when a fire gutted the structure. With new materials procured, the vessel was completely rebuilt at a total cost $97,220, and she was launched on November 7 of that same year. She drew 10' 7", was 91' 8" in length, with a beam of 22' and was powered by a single-cylinder 125hp steam engine. Displaying a single acetylene lens lantern, she was also equipped with a ten-inch steam whistle and a hand operated bell.

As part of a series of a significant offshore light construction projects being undertaken in the Straits area in the late 1920's, the Lighthouse

Service decided to build a permanent station on Poe Reef in 1927. For two years, an 80-man construction crew had been working out of a base camp on Government Island in Les Cheneaux Islands, while they undertook the mammoth task of building the Martin Reef Light. With the completion of that project in the summer of 1927, the entire base camp was loaded onto the lighthouse tenders *Aspen* and *Marigold*, and rebuilt on the north pier at the mouth of the Cheboygan River. With establishment of the camp, construction at Poe Reef Light began on two fronts.

Construction plans called for the placement of a sixty-four foot square wooden crib on the reef to serve as a foundation for the pier on which the tower would be constructed. In order to prepare the reef for the crib's installation, an area first had to be leveled

Poe Reef station in September 1931 showing the station boat on one of the cranes being lowered from the crib deck into the water for a trip to the shore support station at the Cheboygan Front Range light.　Photo courtesy of Terry Pepper

and cleared of all rocks and boulders. For this task, Lighthouse Service Scow #1 was equipped with a steam-powered derrick and a clamshell bucket. Towed out to the reef by the lighthouse tender *Aspen*, and anchored at the edge of the reef, hardhat divers assisted in guiding the scow's clamshell.

Back at the Cheboygan pier with the construction of a skid way complete, the timbers of the crib itself were assembled on top of the skid way. Constructed of dressed 12" by 12" timbers, the crib was a sixty-four feet square and featured tightly crafted half-lap joints throughout in order to provide the utmost in structural rigidity. With the outer walls constructed in an elongated brick pattern, each joint was hand-drilled and bolted, and iron angles added to the corners for even more strength. Finally, the upper exterior surfaces were sheathed with steel plates protruding six feet above the sides. These steel plates designed to cre-

ate the exterior forms into which the concrete of the pier itself would be poured once the crib was positioned on the reef.

With preparatory work complete on the reef, the lighthouse tenders *Aspen* and *Marigold* pulled the completed crib down the skid way, into the water, and thence into the lake to the reef, where it was carefully positioned over the prepared area on the reef. Crushed limestone and rocks were then dumped into the crib from a self-unloading lake freighter until the crib sank to the bottom, resting on the leveled area of the reef. With the crib completely filled with limestone and rocks, Scow #1 was outfitted with a gasoline powered cement mixer, a wooden tower, hopper and discharge chute. With concrete from the mixer dumped into the hopper, the hopper was raised to the top of the tower and dumped into the discharge chute. This chute was then pivoted across the surface of

The Poe Reef Light with an updated paint scheme as it appears in 2012. Note the population of cormorants that occupy it.
Courtesy of Terry Pepper, Great Lakes Lighthouse Keepers Association

was filled with concrete, the next level of forms was added above. Like a giant puzzle, each form created different sections of the ladder accesses on each of the four sides, the arch-topped storage areas within the pier, and finally the wave flare at the top of the pier. This wave flare was a vital component of the crib's design, since it was designed to divert waves crashing against the pier, thus reducing the likelihood of wave action smashing against the tower itself. With the pouring of the final level, anchoring points for the light station structure itself and the posts around the outer edge were cast in place.

With the setting of this final layer of concrete, the bunkhouse on the pier in Cheboygan was loaded onto the *Aspen* and transported to the reef, where it was lifted onto the pier. With the construction of a temporary cook shed, the crew was able to take up residence at the work site, and the workdays grew longer with the elimination of the daily commute from Cheboygan. The crew's attention now turned to the construction of the tower itself.

The station building at Poe Reef was to be an exact duplicate of that which the crew had previously completed at Martins Reef. The main twenty-five foot square structure consisted of a steel skeletal framework to which an exterior sheathing of riveted steel plates was applied. Thirty-eight feet tall, it contained three levels, or "decks", as the crews assigned to the station knew them. The two upper decks were set up as living quarters, while the main lower deck served as housing for the machinery required for powering the lights, heating system and foghorn.

Centered atop the main structure, stood a sixteen-foot square, ten-foot high watch room of similar construction, with a single observation window on each side. Finally, a ten-sided cast iron lantern room was installed on the roof of the watch room, and outfitted with a Third Order Fresnel Lens. The combination of pier and tower provided the Fresnel with a seventy-one foot focal plane, and a visibility range of almost twenty nautical miles in clear conditions. Work was completed at the station and the light exhibited for the first time on the evening of August 15, 1929.

the crib, allowing crewmembers to distribute the concrete evenly until it was filled to the top of the steel plates rimming the crib. By virtue of the base camp's location in Cheboygan, dependent on weather conditions either the *Aspen* or the crew's work boat would transport the crew to the reef at the start of each day's work, returning to transport them back to camp at day's end.

With the final pour to the upper limit of the steel sheathing, the entire top surface of the concrete was carefully leveled through the use of a transit. It was critical that this upper surface be completely plumb, since it was the foundation on which the pier and the lighthouse itself would stand. Once level was established, the first of a series of wooden forms which had been prefabricated back at the camp, were attached to the outside of the structure. As the form for each level

A boat from the Poe Reef Light makes a visit to the Fourteen Foot Schoal Light in September, 1932. Construction on the station was begun in 1930 by the same crew that erected Martin Reef and Poe Reef Lights. At the same time, the obsolete Cheboygan Light was locked up, abandoned and eventually demolished in the 1940s. Courtesy of Terry Pepper, Great Lakes Lighthouse Keepers Association

At some point, in order to eliminate the possibility of the Poe Reef Light being mistaken for the identical all white structure at Martin Reef, the main deck and watch room of the Poe structure were given a contrasting coat of black paint.

With construction at the reef complete in late 1929, the bunkhouse and cook shack were loaded back onto the tender *Aspen*, and returned to Cheboygan, where the camp was readying to begin construction of a new light on Fourteen Foot Shoal. The light was automated in 1974 with the installation of a solar-powered 375mm acrylic optic.

FOURTEEN FOOT SCHOAL LIGHTHOUSE

The Cheboygan Main fog signal recorded its busiest year in 1896, as the keepers were kept busy shoveling thirty-nine tons of coal in order to keep the signals waling for a total of 509 hours. The Duncan Mill burned to the ground in 1898, and with the decision not to rebuild, Duncan City's reason for being disappeared, and the few remaining citizens abandoned the town.

With the construction of the Fourteen Foot Shoal Light offshore in the Straits in 1930, Cheboygan Main was considered obsolete, locked-up and abandoned. With growing vandalism, the old station was considered to be in dangerous condition and the Coast Guard demolished the station's buildings at some time during the 1940's. The Federal Bureau of Recreation conducted a survey of Michigan's coastline for possible State Parks in 1956, and designated Lighthouse Point as part of its proposed "Poe Reef State Park Site." In 1958, the Michigan Department of Natural Resources built the Duncan Bay State Forest Campground on thirteen acres at Duncan Bay Beach, all of which was combined to become the current 1,200-acre Cheboygan State Park in 1962.

With a scant fourteen feet of water above its hard gravel bottom, Mariners recognized the hazard represented by this shoal lurking a mile northwest of Cheboygan Point and close to the main course of entry into Cheboygan Harbor, and while a second-class can buoy had long been placed to mark this danger, it was plain that a more permanent solution was needed.

In 1925, a construction crew was working in the Straits at Martin Reef, and plans had already been drawn up for that same crew to transfer their base camp to Cheboygan at the completion of the work at Martin Reef to begin construction of a virtually identical structure a Poe Reef. With the availability of such an experienced crew in the area, the time was right to provide a more permanent solution at Fourteen Foot Shoal, and plans were drawn up for a new station on which construction would begin as soon as the work at Poe Reef was completed. It was also determined that with the improved lighting that would result from this new station, the seventy-five year old Cheboygan Light would no longer be needed and could be discontinued with the exhibition of the new light.

As a result of recent advances in reliable radio control technology, it was also determined that the new station could have its light and fog signal remotely controlled by the keepers living at the planned Poe Reef Light Station, thereby significantly lowering the cost of operating the new light.

As a temporary measure to better mark the shoal, the can buoy marking Fourteen Foot Shoal was replaced by an acetylene gas buoy showing a flashing white seventy candlepower light every 3 seconds on April 15, 1925.

With completion of the work at Poe Reef in 1929, the work crew turned their attention to work at Fourteen Foot Shoal. While the new light was of a totally different design, and considerably smaller than the twin lights built at Martin and Poe Reefs, the construction of the crib proceeded in much the same manner, with the construction of a wooden crib at the shore station on the Cheboygan Pier. After an area on the shoal was leveled, the crib was eased down wooden ways into the water, and towed to the shoal by the Lighthouse Tender *Aspen*. Once over the leveled area, the crib was sunk to the bottom by filling its empty pockets with rocks and gravel.

This timber foundation then served as a core, upon and around which wooden forms were constructed and filled with concrete loaded from the Lighthouse Service scow. As was the case with both the Martin and Poe stations, the upper edge of the crib was formed into a graceful flare, designed to deflect waves away from the pier, in order to help protect the structures which would be erected on the deck. With the completion of the concrete work, the pier stood fifty feet square, and its deck level fifteen feet above the water.

The steel framework for the single story equipment building was erected at the center of the deck. Standing thirty-four feet by twenty-eight feet in plan, on completion, the entire exterior of the building was sheathed with 1/4-quarter inch steel plates, each riveted to the steel framework beneath. Centered on the roof ridge, a cylindrical steel tower was integrated into the roof, standing six feet in diameter and twenty-four feet above the ridge line. The tower was capped with an octagonal cast iron lantern and outfitted with a flashing white Fourth Order Fresnel lens.

As a result of its relative proximity to the shore, a submarine cable was laid to the station, with

SPECTACLE REEF LIGHT

Spectacle Reef lighthouse showing the single attached fog signal building which was added in 1908.

Left, a view across northern Lake Huron from the Spectacle Reef lantern. This small modern LED lighting system serves mariners from the original location of the station's magnificent Second Order Fresnel lens – one of only five US lighthouses on the Great Lakes so equipped. Center, the Second Order Fresnel lens still in place in the lantern at Spectacle Reef. The lens was removed during automation in 1982 and is now displayed at the Great Lakes Historical Society in Vermilion, Ohio. Right, the first floor radio room as it appeared in 1968.

Left, the second floor kitchen as it appeared on September 23, 2009. Right, a view down from within one of the interior stairways. There are flights of stairs similar to this connecting each level, each with its own door. The door to the left accessed stairs leading to the level above, and the door to the right lead to the level below. Steel doors at each level helped prevent the spread of fire to the level above.

Photos courtesy Terry Pepper, GLLKA

CHEBOYGAN AREA MEN (AND WOMEN) WHO LIT THE LIGHTS

Lawrence William Clark[1] was born Aug 19, 1873 in Forest, Ontario, Canada. He first worked for the Detroit & Cleveland Steamship line. He married Amelia Karg at Sand Harbor in 1896 and shortly thereafter applied for naturalization in 1897 in Cheboygan. After his marriage Lawrence joined the Lighthouse service. He served many positions including: 2nd Assistant at Fourteen Mile Point, 1st and 3rd Assistant at Spectacle Reef, and 2nd Assistant at Big Bay Point Lighthouse. In 1928-1930 he was keeper at Martin Reef and his son, Stanley was 2nd Assistant. From 1928 to 1933 Lawrence was a fireman at the Water Works plant in Cheboygan but then he returned to the Lighthouse Service where he was keeper of Poe Reef from 1930-1936.

Lawrence William Clark

His first wife, Amelia, died July 24, 1920 in Cheboygan and he then married Hilda Lundberg on June 9, 1921, in Cheboygan. His children were all from his first marriage. His daughters were Della Rana (1897-1990), Mable Ellen, (1898-1992), Eunice (1902-1995), and Naomi (1907-1912). His son, Stanley William Clark (1900-1966) married Myrtle Daisy Greenless on Nov 24, 1921 in Cheboygan. Stanley also served at Spectacle Reef and Martin Reef lighthouses.

George Cleary was born in 1859 and died 1954. He was appointed keeper at Walker Lighthouse, Bois Blanc Island, in October 1890 and served there 35 years. He was the first captain of that station. His children were John William Cleary, Viola (Mrs. Frank Merritt), Grace, Francis (Mrs. Henry Quintal, and Evangeline (Mrs. William Muller).

Charles Corlett[2] His obituary tells that "Charles was born in Chardon, Ohio on July 22nd, 1853. When he was a small boy, twelve years old, he moved to Beaver Island, Michigan with his parents. Six years later they came to Cheboygan which had since been his home until 8 years ago, Mr. Corlette having been light keeper of the White Shoal lightship for twenty years. After twenty years of service he was promoted to the North Manitou light at Leland, Michigan, where he served for three years. The past 6 years he served at the Range Lights at Manistique. Forty-one years ago he was married to Miss Elizabeth Barber of this city. [Cheboygan] To this union eleven children were born of which three daughters and five sons are left with the mother to mourn the loss of husband and father. The children were Robert, Kneale, Arthur and Charles all of Manistique, and John of this city, Mrs. Angus Philips of Saginaw, Mrs. Charles Faulkner of Tacoma, Washington, and Mrs. Philip Rollin of Raymond, Wash. He was also survived by two sisters, Mrs. Andrew Trombley and Miss

---

1 Information and photos from Marcia Simmons, his great granddaughter
2 *Cheboygan Democrat*, Nov. 12, 1920.

Alice Corlett of this city and a brother Daniel of Seattle, Washington."

Maynard Stanley Corlett[3] was born Aug 22, 1857 in Ohio and died March 20, 1911 in Cheboygan. He married Nellie Budwine who was born on Beaver Island. He was first master of Gray's Lightship LV57 from 1892 until he died in 1911. A newspaper clipping from an interview with his wife tells her memories of being a keeper's wife.

Mrs. Maynard Corlett, 90 years old, looks at food prices in papers and recalls how she raised a family of eight children in Cheboygan on $52 a month. That was the salary paid her husband by the government when he was Captain of the lightship at Gray's Reef. Getting by meant economical shopping. "My husband would go from store to store in the winter getting prices, she recalled, and sometimes he would be able to buy a quarter of beef for 6 cents a pound". Mrs. Corlett made all the children's' clothes and milked two cows morning and night while the children were small. Raising the family was pretty largely her job for during the years that her husband was in commercial fishing; he would go out in the spring and not come back until fall. In the 18 years he was on the lightship, things were better, for he was on duty 10 days and home 10 days.

The pleasant, friendly woman with the pretty hair is visiting her son and daughter- in- law, Mr. and Mrs. Dan Corlett at their home on Littlefield Street. She divides her time between her children, spending much of it with a daughter, Mrs. D. H. Wood, of Charlevoix. Mrs. Corlett spends a lot of her time reading, which is something of a surprise, considering that she had benefit on only a three grade school, when she was a girl. She lived on Beaver Island and the isolation kept teach-

ers from staying long. School consisted of a three month winter term, she said, and a three month spring term. She developed a good reading knowledge and enjoys magazine articles.

After her limited education she made up her mind that her children would have good schooling. Her children shared her interest in learning and three became school teachers. When her husband died, two daughters, Julia and Margaret, had credits enough so that they were able to quit high school, Mrs. Corlett reminisced, and to enter County Normal. Another daughter, Jessie went on and graduated from high school, all three becoming teachers. The Cheboygan Mrs. Corlett first knew was a Cheboygan of horse drawn vehicles. Mrs. Corlett used to rent a horse and buggy from Ming's Livery stable and drive out in the country to bring one of her teacher daughters home for the weekend. Early Cheboygan was a great center for sailing craft as fleets of schooners tied up here along with steam tugs and their barges for lumber. Captain Corlett had his own 35 foot boat. In those days, water was deep up Smith Creek, and the captain could sail his boat right up to the First Street Bridge. Mrs. Corlett was a wheelsman and steered boats for her husband. Smith Creek, now in summer, is just a dry ditch.

She was born on Beaver Island in a Mormon built house, and recalls stories of how her father- in-law was chased off the island by Mormons, escaping at night in a boat, taking his cow with him. Indians lived on Garden Island, three miles from Beaver, and sometime they would come over and beg for food. After marrying she came to Cheboygan to live, but spent two years at Detour while her husband was doing commercial fishing. She moved around with him by sailboat while he set pond nets.

---

3 Information from his great granddaughter, Kay Forster, includes newspaper clippings, no date, circa 1951.

At times she would be left alone with her children on one of the islands, and at such times might put the youngsters in a rowboat and row to one of the other islands to pick berries. The fishery which employed her husband also hired Mrs. Corlett to cook for the fishing crew, a job which meant baking 15 loaves of bread every other day. All of this work was in addition to caring for her own family. She had three small children at that time. Blessed with a keen mind, now after 90 years of life, Mrs. Corlett enjoys writing letters. She averages close to a letter a day to relatives. Becoming 90 years old is a happy event, when a person can be as spry as Mrs. Corlett and have the love of a fine family.

Bois Blanc Island Lighthouse.
Courtesy of Terry Pepper, Great Lakes Lighthouse Keepers Association

James Davenport[4] was born April 1, 1847 and died October 18th, 1932 at the age of 85 years. He was born on Mackinac Island, one of a family of fourteen children. Mr. Davenport was in the United States Lighthouse service for nearly fifty years, being appointed assistant keeper at the Waugoshance light in 1870, transferred in 1874 to Petite Point, Au Sable Light House; transferred to McGulpin Point as keeper in 1879 and in 1907 was transferred to Old Mission Lighthouse. He retired in 1912.

William Drew, the son of John Drew and Margaret Lasley, was born in 1835 on Mackinac

Island. Williams's grandmother was Indian and his father, John was a trader working with Edward Biddle on the Island. William married Caroline Roulette there on Oct 1, 1846. He was the first lighthouse keeper at the Cheboygan Light on Duncan Bay. This lighthouse was built in 1851. He was succeeded by Jacob Sammons as the next keeper. By the 1860 census William had moved to Detroit, as had most of his siblings.

John Duffy was born 1864 in Ireland and naturalized in 1886. The 1900 census shows him as a Cheboygan light keeper. In 1910 he was living on Water Street and listed as a light keeper. In the 1920 census his sons, Earl and John were listed as serving on lightships.

Earl Duffy was born in Detroit on August 1, 1895 and came to Cheboygan as a child with his parents. His father, John Duffy was a lighthouse keeper in Cheboygan for many years. Earl married Gladys Amlotte April 14, 1927. He was a veteran of World War I and II in the Coast Guard. He served in Lighthouse Service until his retirement. He died May 1976 in Cheboygan. This *Life Magazine* article tells about his career.

Earl Duffy climbed aboard a Coast Guard launch manned by a young seaman and it was lowered from its perch 20 feet above the water down the side of Poe Reef lighthouse into Lake Huron. It was the last trip to shore for Poe Reef's last civilian keeper, who had spent 17 years tending this particular light. But it was more. Earl Duffy is part of a whole era that is in the seaman's phrase, "swallowing the anchor'. No civilian lighthouse keepers have been hired since 1939, when Franklin D Roosevelt announced that the Coast Guard would take control of the nation's aids to navigation. Although civilians in the service at the time would

4 *Cheboygan Daily Tribune*, June 19, 1932.

5 *Life Magazine*, Nov. 22, 1968.

Spectacle Light

retain their jobs, only 10 of them are still at work and when the last of them retires or dies, America will have ended another of its legends.

Earl Duffy, the son of a keeper, reared in a lighthouse only a mile from Poe Reef has spent almost 40 years in the service of lights. In the launch, wearing his pea coat, he looks compact and durable, like a bundle securely wrapped for a long voyage. His shoulders are perpetually hunched as if to keep the cold winds from the Great Lakes from going down the back of his neck. This is a solid man. It is not surprising that a whole era changed its ways before Earl Duffy changed his.

On the night before his retirement Duffy had sat in his lighthouse with two visitors and reminisced. One visitor was Carl Hagstrom, another civilian keeper, who had shared some of his years on Poe Reef. Hagstrom remarked, "Even when I started here in the 20's not all of us had power boats. Many times I rowed six hours to get to shore and when I got there my hands were so blistered they stuck to the oars. You had to be careful. If we rowed straight into a sleet storm and didn't keep moving you could get a sheet of ice on your back that would freeze you to the seat. On Poe Reef weather was always the enemy. The keepers endured it and the constant hard work without complaints. "

"For those old kerosene lights we had to pump up the pressure to 70 or 80 pounds with a hand pump" Duffy said. "But that was a wonderful light, I tell you. And then to keep the light revolving we wound the clock 328 times every four hours night and day but the real job was getting up steam for the foghorn," Hagstrom said. "Yes" said Duffy, "That is how we took baths in the water that circulated around the foghorn engine. When the pipes got hot we'd open a valve and drain some water. You got baths when the fog rolled in." "You stood watch all night," Hagstrom recalled. "And in the day would come the cleaning. On Poe Reef we had an old French Light made of crystal prisms. Those prisms must be cleaned, a job that takes 3 men a full day. When we were finished our fingers would be so sore we'd have to tape them. I'd like to see some of those young fellows in the Coast Guard working till their fingers had to be taped."

"When my father was keeper", Duffy adds, "He made us take off our shoes when we came inside so we wouldn't dirty the lighthouse. Those old timers were different. If the Service didn't give them enough cleaning supplies they took money out of their own pockets to buy them."

Patrick Eustice[6] was born Dec 14, 1861 in Hamilton Ontario. He moved to St. Ignace where he was chief marine engineer of the Arnold Transit Co. passenger boats for 25 years. Somewhere between 1892 and 1894 he moved to Cheboygan where he raised his family. He took up duties with the United States government in 1912 as engineer of the lightship at Martin Reef and later on the North Manitou Light. He retired from service in 1931.

---

6 Information from his great granddaughter, Sally Eustice Humphrey

Captain Joseph Fountain
Courtesy of Terry Pepper, Great Lakes Lighthouse Association

Captain Joseph Fountain[7], a well-known light house keeper of the Great Lakes, passed away at his home at Gros Cap last Friday from pneumonia. Captain Fountain was 66 years of age, having been born in Mackinac Island, August 28, 1843. When a young man he entered the U.S. Lighthouse service, his first appointment being at Skilligalee light. He was then placed in charge of the light at Fox Island, then the Beaver Island light, then at Seul Choix and finally transferred to the St. Helena Station, where he was in charge for about 20 years, until his honorable retirement from the service.

Carl Hagstrom[8] was born Dec 18, 1895 in Cheboygan, the son of Charles and Anne Hagstrom. He served in the U.S. Army as a private during World War I. He married Garnet Thomas who died in 1959. He then married Olive Barr Proctor. He served 30 years as a lighthouse keeper, serving

seven years at Whitefish Point on Lake Superior and 23 years on Poe Reef off of Cheboygan. Following his retirement he worked as a carpenter in the Cheboygan area. when he died, he was survived by his wife Olive, daughters Mrs. Earl (Carol) Carmody, Betty Joan Bialk, four sons, Charles, Kenneth, Donald and Carl, and three stepdaughters: Mrs. Cyril (Gerty) Rocheleau, Mrs. Cliff (Mae) Kortman, and Mrs. Howard (Shirley) Barrette.

Charles Antoine Hamel was born May 25, 1825 in Berthierville, Quebec and died June 8, 1908 in Tacoma, Washington. He married Mary Bergeron May 22, 1848 on Mackinac Island. He served as lighthouse keeper on Bois Blanc Oct 1866 until June 1867. In the 1880 census his children were living in Burt Township, Cheboygan County.
Fred Louis Kling was born 1871 and died Aug 20, 1945 in Cheboygan. The Cheboygan newspaper of Aug 1, 1929 reported that he had for some years been keeper of the Cheboygan Main Lighthouse at Lighthouse Point and that he had received a letter advising him that he had been nominated for appointment to the position of Keeper of Poe Reef light station. It said he was to report for duty on August 7th to familiarize himself with all machinery, radio, beacon and radio telephone apparatus from foreman John Sellman and mechanics who were installing the equipment. He was to have two assistants, Louis Hudak, who had been working with him at the Main Light Station and second assistant Carl Hagstrom who had been at White Fish Point the last few years.

Fred Louis Kling[9] was born 1871 and died Aug 20, 1945 in Cheboygan. The Cheboygan newspaper of Aug 1, 1929 reported that he had for some years been keeper of the Cheboygan Main Lighthouse at Lighthouse Point and that he had received a letter advising him that he had been nominated for ap-

7 *Cheboygan Democrat*, Dec 5, 1919.
8 *Cheboygan Daily Tribune*, Sept 7, 1982.
9 *Cheboygan Daily Tribune*, Aug. 1, 1929.

Clarence Land
Courtesy of Terry Pepper, Great Lakes Lighthouse Association

Ivory Littlefield
Courtesy of Terry Pepper, Great Lakes Lighthouse Association

pointment to the position of Keeper of Poe Reef light station. It said he was to report for duty on August 7th to familiarize himself with all machinery, radio, beacon and radio telephone apparatus from foreman John Sellman and mechanics who were installing the equipment. He was to have two assistants, Louis Hudak, who had been working with him at the Main Light Station and second assistant Carl Hagstrom who had been at White Fish Point the last few years.

Clarence Land was born May 16, 1905 and died March 28, 1966 in Cheboygan. He first entered Lighthouse service as a Mechanic in the early

1920's. When the lighthouse service was turned over to the Coast Guard, Clarence stayed on as a civilian keeper at the Cheboygan Front Range light until his death in 1964. Clarence was so well respected that he was posthumously awarded the Albert Galatin Award, the U.S. Treasury Department's highest career service award, which was presented to his wife Marie on the deck of the icebreaker Mackinaw.[10]

Ivory Littlefield[11] was born Sept 16, 1835 in Rome, Maine and died Sept 1, 1894 in Cheboygan. He was educated in the village schools of his native town and at the outbreak of the war enlisted as a private

10 Terry Pepper, GLLKA
11 *Cheboygan Democrat*, Sept 1, 1894.

in Co. K, 31st Maine volunteers, in which company he served until the battle of Cold Harbor, where he lost a leg. He spent several years in California and removed to Cheboygan in 1868, where he has ever since resided. He was a member of Ruddock Post G.A.R. He was keeper for the Cheboygan Range Light from 1883-1894.

Philancy "Fannie" Littlefield was listed as one of 53 women in Michigan to be either a Lighthouse keeper or assistant keeper. She was listed at the Cheboygan River Range Light in 1894. She was born at Moosehead Maine and at the age of 18 married Ivory Littlefield. He was a veteran of the Civil War. Immediately after their marriage they came to this city. At that time there was no railroad into Cheboygan and practically all supplies and transportation came to this city from Petoskey, by stage and wagons. There was a railroad into Petoskey but not north of that point. Mr. Littlefield drove stage until the railroad came into Cheboygan, then he was given the job as tender of the range lights here, a government duty performed until his death.

Jane Barr of Cheboygan was listed at the Cheboygan Crib light from 1879-1880.

Charles Louisignau[12] The *Tribune* gave this retirement announcement of Charles Louisignau.

After forty six years of continuous services and leaving behind him an unblemished record, Charles Louisignau retired from the United States government lighthouse service, Friday, closing his career at the Dummy light. Mr. Louisignau has attained his 65th birthday, and it was up to him to elect whether he should retire now or continue in the service for five years longer, but on account of his defective hearing, and injury to his shoulder a few years ago, he concluded to retire on his 65th birthday on a pension. He has a splendid home on south B Street where he

and Mrs. Louisignau can enjoy home life.

Mr. Louisgnau was born at Mackinac Island in 1859 which place supplied most of the lightkeepers of this section on account of every man brought up there became an expert sailor, which is necessary in the service. He enlisted in the service in 1879 when he was commissioned assistant keeper of Skilligalee Light, his commission being signed by J. C. Watson, commander U. S. N. The salary at that time was $400 a year.

In 1883 he was transferred to the Cheboygan light, succeeding Adolph Gans. For thirty three years he was keeper of this station and during that period he had only three assistants, which goes to show that there was perfect harmony which is not often found. After retiring from the position of keeper of Cheboygan light, he went to Windmill Point light, Detroit River, where he remained for three seasons and then returned to Cheboygan to take charge of the Dummy Light at the entrance to the harbor. It was while at Cheboygan light that his hearing became impaired on account of the fog whistle. If there is a man in the light service who has earned what retirement carries with it, it is Mr. Louisignau. The dummy light is temporarily in charge of Charles Chevalier until a regular man is appointed by the inspector. Charles died Nov 10, 1932 at his home in Cheboygan.

Walter Marshall[13] was born on Mackinac Island, the son of officer left in charge of the fort. His brother was keeper of the Mackinac City light for many years. He first got a job on a tender for the United States Lighthouse Service in 1872. And it was on this ship that among other things, he helped to haul the stone from which Spectacle Reef Light was built. The light stands on a foundation 92 feet square built of rock and gravel that rests on a bur-

12 *Cheboygan Tribune*, June 9, 1924.
13 *Cheboygan Daily Tribune*, April 6, 1931.

ied reef 24 miles offshore from Mackinac. In 1882 he became third assistant keeper there.

"In those day" he says, "We used lard oil in the big lamps and had to keep another burning under them to melt the lard. There were four men with four hour watches each and in rough weather all of us had all that we could do." The engine house was not connected with the light tower and during the late fall storms, the waves that washed over the piers froze almost as soon as they struck. Between wind and water, ice and sleet, it was impossible for the men to get from the light tower, where their living quarters were, to the engine house, where they must tend the fires, unless ropes were fastened around their waists and secured to the iron work on the tower. A sailboat was used to make such trips to land as were necessary. In the late fall when we'd head in shore for the winter the ice was often so piled around the base of the light that we couldn't launch our boat. We'd often keep a steam hose going on it for 48 hour or so to thaw it.

Capt. McIntyre[14] Tuesday morning Cap. McIntyre, of the Simmon's Reef Lightship, came to Cheboygan and reported that Capt. Sam Dodd was missing and was supposed to be drowned. Tugs were chartered and men went to the scene of the disaster, but could find no traces of the missing, but when they got back at night they were glad to learn that the captain had been heard from and was safe at Glen Haven. It seems that Capt. Dodd went sailing Sunday morning in an unseaworthy old tub he had made from a yawl, going to "the Shanks" (Waugoshance Light house). Coming home a lively gale was blowing and when about two miles from his ship, the boat's sails were carried away, and he was thrown into the water. A passing schooner picked him up, and left him at one of the Manitous; from there he made his way to the mainland and telegraphed his wife.

Captain Harry McRae An April 12, 1937 article in the *Tribune* talked about the Gray's Reef Lightship being replaced by a new lighthouse. It said the new lighthouse will be manned by a crew of the lightship who will find solid concrete floors a change from the tossing decks to which they have been accustomed for many years. Heading the personnel will be Capt. Harry McRae; other members of the crew include Peter Gallagher, first mate, Angus Phillips, Chief engineer and Phillip Sharkey, assistant engineer. Captain McRae and Engineer Phillips are former Cheboygan residents and are both well known here. They lived here until a few years ago when they were transferred to lightship duty near Charlevoix, and made their homes at Charlevoix. Mrs. Alwyn Sangster and Mrs. Wallace Burrell of Cheboygan are daughters of Mr. Phillips.

Bert Thomas Proctor was born in Cheboygan, Dec 10, 1893. He worked on Great Lakes vessels, including several years as wheelsman on the lake liner, *North American*. He spent 16 years in lighthouse work, stationed at Standard Rock in Lake Superior, Martin's Reef and Round Island. He served at the Round Island Lighthouse from 1938 till 1947. His family spent the summers there and these memories are shared by his daughter, Gertie Rocheleau.[15]

Life on round Island lighthouse in the thirties did not have any of the amenities that we take for granted today; such as lights, running water, radio, showers, etc.

We, as dad being the assistant keeper, had to live on the third floor and we were always reminded, whenever we went outside to take the bucket and bring water back with you. We had to dip the water from the lake and then put drops in to purify it for drinking and cooking. When it came time to do the laundry, my father made a brick stove to heat the tubs of water on the beach. There was a stand

---

14 *Cheboygan Democrat*, May 5, 1894.
15 Correspondence with Gertie Rocheleau

that held two tubs, one the soapy water and one for rinsing, with a wringer in the center, which we had to turn by hand to wring out the water from each item, first the soapy water into the rinse water. We girls each had to take our turns doing the labor.

We were at the island in the summer only, July and August, during the school vacation. It was a time to be together as a family, as my father, as most lighthouse keepers were, was gone nine months of the year. At the crib lights, those on the lakes, the men were given five days each month to go home. At the land based lighthouses the families could live. Some land based lights had bigger homes and buildings. The men were taken from the lights in November and brought back in March.

We, as children, did not have much to entertain us, other than reading, playing board games going outside—we would walk the beach every day to see what new treasures we could find washed up on the beach. We also could look for berries in the woods. We had no other children to play with, only if some cousin was allowed to come for a visit.

My father was kept very busy with the maintenance of the light and the machinery that operated it. Also, with the painting of the rooms and the engine room. He and the Assistant keeper took watches keeping sure the light was always lit. The keeper also kept a log of each day of all activities or any unusual happening. There were occasions when some of the little sailboats would venture out and if the weather turned bad, would be in trouble, and dad would go out in his little skiff and tow them back to Mackinac Island.

One story, he told us, that the fog horn was blowing and he was on watch and looking out, saw a freighter headed for the light. He blew the signal for Dan-ger! Danger! In time for the ship to avoid a collision!

Another time the cruise ship D & C, became grounded on Round Island in the channel between Mackinac Island and Round Island. It took several tugs to pull it loose. Dad mentioned someone was going to be in trouble, as it hadn't been foggy, just a clear night.

The salary in those years was nothing to what we are paid now. My father was paid $125 a month at that lighthouse. So mother had to do a lot of canning to help save on groceries. Even at that time it was too expensive to buy many groceries on Mackinac.

I had my first job at Mackinac Island when I was thirteen. It was at Mrs. Emmert's Tearoom, behind Horn's. She served meals to the businessmen and carriage drivers. She was an excellent cook. I stayed the summer and had a room there. It was only a mile from Round Island, but I was so lonesome. We survived somehow and it made for some good memories.

John Smith Riggs[16] was the first white child born at Fentonville, Michigan on Dec 10, 1829. His father, Lauren Riggs, was an Indian trader who first owned property at what became Dodge's Point at Mullett Lake. He later lived at the Burt Lake Indian Village. When a young man he went west, but later returned to Michigan and came to Cheboygan where he was married on Nov 23, 1857, to Catherine McLeod, the wedding being performed at the old H.W. Horne home. (She was the widow of Alexander McLeod.) Shortly after the war broke out John enlisted in Company H, 2nd Michigan Volunteer Calvary, with which he served until the close of the war, when he was mustered out, returned home and went back to the work of keeping lighthouse, a job that he was engaged at when called out for service. After tending Cheboygan light for a couple of years he was then appointed

16 *Cheboygan Democrat*, March 14, 1910.

deputy revenue collector at Detour, where he was stationed for one year, then was appointed lighthouse keeper at the point where he remained for four years, then returned to the Cheboygan light. After remaining here for some time he became tired of the work and went into the northern peninsula being located at Escanaba most of the time, but again returned to Cheboygan after an absence of 17 years and assumed charge of the Cheboygan light, being in the service this time for 10 years.

Mrs. John Riggs[17] "age 73, died last Friday evening at the home of James Pennman. The deceased was a resident of Cheboygan for many years. Her husband was keeper of the Cheboygan Light at the breaking out of the Civil War, and went to the front. During his absence she took care of the light. The deceased leaves two daughters to mourn her, Mrs. A. Schall and Mrs. J. Pennman. Mrs. Riggs maiden name was Catherine Barron and she was first married to Alexander McLeod."

Jacob Sammons was born June 11, 1804 in Syracuse New York and died Oct 27, 1859 in Cheboygan. He was a canal boat captain, a farmer, a cooper, a land developer and much more. It was Jacob and his wife, Chloe Dutton, who are noted as being the first white family to start the city of Cheboygan. He first came to Cheboygan in the fall of 1844. He built barrels, helped build the first steam saw mill, farmed and in 1855 he was appointed keeper of the Duncan lighthouse. He retained this position two years. His son, Charles was born in the lighthouse.[18]

Capt. Sinclair[19] "who goes next week from Thunder Bay light to be keeper of the Cheboygan range lights, is one of the oldest and best men in the service. He has served 22 years, ten years at Fort Gratiot, and twelve and a half years at the island. The Captain is 65 years of age, still hale and hearty, but has for some years desired a post on the mainland and in or near some city. Some time ago he made application for such a change, and owing to his long service the officers of the department have been looking for such a location as he desired, and have found it at Cheboygan. The Captain's many friends in Alpena regret to have him leave us and will hope for his continued good health and good fortune."

Captain William J. Stewart[20] "arrived at his home in the city Saturday morning from the Petoskey hospital where he has been confined for eight weeks. He is looking quite pale and somewhat thin after his long confinement, as his work on a lightship out of Charlevoix had colored him as brown as a berry. William Stewart served as Mate on LV56 at North Manitou and later served as Master when the same lightship was stationed at Gray's Reef."

Capt. August Todd was born in New York State March 26, 1808; was educated in Ohio, and at the age of 18 began sailing, and was on the water for twenty years. Capt. Todd, widely known at one period throughout the lakes as commander of vessels and steamcrafts, resided at Mackinac since his retirement from the lakes. He came to the Island of Mackinac, and began the general merchandise business, which he followed until 1855; was with the light house business five or six years; was Village President for nine years; was School Director and School Trustee, and filled several other offices. Capt. Todd was married to Miss Sophia Hamel. They had eight children. He died Oct 2, 1873.

---

17 *Cheboygan News*, March 20, 1901.
18 *Cheboygan Daily Tribune*, 1929 Jubilee Edition
19 *Cheboygan Democrat*, Oc.t 18, 1894, reprinted from the Alpena Pioneer.
20 *Cheboygan Observer*, May 2, 1929.

Capt. August Todd[21] was born in New York State March 26, 1808; was educated in Ohio, and at the age of 18 began sailing, and was on the water for twenty years. Capt. Todd, widely known at one period throughout the lakes as commander of vessels and steamcrafts, resided at Mackinac since his retirement from the lakes. He came to the Island of Mackinac, and began the general merchandise business, which he followed until 1855; was with the light house business five or six years; was Village President for nine years; was School Director and School Trustee, and filled several other offices. Capt. Todd was married to Miss Sophia Hamel. They had eight children. He died Oct 2, 1873.

BOIS BLANC ISLAND LIGHTHOUSE ALBUM

Emily Ward taken long after she saved the illuminating apparatus at Bois Blanc Island light station as a young girl in 1837.

This new steel-framed boathouse which was erected at the Bois Blanc Island light station in 1910 by Chief district Engineer Ralph Russell Tinkham, who went on to serve as Chief Engineer for the Lighthouse Service. Courtesy Terry Pepper, GLLKA(3)

Landscape oriented view of the Bois Blanc Island light station.

21 *History of the Upper Peninsula*, Western Historical Company, A. T. Andress, Chicago, 1883, p. 361.

CHEBOYGAN ANSWERS
LINCOLN'S CALL TO COLORS

BY SALLY EUSTICE HUMPHREY

In April of 1861, following the attack on Fort Sumpter, President Abraham Lincoln issued a call for 75,000 volunteers to join the army of the North. Fourteen men from Cheboygan quickly enlisted and became part of Company F, Third Michigan Cavalry. This group was organized in Grand Rapids in September of 1861, and was mustered into service on October 4, 1861, with 1,160 officers and enlisted men.

The regiment went to St. Louis, Missouri, under the command of Colonel Robert H. G. Minty. They were then sent south to the Shiloh Battlefield in March and took part in the Siege of Corinth, Mississippi, in May of 1862. By 1863 they were stationed in Tennessee and Mississippi. After a one-month furlough in Michigan and then reenlisted

---

1 The Pine Hill Cemetery photos in this section, as well as the GAR monument in Washington Park were all taken by Doug Dailey for the Cheboygan History Center.

in January of 1864. They were sent to Arkansas to act as scouts and to secure food and supplies. They helped in the taking of Mobile, Alabama, and Baton Rouge, Louisiana, in 1865, and in July of 1865 they followed General Philip Sheridan to San Antonio, Texas, to help guard the Mexican border. The Third Michigan Calvary was disbanded in 1866.

Who were these men who went and why did they go? Cheboygan's population was less than 500 and the first permanent family home had only been established 16 years before. Many were young and probably seeking adventure. Others had grown up in the shadow of Fort Mackinac or descended from families with a military tradition. For whatever reason, they served their country well.

John Vincent, a local boat builder and his son **Benjamin** both enlisted. The father was 46 when he joined and he mustered out on August 8, 1862, at Camp Dennison, Ohio. The cavalry life was too hard on his rheumatism. His son Benjamin stuck it out until the end of the war when he mustered out at San Antonio, Texas. A newspaper stated that John was being admitted to the Soldier's Home at Grand Rapids. "He was a brave old soldier, not alone amid the rain of shot and shell when the nation's life was in peril, but in everyday life. . . The splendid work that Mr. Vincent and his beloved wife did for Cheboygan people in the old days when the whole town had the small pox and with no doctors, no medicine and no help, was as heroic, as any battlefield ever produced. Now that Mrs. Vincent has gone to her reward, we are glad that the old man will have a splendid home and all the comforts of life he just deserves."[2] His son Benjamin returned from the war but was killed by a lightning strike at Cecil Bay. He and his brother were repairing pond nets in a shanty and were instantly killed when lightning struck the wood building and it burned.[3]

Philip O'Brien

Philip O'Brien, age 42, enlisted as a private. He was born in County Clare, Ireland, and as a young man had served with the British Army in various parts of the world. He came to Cheboygan and married Margaret Hughes, crossing the ice to St. Ignace in February of 1851 to be married by Fr. Perriett. Margaret's brother–in- law worked at the water mill and her sister ran the mill boarding house, with Margaret's assistance. After their marriage, Margaret and Philip took up a homestead which later became part of the city. It was said Philip was the first white settler above the dam. Ten years after their marriage, Philip mustered in as a private in Captain McCloud's Company F, Third Regiment Calvary, and was assigned to horse artillery. He was wounded in action at Corinth, Mississippi, on October 4, 1862, which resulted in the amputation of his right arm. He continued to serve until he mustered out at Brownville, Arkansas, on October 24, 1864. O'Brien returned to Cheboy-

---

2 *Cheboygan Democrat*, February 19, 1902.
3 *Cheboygan Democrat*, June 13, 1885.

gan where he purchased land which later became known as O'Brien's Grove where St. Paul's Methodist Church is located today. Part of their property was used as the Cheboygan State Park, across from today's county fairgrounds, and managed by their son, Charles Henry O'Brien. O'Brien's Drive was also part of the homestead. Philip lived to be 95 years old.

Joseph Marcel Jerue was born in St. Michaels, Quebec, in 1834. He first came to Cheboygan in 1856. He was first employed by the government in the lake survey and later worked for Lorenzo Backus who owned a saw mill on the banks of the Cheboygan River. When the war broke out he enlisted in Company F, Third Michigan Cavalry. He came home on a furlough and married Cecelia Recolla who was born and raised on Mackinac Island. After the war they took up a homestead at Mullett Lake and became farmers. "In 1866 he settled on his farm at Mullett Lake, the country then being a dense wilderness, not a road had yet been laid out and there were nothing but Indian trails for the pioneer to follow."[4] His obituary said he was "once the most prosperous farmer in Cheboygan County."

Anson Dodge, enlisted as a private at age 21. He was the son of Edwin Almerton Dodge who in the 1860's had purchased the property that became Dodge's Point and the Mullett Lake Golf Club. Anson became attached to the 9th Illinois Cavalry and was discharged at Detroit on October 12, 1864. He came back to Cheboygan where he married Sylvia Jane Gee on January 28, 1866. He became a farmer and later moved to Saginaw where he died in 1918.

Myron Sammons was born about 1840 in Illinois to Jacob and Chloe Sammons. It was his family that built the first permanent residence in Cheboygan. Myron enlisted at age 21 as a private and served through the war, mustering out January

27, 1866, at San Antonio, Texas. He got his honorable discharge at 10:00 AM and died of typhoid fever an hour later.

Luke Ruddock enlisted at age 19. He mustered out on June 2, 1865, at Baton Rouge, Louisiana. He returned to Cheboygan where he married Margaret Clark in 1873. They lived in Burt Township where he was employed as a sawyer. Luke died in 1882, and when the GAR Post was formed in Cheboygan, it was named in his honor.

Henry Bartholomew was involved in the family coopering business in Cheboygan. They made fish barrels that were used to ship salted fish to Chicago and markets in the east. He mustered out on a disability discharge on May 8, 1865, in Saint Louis, Missouri, and returned to Cheboygan for a while, eventually moving to the New York area. His brother, Theodore, later enlisted in the Seventh Michigan Cavalry on February 27, 1864, and was mustered out in Salt Lake City, Utah.

Oliver Spooner was the son of Peter Spooner. He was born in 1839 in St. Martine, Chateauguay, Quebec and came to Cheboygan with his family. He enlisted in Company D, Third Cavalry on October 12, 1861, and mustered out at San Antonio, Texas, on February 12, 1866. He married Lucinda DuFresne, while on furlough, in Potsdam, New York. After the war he lived in Duncan and worked in the saw mill for many years. In 1910 he was living at the Grand Rapids, Michigan Soldiers' Home, age 71.

Jacob Wilson was born in New York and came to Cheboygan where he married Julia Penman. He enlisted in Company F, Third Michigan Calvary and rose to the rank of sergeant. His obituary said "up to a few days ago he was to have been seen in John R. Clark's store listening to the veterans who would congregate there and talk of the present war."[5] He was buried with military honors, the casket wrapped in a flag, and the handsome colors

4 *Cheboygan Democrat*, January 20 1908
5 *Cheboygan Democrat*, May 21, 1898.

of the GAR post were draped with crepe.

Austin W. Strang was the son of Cheboygan's fish inspector, Daniel Strang. He was born in October, 1842, in Ohio. He joined the Third Michigan Cavalry and mustered out February 12, 1866, at San Antonio, Texas. After the war he moved to Clinton Rock, Wisconsin, where he died in 1925.

James Lewis was born in 1843 in Mackinac County, Michigan, and enlisted for three years at age 18. He was discharged for disability at Jackson, Tennessee, on April 24, 1863. He later lived in Addison, Michigan.

Cyril Riendeau, born in 1840 in Canada, enlisted as a private on January 10, 1861, in Company F, Third Michigan Cavalry, from Cheboygan. He mustered out on August 31, 1862, at Tuscumbia, Alabama. Nothing further is known of him other than his name seems to match census information in Quebec after the war.

Clovis Vanyea headstone.

Following the end of the Civil War, many veterans moved to Cheboygan County. Some had family ties nearby, and others were looking for jobs in the sawmills and lumbering industry. The government granted up to 160 acres to veterans if they would agree to homestead unimproved property. The allure of "free land" brought many to the county. Some came in family groups, some by themselves. Some came at the invitation of men with whom they had served.

One extended family group that came was the Vanyea family from Malone, Franklin County, New York. They included the following:

• **Frank Vanye**a, private in Company E, 60th New York Infantry
• **Clotus Vanyea**, Company A, 98th New York Infantry and 60th New York Infantry
• **Nelson Bourdeau**, husband of Permilia Adella Vanyea, who joined the war age 16
• **John Vanyea**, Company D, New York 147th Infantry
• **Akin Capstraw,** husband of Jane Vanyea, Company H, 98th New York Volunteers.

The highest ranking Civil War officer to be buried in Cheboygan County was **Henry Greene**

6

6 GAR (Grand Army of the Republic) markers are used to mark Civil War grave sites. The G.A.R. (Grand Army of the Republic) was a fraternal organization for veterans of the Union Army. It was founded in 1866 and dissolved in 1956 when it's last member died.

*Brevet Bridgadier General
Henry Greene Davis*

Davis. He was born in 1819 in Addison, Vermont, and enlisted as a First Lieutenant in the 29th Indiana Infantry in Elkhart, Indiana. He rose to full Captain, and then Full Lieutenant Colonel of the 101st Colored Infantry on September 2, 1864. He then became a Brevet Colonel and Brevet Brigadier General USV on March 13, 1865. He was with General Grant at the Battle of Shiloh, Look Out Mountain, Chattanooga, and Chickamauga. He served as Commander of the Department of Mid-Tennessee as Brevet Brigadier General. After the war he moved to Cheboygan, with his wife and daughter Carrie. He died in 1898 and was buried in Pine Hill Cemetery. His son-in-law, Edwin Zina Perkins, held the office of Cheboygan Circuit Court Commissioner, Judge of Probate and County Treasurer. Edwin was then elected a Representative from Cheboygan County and later served in Congress.

Captain Edward A Bouchard[8] was born on board the schooner, Supply, near Green Bay, Wisconsin, on December 1, 1836. He attended primary school on Mackinac Island and attended Hiram College in Ohio while sailing in the summer months. In 1860 he was appointed Mate of the schooner, *Albatross*, and when the Civil War began he joined the Navy, enlisting in Chicago. He was assigned to the *USS Hartford*, the flagship of Admiral Farragut, who was in command of the West Gulf Squadron and was thus able to participate in the capture of Forts Jackson and San Philippe and the city of New Orleans. He then went up the Mississippi to take part in the battle of Mobile, Alabama. He was transferred to the *Kickapoo*, on which he served to the close of the war. He was honorably discharged from the Navy at New Orleans on July 27, 1865, holding the rank of Surgeon's Steward in Charge.

After the war he returned to Mackinac Island and was appointed master of the screw schooner *U.S. Grant*. He also sailed the *Frances Adah* and then the steamer *Islander*. In 1873 he sailed the passenger steamer *Grace Dormer*, which was destroyed by fire on July 3rd. He finished the season on the *Islander*. He then became master of the steamer *Kittie Reed*, the Mate of the lake tug *Leviathan*, Mate

7 Photo of Henry Greene Davis from website generalsandbrevets.com
8 *St. Ignace Enterprise*, May 20, 1925.

USS Hartford, Flagship of Admiral Farragut. Captain Edward Bouchard, of Cheboygan, sailed on her during the Civil War.[9]

and Pilot of the steamer *Norman*, Mate and Pilot of the steamer *Passaic* and Master of the *Conisteo*. In 1879 he helped establish the inland water route between Cheboygan and Petoskey on the steamer Van Raalte. He later ran the steamer *Messenger* to Manistique, and the *Van Raalte* between Harbor Springs and Manistique.

Captain Bouchard decided to return to civilian life and was appointed Cheboygan City Marshall for a two- year term. He was then appointed Superintendent of the Cheboygan shipyard, which was engaged in repair work. He then became Master of the tug *Duncan City*. He was elected Justice of the Peace and then re-elected three times. He died at age 78, in Cheboygan, and is buried in Pinehill Cemetery.

The cannon in front of the Cheboygan County Court House came from the USS Hartford which was the flagship of Admiral David G. Farragut. It was used during the battles of New Orleans, Vicksburg, Port Hudson and Mobile during the Civil War. It is a Dahlgren gun, designed by John

Adolphus Dahlgren, who was the Chief of Naval Ordnance. These guns were first cast in 1850 and 1,185 were made. Only 53 survive today, and one of those is here in Cheboygan. The 9 inch cannon in Cheboygan was cast by Cyrus Alger & Co, #225. Each of these type cannon weighed 9,200 pounds and fired a 170 pound shot. They could also fire multiple charges of smaller grape shot.

Cheboygan's cannon was first located near the front door of the old courthouse at Court & Main Streets. When that courthouse was torn down and replaced by the new County Building, the cannon was placed in front of the new courthouse on South Main Street. There are also three of these cannons in the Marina Park at Mackinaw City, and one each in Petoskey, Harbor Springs and Gaylord. The guns were brought to northern Michigan in the winter of 1904-05 from Mare Island Navy Yard in California. Credit for bringing the Farragut guns to Northern Michigan is given to Congressman George Alvin Loud. Edward Bouchard assisted in making local arrangements to get the cannon placed in Cheboygan.

9 Photo from *Civil War Naval Chronology*, 1861-1865, Naval History Division of Navy Department, Washington, DC, 1871. VI, 362.
10 Dave Garthus, *"The Other Gun in Cheboygan Has a Rich History,"* *Cheboygan Daily Tribune, Senior Living Section,* October, 2007, p. 4.

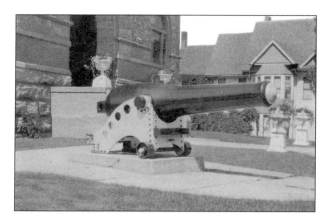

Cannon in Front of "Old Courthouse" once located at corner of Court and Main.

Thompson Gym was the headquarters for the GAR in Cheboygan.
Photo courtesy Patricia Wight Geyer Collection

The last of Cheboygan's "Boys in Blue" to die was Judge William N. Cross. He died August 14, 1937, at age 93. He was born in St. Lawrence County, New York, and enlisted in the 106th Regiment of New York Infantry. He was in Confederate prison camps at Danville and Libby, Virginia. When he came to Cheboygan, he took up the study of law at home and was admitted to the bar. He also entered politics and served as county clerk, twelve years as a probate judge, and twelve years as circuit court commissioner. He was a life member of the Masons and was credited with being the oldest member of the lodge in the state at his death.

The Thompson Gym was located on the corner of Main and Pine Streets where the new Cheboygan Brewery was just built. The bottom floor was used as a gym, auditorium, and community hall while the upstairs included the smaller meeting rooms and offices of the various service and legion groups that served from Cheboygan. The G.A.R. Room was located on the second floor. They held their meetings and kept records there. The original GAR Charter, issued on February 8, 1884, hung in that room. It had the names of 27 members. In October of 1897 the GAR Ruddock Post had formed a committee with Company H and they were seeking a site to build an armory for the joint use of the old soldiers, the Women's Re-

lief Corps and the young soldiers of Company H.

In 1920 the Armory was rented to the American Legion and became known as Memorial Hall. It was administered by the Legion until acquired by the Cheboygan Board of Education. During the time the Legion had charge of the hall many activities were sponsored by the Post. They held classes for children of the city. They sponsored basketball, volley ball and handball teams.

The building burned down in early 1942. This was very unfortunate for the community as it ended many of the school sports activities until a gym was built at Cheboygan High School. It is frustrating to the historians because most of the American Legion, GAR, WW1 and Women's Relief Corps records were lost in that fire.

Henry Frank Stinchfield was born in Bangor, Maine, in 1847, and enlisted for service in the Civil War in 1863 as a bugler at age 17. After the war he moved to Alpena and later Cheboygan where he was involved in lumbering and farming. After the death of his first wife, Abbie Nuite, he married Ada May Sherman in 1901. She was the last Civil War widow to die in Cheboygan County, passing away in 1980 at the age of 100.

The large rock used to make the GAR Monument in Washington Park came from the Stinch-

---

11 *Cheboygan Daily Tribune*, August 14, 1937.

field farm. Ada was very active in the Women's Relief Corps which is the organization that helped raise funds and see to the care of the veterans and their families. They sponsored the plaque to mark the monument.

ANTHANY BONDY
CIVIL WAR VETERAN

Grave marker of Anthany Bondy at Pine Hill Cemetary in Cheboygan.

The following story of Civil War Veteran, Anthany Bondy, was written in his obituary in 1919. It is stories like this that show us the pioneer spirit that founded Cheboygan.

Mr. Bondy was born at Ecorse, Wayne County on the 17th day of February , 183. Mr. Bondy resided with his parents, who were of French descent, and were among the early settlers of Wayne county, until he grew to manhood, when he was married and lived in Ecorse until 27 years of age, when during the year 1862, he heard his country's call for defenders and shouldering his musket, started for the front, with his company, leaving his wife and two small children at home.

He enlisted in August 1862 in the twenty fourth Michigan infantry, recruited at Detroit, which afterward became famous for its valor in the Great War, and earned for itself the name of the Iron Brigade. Mr. Bondy was a member of Company F. He was with the regiment continually until June 1864, when he was wounded and was sent home. He was in the thick of many engagements of the regiment, such as the Battle of Frederickburg, the Chancellorsville Campaign, the Battle of Gettysburg, and with Grant, during his Memorial Campaign and in the Siege of Petersburg in 1874, where he was wounded.

After the close of the war, Mr. Bondy moved his family to Cheboygan County, taking up a homestead on the banks of Mullet Lake, where by hard work and the attendant hardship upon pioneering, he and his faithful help mate succeeded in wresting a fine home from the virgin forest. They came up from Wayne County by boat and were landed with their household goods at Duncan, from which place they went to the land which had been assigned to them, and began work. After

a log house had been built, they began to clear up the land and by keeping constantly at it, soon had crops growing.

When they came here, their belongings were loaded upon a tug and taken up the river and dumped off in the wilderness at what was known then as Bismarck Landing, which was near where Aloha is now situated. There were three or four families, the Ball's and Andrew's and another family or two on that side of the lake when Mr. Bondy and his family arrived and their nearest and most numerous neighbors were the Indians.

There was nothing to Cheboygan at that time and Mr. and Mrs. Bondy have watched the growth of the city and the shaping of the surrounding country from a veritable wilderness to a community of great pride. In 1896 they sold their farm and bought a home in the city [Cheboygan], where they have since resided.

CHEBOYGAN G.A.R. PROJECT

Grand Army of the Republic medal front side, left, and back side, below.

A project is underway to record the lives of all Cheboygan County Civil War veterans. The Cheboygan County History Center is collecting obituaries, copies of documents, and photos. These will be available for research and display. It will include published lists of veterans, GAR and Women's Relief Corp information. If you have information or would like to be involved contact the Cheboygan County History Center. When this project is completed, copies will be available at the History Center and all Cheboygan County Public libraries.

HISTORY OF THE EARLY
BLACK RIVER SETTLEMENT 1880-1960

BY DALE D. FRANCE

Black River, Cheboygan, Mich.

Early settlement along the lower part of Black River in Cheboygan County was a very interesting part of Michigan history. The Black River is a branch of the Cheboygan River, which connects Mullett Lake with the Straits of Mackinac. The Black joins the Cheboygan River about three miles inland from the City of Cheboygan, which is located on the Cheboygan River. Black River angles off to its headwater, Black Lake, about twelve miles to the south east.

This lake has numerous rivers and creeks flowing into the lake from as far away as twenty miles to the south. Each of these streams was the highway which enabled thousands of logs to be transported out of the interior during the lumbering days. As the logs flowed into the lake, they were put into booms which were towed to the mouth of Black River. Here they were released to be carried by the current, down the river to the saw mills.

---

1 This paper was written for a Michigan History Class at Michigan State University in 1958. The information was gathered from personal interviews with relatives and neighbors: Charles France, Frank Stinchfield, Jr., Ada Stinchfield, and Fred St Antoine.
2 Postcard courtesy Patricia Wight Geyer Collection

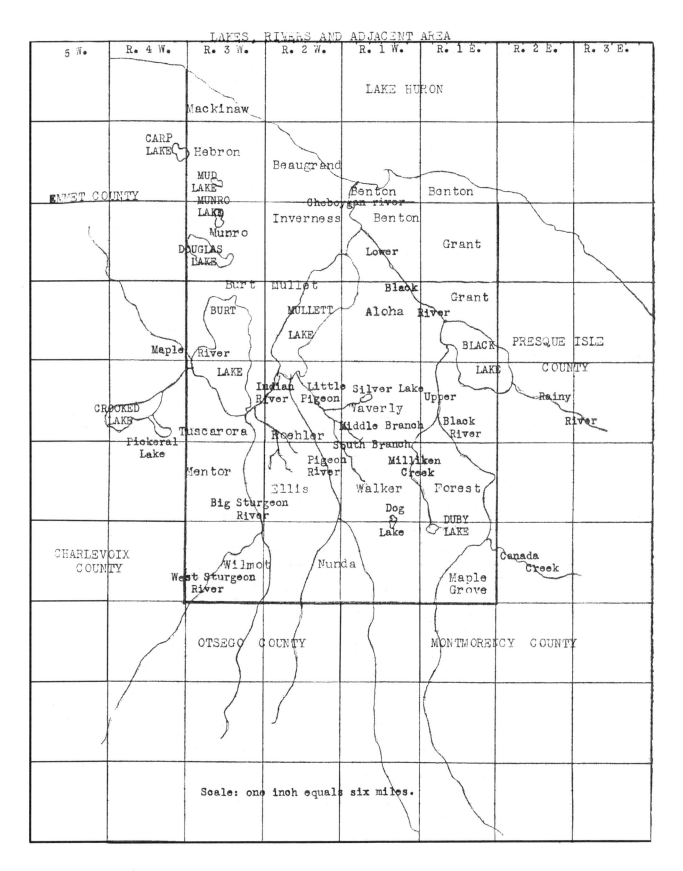

Map taken from a thesis by Lloyd M. Atwood, Cheboygan as a Nineteenth Century Lumber Area. 1947.

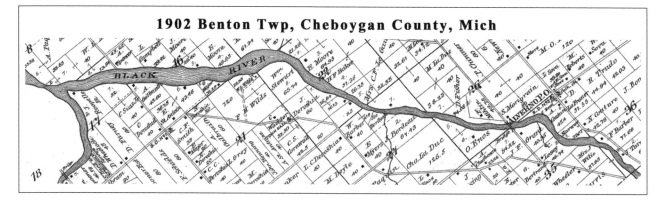

1902 Plat Book, Black River.

The last three miles before it dumps into the Cheboygan River, the Black River widens and becomes quite deep. From this point tugs were able to haul lumber out to the straits on barges, and supplies were brought back in. Because of this, saw mills were built and settlers began to build homes along its banks.

A traveler starting up Black River in 1880 would have found about a dozen homes and two saw mills. The first saw mill was at the fork of the Cheboygan River and Black River. It was called the Emery-Stinchfield Mill, named after its owners. On the southeast bank of the fork was a log cabin facing the Cheboygan River. It was owned by an Englishman by the name of David Hudson. David was one of the earliest settlers on the river and had married an Indian woman. He worked in the woods in the winter, rode the logs down river in the spring, and had the reputation of a fighter who had never been beaten.

Further up the river, about a half mile was the Matoon Mill. It was known for having the first circular saw in the country. This mill made up a small village. Besides the mill itself there was a cook's camp, a men's camp, an office, a store, and a large barn where the company kept about thirty horses. Off to the west of this cluster of buildings, on a high bluff, stood the Amos Galbraith home, an expensive looking home with fancy moldings around the roof and windows. Galbraith had come

from Alpena and was one of the owners of the mill.

The next house was the Joe St. Antoine place, a quarter of a mile up the river, sitting back about four hundred feet from the river, on a high bluff, overlooking a bay. This was a new house of finished lumber, but the log house where his family had previously lived still stood behind the new house and was used for a stable.

Cross Farm.

Further up the river was the George Major house, which was only a log cabin. Frank Wilds and Bill Cross built homes next to each other in a hardwood grove about a mile up the river from the Matoon Mill. They later sold their land to the Keeney Seed Company which turned it into one of the most prosperous farms in the area. A quarter of a mile beyond the Cross home was the Stuart

1 Warren P. Cross, *A Man From Michigan, A homespun Story and Yarn of Early Times in Michigan*, 1965, p. 19.

Earle Farm, near the Mograin Bridge at Black River, c 1880.   Collection of the Historical Society of Cheboygan County, Inc.(2)

house and beyond that a quarter of a mile further were the homes of Joe Deroshia and his father, side by side.

All of these people settling along the river were lumbermen except Joe Deroshia and his son, who were carpenters. The Deroshias worked in Cheboygan, commuting by boat. They would row down river and back up each night, a total of ten miles. Joe Deroshia Jr., had a large home of finished lumber, which still stands today and is owned by his daughter and son-in-law, Frank Stinchfield Jr., son of the mill owner. Frank is retired from Buick. The log home of Joe Sr., also still stands and though it is used as a chicken coup now, it looks as sturdy as the day it was built.

The river in front of these two homes was the center of a great deal of activity during the spring and summer. A boom company had built a sorting gap, because it was here that the river widened and there was relatively slow current the rest of the way down river. The sorting gap consisted of a catwalk, floating on logs, strung out across the river which was chained to each bank. Built along the catwalk were small shanties where a tally was often taken. As each log was pushed through an opening in the catwalk, it passed into the boom of the company to which it belonged, according to its mark. When a boom was filled it was hauled by tug to the owner's mill. At this time there was over a dozen sawmills in the area where logs might be hauled.

In the 1880's nearly all the settlers along the river were lumbermen and only a few did any farming at all. The farming that was done was only on a small scale. At first, most of the settlers just raised vegetables for their own use. These gardens were the responsibility of the wife and the growing chil-

Family portrait of the Deroshia Brothers.
Courtesy of Darlene Holling

Sorting Gap on the Cheboygan River, near the Black River fork.
Courtesy Ellis Olson

Photo of the Robinson Mill on east side of the Cheboygan River across from the tannery. Note the orchard across the river. The lower right shows a pile of bark—probably hemlock bark for the tannery.

Collection of the Historical Society of Cheboygan County, Inc.

dren too young to work in the saw mills.

By the end of the 1880's the river mills began to shut down because of the stiff competition of the bigger mills of Cheboygan that were located on the straits. These mills were not only better located for shipping lumber because the large lake vessels could load right off their docks, but as the supply of timber was declining in the surrounding area they could supplement their supply with logs from Canada and the upper Peninsula. The location of these mills was such an advantage, a few of them were able to continue operating until the 1920's.

After the early 1890's, the Black River settlers began clearing their land and farming in the sum-

mer, going back to lumbering hardwood only in the winter. Some would spend the winter cutting pine in the Upper Peninsula away from their families in order to have enough money to begin farming in the spring. One sad example of this was Arthur Galbraith, son of Amos Galbraith. Arthur was the head of a family of six and spent the whole winter working in the woods near Newberry to buy seed and equipment for spring farming. On Arthur's return trip in the spring, his wallet was lifted in a railroad station, and he returned home without a penny to show for his winter's work. Many others lost their money nearly as quickly in the saloons of Cheboygan. After spending winter in the woods they would walk past their homes and families without stopping until they had patronized a good many of the forty six saloons that were in Cheboygan at that time.

Most of the early agricultural produce was sold locally to feed the men of the saw mills and lumber camps. A farmer could also earn money renting his team for clearing land and building roads. But as the saw mills decreased, the farms increased and they had to begin raising crops that could be shipped out. Farmers of southern Michigan were raising grain, but the northern season was not long enough to permit a very high yield. By about 1900 the Keeney Seed Company established a branch in Cheboygan and began letting out contracts to the farmers to raise seed for them.

The soil along Black River seemed highly favorable for raising peas and most of the farmers began contracting for seed with the Keeney Company. The company bought the land owned formerly by Frank Wilds, Bill Cross and Stuart. They built a huge, hip roofed barn, five hundred and twenty feet long and about seventy feet high. The barn was well ventilated, which was needed to dry the peas for thrashing. The procedure for picking seed peas was pulling out the whole vine and storing it until it was dry enough to thrash. After the peas had been thrashed they were hauled to town where the company owned a seed elevator and warehouse, where the peas would be screened. The number one seed peas would be shipped out to be sold for seed and the culled peas returned to the company farm where it was fed to herds of hogs that ranged in number from six hundred to a thousand.

Many of the farmers along the river worked for the Keeney Company on the farm and in the

Keeney Seed Elevator and Storage Building which was located on the corner of Lake and Huron Street. Collection of the Historical Society of Cheboygan County, Inc.

elevator while at the same time they would get contracts from the company to raise seed on their own farms. The company would give them so much seed to plant and at the end of the season the farmer would bring in the threshed peas from his crop to the elevator. The peas would be screened and the amount of seed the company had advanced him in the spring would be deducted. From the remaining peas that were number one grade, the farmer would receive anywhere from a dollar and a quarter to two dollars a bushel.

When the land was new, a farmer could expect a yield of about thirty bushels of number one grade peas to the acre. Because the farmers raised this same crop year after year, without any crop rotation or attempting to put anything back into the soil, the yield began to fall off about 1910. Some of the farmers began using what new land they had left and others began raising green peas for a canning factory that had been built in Cheboygan. This was located next to the railroad tracks, just west of Cuyler Street and south of Court, behind the present day, Cheboygan Co-op.

By 1915 the Keeney Company changed the

Cheboygan Pea Canning Company, located south of Court Street, along the railroad track.

Collection of the Historical Society of Cheboygan County, Inc.

company farm to general agriculture. That same year it planted about fifty acres with apple orchards. When these orchards reached maturity its apples were shipped to New York and the east coast. The Keeney Company also began raising cattle, renting pasture from a two thousand acre ranch about twelve miles away, leaving the rest of the farm to raise feed for the winter and the dairy cattle. To support a large operation like the Keeney Farm nearly all the neighboring farmers were employed by the company because at this time there was little labor saving machinery available. For example, maintenance of the orchard required two men full time for pruning, replanting and disease control. At harvest time twenty five to fifty men, women and children were hired for picking the apples.

The rest of the farming operation required a crew of about twenty men during the summer. There were large crops of silage corn raised to feed the cattle during the winter. This would keep three

to five men busy most of the summer cultivating it with one horse cultivators. The rest of the crew would be used in spring for preparing the soil for planting, then haying, thrashing, (wheat, oats, barley) and silo filing. Most of these men worked for sixteen dollars a week, which was six ten-hour days. There was no such thing as workmen's compensation. If a man broke an arm, he was out of work and had a doctor bill to pay.

In spite of these conditions they were happy and thankful for their jobs. This was before the automobile age and most of the recreation was dancing or card playing parties of which each family would take turns entertaining the rest of the neighborhood. The chief means of transportation was the horse. Most everyone in the neighborhood could recognize his neighbor's teams of horses by the tone of the sleigh bells. At that time the horse was the family's most prized possession and nothing was too good for their horse's appearance. In

Steam tractor at the Riggs farm set up to tresh a load of hay in the nearby barn. The farm was located on South Extension Road in Inverness Township. Riggsville was established by the Riggs brothers in 1860. A post office opened there in March, 1880.

Collection of the Historical Society of Cheboygan County, Inc.

the winter the roads were rolled in order to pack the snow so the sleigh would not sink deep and the horse would not have to wade through the drifts. Each one in the neighborhood would take his turn rolling the road, and when he finished he would leave the roller at one of his neighbors. It became a habit that wherever the roller was left, the rest of the neighborhood would gather at that house for a card party later that night.

About 1925 the Kenny Farm began a different type of farming, that of fattening Montana lambs. In the fall of the year they would receive by railroad, about five hundred spring lambs from Montana. The company would ship in carloads of grain which would be culls from the other branches of the seed company to be used for fattening the lambs. The lambs were grained heavily all during the winter and the next summer until they were

Horse drawn plow used to clear snow on roads.   Collection of the Historical Society of Cheboygan County, Inc.

sold for mutton. In the spring, sheep were sheared, enabling the company to profit from the wool, besides the gain of weight of twenty to sixty pounds of the lambs. This was not as profitable as it may seem, because a high percentage of sheep died as a result of the heavy feeding.

By 1929 profitable farming became more difficult and the Kenny Company began leasing the farm. This forced a hardship upon the whole community. All of the neighboring farmers were now forced to live off their own farms without the part time employment of the Kenny Company. To add to the trouble of these farmers, was a national depression. During the thirties many of the farmers closed down entirely. When World War II came, more of the farmers left the farms and moved to the city to get the high wartime wages. After the war was over a few returned and began farming, which they believed to be a cleaner life than in the city. But before long they found profits too small for ten to fifteen hours a day of hard labor, so they returned to the city.

Today many of the farms along Black River are lying dormant and the fences are falling down. Along the river road there are a few new homes built near the old homesteads. There are still some signs that the area may live again, because speculators are again buying land along the river. Some of the old farms have already been subdivided with lots along the river with hopes of attracting the attention of the resort population as a place to retire or for a summer home. Whatever the fate of the Black River Country, only the future can tell, but whatever it is, it can never be as colorful and as exciting as its past.

Sheep from Ravilli County, Montana.

Editor's Note: *Dale France wrote this paper when he was in college in 1958, more than 50 years ago. He still lives on the Black River and has watched the changes continue. He has seen the area turn from farming to resort to permanent, year round housing. Dale has a great appreciation for history and it is his desire that new residents moving into the Black River area know about the early years on the river.*

Cheboygan Brewing History

By Phil Porter

In 2009 a small group of Cheboygan residents conceived the idea of establishing a microbrewery in their hometown. Intrigued by the idea that there had been an historic Cheboygan brewery and with a desire to reconnect with these brewing roots, the group decided to name their venture the Cheboygan Brewing Company and begin brewing beer in 2011, exactly one-hundred years after the town's last brewery closed. The new brewery was constructed on the corner of North Main and Pine streets, just a few blocks from the site of the original Moloney Brothers brewery which was situated on the west bank of the Cheboygan River at the intersection of North Main and Court streets.

From the beginning, the brewery partners have been committed to sharing the history of brewing in Cheboygan as part of their mission. To this end, a small museum was included in the public area of the new brewery. The purpose of this paper is to provide an historical narrative that will be used, along with historic photographs and objects, to create the museum. This information will also be shared with the public through the Cheboygan Brewing Company website and this Cheboygan County History Center publication.

Charles and Peter Hentschel established Cheboygan's earliest commercial brewery on the west bank of the Cheboygan River just south of the Cheboygan city limits. The Hentschels purchased the property in July 1872 and established their brewery soon after. Boasting a beer of the "finest quality, equal in every respect to Milwaukee or Toledo Lager," the brewery was known vari-

ously as "Cheboygan Brewery," "C. Hentschel and Bro. Brewery" or "Hentschel Bros. Brewers." The brothers were natives of Prussia who employed a young immigrant from Wirtemberg, Germany, H. Tiedemann, to assist as brewer. The brewery produced a modest output of 500 barrels per year.[1]

The Hentschel brothers sold their Cheboygan brewery and property in September 1881 to August Quast and Charles Schley who reestablished the brewery under the name Cheboygan Brewery and Bottling Works. The 36-year old German-born Quast, who owned and operated a saloon on Detroit's Michigan Avenue, and Cheboygan-resident Schley, hired Adolph Hauck to manage the brewery. Hauck, the 21-year old son of German-born

---

1 Cheboygan County Register of Deeds Office, Liber D, pp. 203-4, Liber E, p. 212. *Cheboygan Democrat*, April 14, 1881. *Michigan State Gazetteer and Business Directory*, 1879, 1881, Michigan State Library, Lansing, MI; American Breweries, Donald Bull, Manfred Friedrich and Robert Gottschalk, Trumbell, Ct.: 1984. *The Register of United States Breweries 1876-1976* (Volume I & Volume II) by Manfred Friedrich and Donald Bull; Printed privately by Holly Press, Stamford, Connecticut (1976).

immigrants, had previously worked as a bartender at Frank Paronts saloon in Detroit. Charles Eberhardt, also just 21 years old and the son of German-born immigrants, served as the company brewer. In June 1883 Schley sold his share of the property and business to Quast who continued to operate the brewery under his name until he shuttered the plant in 1884.[2] Quast's decision was undoubtedly influenced by the success and competition provided by James F. and Patrick X. Moloney's Northern Brewery.

The Moloney family arrived in Cheboygan in the late 1870s and, for nearly a century, established themselves as business and civic leaders who made considerable contributions to the community. James L. Maloney emigrated with his family from Ireland to Canada, through Quebec City, in the mid- 1850s. James and his wife, Ellen O'Neil, were natives of Tipperary where several of their nine children, including James F. and Patrick, were born. The Maloney family lived in Amherstberg, Ontario for a while before moving to Detroit where James started a grocery business assisted by sons John and James F. Maloney. In 1877 their brother, William, established a brewery in Detroit under his name. The business, later named Vienna Brewing Company and featuring English ales and porters as well as German lagers, was the family's first venture in the brewery business. In the late 1870s James F. Moloney moved to Cheboygan where he ran a saloon in 1877 and, two years later, opened a grocery store. His brother Patrick joined him in the grocery business which they jointly operated until they launched the brewery in 1882.[3]

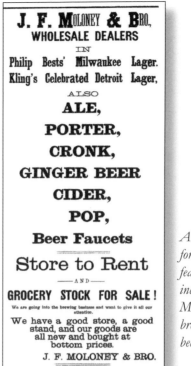

An 1882 advertisement for the Moloney Grocery featuring several beers including Philip Best's Milwaukee Lager, the brewery that eventually became Pabst.

James F. Moloney

The opening of a brewery, or any business, in Cheboygan in the early 1880s coincided with tremendous growth and prosperity in the community.[4] Northern Michigan's lumber industry spawned the construction of sawmills beginning in the 1840s. By 1880 Cheboygan, with it wide river and nearby Duncan City with its well-protected bay, boasted dozens of mills with hundreds of employees cutting and shipping millions of board feet of lumber every year. The success of the lumber industry attracted settlers and other businesses including banks, grocery stores, blacksmith shops, foundries, saloons, and hotels. In 1881, the Michigan Central Railroad established service to Cheboygan and, the following year, extended its tracks to Mackinaw City. Rail service put Cheboygan on the main transportation route between Detroit

2 United States Federal Census, 1880; *Cheboygan Directory 1884*, excerpted from the *Directory of Big Rapids, Mecosta County, Cadillac, Cedar Springs, Cheboygan...* Published by R.L. Polk and Co. Tribune building, Detroit, Mich. 1884, MI Gen Web; *Michigan State Gazetteer and Business Directory, 1883*. Cheboygan County Register of Deeds Office, Liber H, p. 23, Liber H, p. 57.

3 Genealogical information about the Moloney family is found in several sources including *Descendants of James L. Moloney*, manuscript provided by Sally Eustice Humphrey and the Cheboygan Historical Museum; *A History of northern Michigan and its People*, Perry Powers, The Lewis Publishing Company, Chicago, 1912; *Memorial Record of the Northern Peninsula of Michigan*, The Lewis Publishing Company, 1895. *Michigan State Gazetteer and Business Directory, 1877, 1879, 1881*. *Brewed in Detroit, Breweries and Beers Since 1930, Peter Blum*, Wayne State University Press, Detroit; 1999, pp. 97-100.

4 Additional information on the history of Cheboygan can be found in *Among the Sturdy Pioneers, The Birth of the Cheboygan Area as a Lumbering Community, 1778-1935*, Matthew J. Friday, Trafford Publishing, Victoria, B.C., 2006.

and Mackinaw and brought additional businesses, settlers and an ever-growing number of tourists and summer residents to the area. The influx of businesses and settlers swelled the population of Cheboygan County from 2,196 in 1870 to 11,986 in 1890. All of which boded well for the Moloney brothers as they launched their brewery.

James and Patrick chose the west bank of the Cheboygan River at the junction of South Main and Court streets as the location for their brewery. They established the firm under the name J. F. Moloney and Bro. and, initially, called their operation the Northern Brewery. The brothers hired Charles Schmidt, an experienced brewer from Cincinnati, to oversee beer production.[5] By nature, breweries require a tremendous amount of fresh water, and the Moloney's connected their plant to the city water works, which began in 1882.

The original brewery, which produced about 40 barrels a day, consisted of several buildings that provided space for a malt mill, mash tub, brew kettle, office, engine room, cooler, ice house, beer bottling, and a dwelling. The facility was initially lit with candles and kerosene lamps and powered by a steam engine fueled by wood and coal.[6] The brewery followed a seasonal pattern with a peak in production during the summer months when a cool beer was appreciated by both residents and vacationers. In winter, the Moloneys kept a crew of ice cutters busy harvesting and storing the vast amount of ice that was required for the brewing process prior to modern refrigeration. The lagers, ales, porters, and other beers produced by the Moloneys were well received by northern Michigan customers.

In February 1890 the Moloney brothers divided the brewing and bottling activities of the com-

Northern Brewery at S.Main and Court Sts.   Collection of the Historical Society of Cheboygan County, Inc.

5 *Cheboygan Democrat*, September 16, 1882.
6 *The Traverse Region, Historical and Descriptive, with Illustrations of Scenery and Portraits and Biographical Sketches of Some of its Prominent Men and Pioneers.* Chicago: H.R. Page and Co, 1884. Sanford Fire Insurance Map, Cheboygan, Michigan, 1884.

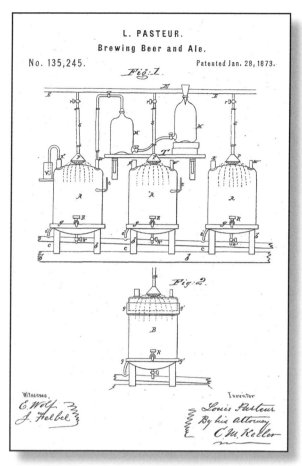

Louis Pasteur's process for purifying beer and ale.
A.M. Photo-Lithographic Co., NY

and covered with tin foil. Labels were glued into place and the bottles were moved to the cool cellar to await shipment.[8] Patrick generated additional income at his new location by bottling a variety of other products including carbonated waters, ammonia, blueing, and a wide variety of soft drinks including his popular "Imperial Ginger Ale."[9]

Bottle label for the Cheboygan brewing and Malting company High Grade Export.

pany. James purchased his brother's half interest in the brewery and, in May, incorporated the business under the name "Cheboygan Brewing and Malting Company." The bottling plant at the brewery was closed and Patrick started a "steam bottling works" on the corner of Main and Nelson streets.[7] The split seems to have been amicable as Patrick continued to bottle his brother's beer, which was transported to the site in barrels and bottled under the watchful eye of the brewmaster who made sure that the bottles were carefully washed and rinsed prior to filling. Once filled and corked, the bottles were steamed in a huge vat to prevent fermentation, after which the corks were wired into place

With Patrick gone from the company, James Moloney turned to other relatives to help him run the brewery. His brother-in-law William Alliar (married to his sister Bridget) served as secretary-treasurer until 1901. Sylvester "Vet" Moloney, James' 21-year old son, joined the company as bookkeeper in 1896 and took over as secretary-treasurer in 1901, a post he retained until the company was sold four years later.[10]

In 1905, after more than 20 years in the brewery business, James Moloney decided to sell the Cheboygan Brewing and Malting Company.[11] Moloney and his fellow stockholders held their last meeting on February 1 and adjourned to Minneapolis where, on the same day, they transferred their stock to the new owners. On February 7 the new board of directors elected Albert Massolt president, M.S. Rutherford vice president and Siegmund Wilhartz as secretary and resident manager.[12]   Mas-

---

7   Cheboygan County Register of Deeds Office, Liber X, pp. 4-5, Liber U, p. 571.
8   *Cheboygan Democrat*, August 1897
9   *Cheboygan City Directory*, 1908.
10 United States Federal Census, 1893-94, 1895-96, 1897, 1899, 1901, 1903-04, 1905.
11 James established and became president of the new Cheboygan County Savings Bank and his son Vet joined his father as a bank director and became involved in real estate and insurance businesses

Cheboygan Brewing and Malting Company beer cart in front of the company offices on Main Street, 1908.

Collection of the Historical Society of Cheboygan County, Inc.(4)

solt's father owned and operated a bottling business in Minneapolis and Wilhartz had recently served as secretary and manager of the Standard Brewing Company in Mankato.[13] Wilhartz filled out his staff by hiring Joseph Moloney, James' son, as his assistant manager, and William Keinath as brewmaster.[14]

The new owners immediately made plans to expand and improve the brewery and, in mid-April, met with Cheboygan "saloon men" at the armory to explain their ideas and give them an opportunity to invest in the new venture.[15] President Massolt spent considerable time in Cheboygan during the first year overseeing the new construction. Improvements included installing electric lights and doubling the size of the plant by adding a new ice house, expanding beer storage, and construct-

Brewery asstistant manager James Moloney.

ing an office and bottling works across the street on the south corner of Court and Main streets.[16]

The new company, preferring to keep the entire operation in house, cut ties with Patrick Mo-

---

12 *Cases Decided in the Supreme Court of Michigan from June 8 to September 27, 1910,* James Reasoner, State Reporter. Vol 1, 62, First Edition, Chicago: Callaghan and Co., 1911.

13 *Men of Minnesota: A Collection of the Portraits of Men in Business and Professional Life in Minnesota.* Minnesota Historical Company, 1902, p. 526. *Land of Amber Waters: The History of Brewing in Minnesota,* Doug Hoverson, University of Minnesota Press, pp. 243-4, 255.

14 *Cheboygan Democrat,* Souvenir Issue, September 20, 1906.

15 *Cheboygan Democrat,* April 17, 1905.

16 *Michigan State Gazetteer and Business Directory,* 1907

Siegmund Wilhartz managed the brewery until 1909. Below, a 1911 advertisement in the Cheboygan Democrat.

loney who continued to bottle other products but ceased bottling beer for the Cheboygan Brewing and Malting Company in 1905. Beer was pumped from the brewery to the new bottling plant through a pipe that ran below Main Street.[17] The company's new bottles featured "crown cap" closures, a device invented by William Painter in 1892 and still, with few changes used on many beer bottles today. In 1907 bottled beer from the brewery was selling for $1.25 for a dozen quarts and $1.50 for two dozen pints.[18]

The new ownership not only expanded the facility but also added new beers and aggressively marketed their products. "Silvo" and "Bohemian" became the brewery's trademark beers and most popular brews. A series of advertisements appeared in local newspapers promoting the purity, quality and medicinal advantages of the company's beers. In a tongue-in-cheek challenge to the Joseph Schlitz Brewing Company's promotional slogan "The Beer that Made Milwaukee Famous," the Cheboygan brewery claimed to produce "The Beer that Made Milwaukee Jealous."

Siegmund Wilhartz managed the brewery until 1909 when Dietrich W. Thoma became president and treasurer of the company and A.R. Riebeth was appointed secretary. Joe Moloney continued to work for the company and assist with the opera-

tion of the brewery. This management team operated the plant until it closed two years later.[19]

Cheboygan brewers, beginning with those who worked for Hentschel and Quast, were primarily of German origin. In the mid-nineteenth century, American beer tastes were beginning to change from British-style ales, porters, and stouts to lagers. German immigrants, who flocked to the United States as a result of civil unrest and military revolution in their homeland in 1848, brought their recipes for lager, a pale beer with a distinct hop flavor that soon became popular throughout the United States. Lagers were sometimes referred to as "Bohemian" style beers while the darker Bavarian-style beers were named after the Bavarian cities of Munich (Munchen), Wurzburg, or Ulm.[20]

Cheboygan Brewing and Malting Company c. 1908 featuring "Silvo Bottle Beer"

Brewers working for the Moloney brothers included Charles Schmidt (1884) and John Zaiger who oversaw the brew pots from the late 1890s to the turn of the century. Zaiger was born in Wuertenburg, Germany and immigrated to the United States in 1881. A graduate of the American Brewing Academy in Chicago (later the Wahl-He-

17 *"Historic Building Coming Down Soon,"* Gordon Turner, *Cheboygan Tribune,* September 22, 1986.
18 *Cheboygan Democrat,* November 8, 1907.
19 United States Federal Census, 1909-10, 1910-11
20 *Brewed in Detroit, Breweries and Beers Since 1930,* Peter Blum, Wayne State University Press, Detroit; 1999, pp.42-44.

Advertisement from 1909.

ers continued to produce "Blue Label" and added new brews including "Cheboygan Bohemian," "Wurtzberger," "Export," and the very popular "Silvo." [23]

Little is known about the extent to which Cheboygan beer was distributed in northern Michigan. Certainly it was a staple in the community, both for private consumption and in the town's many saloons. James Moloney's brother John, a liquor distributor in Sault Ste. Marie, sold both Pabst and Cheboygan Brewery products.[24] In 1884 the Moloneys established a second bottling plant and branch office in St. Ignace.[25] Here company representative Napoleon Rapin made deliveries with his horse and wagon. By 1907, however, manager Sig Wilhartz, claiming that they were "taxed to the fullest capacity to support Cheboygan and the immediate locality where their trade has enjoyed a phenomenal growth of late," closed the St. Ignace operation and ordered Rapin to ship the delivery horse to Cheboygan.[26] Though current research does not provide documentation, it is reasonable to assume that the breweries products were sold in

nius Institute of Fermentology), Zaiger oversaw the production of both an export (a pale lager) as well as a porter (a dark, stout-like beer of British origin.) The Moloney brewery also produced beers with the brand names "Perfecto" and "Blue Label." [21] After Zaiger left the Cheboygan Brewing and Malting Company he cofounded a brewery in Petoskey that eventually became a distribution enterprise called Zaiger Beverage Company. The company continues today under the name Bayside Beverage Corporation.

William Keinath became brew master after Wilhartz took control of the brewery in 1905. Keinath was replaced by Herman Scheltle who, like Zaiger, was a graduate of the Wahl-Henius school. Scheltle remained in this position from 1907 to 1911 when he returned to the Chicago-based brewing school to join the staff. Both brew-

Cheboygan Brewing and Malting Company "Bottling Department" and office on Main St. across from the brewery, c. 1910.
Collection of the Historical Society of Cheboygan County, Inc.

---

21 *Cheboygan Democrat*, October 30, 1897; *Cheboygan City Directory 1884*, Op. Cit.; *Plat Book of Cheboygan County Michigan*, Beaugrand Township, P.A. and J.W. Myers, Surveyors and Draughtsmen, Minneapolis: The Consolidated Publishing Co, 1902.
22 *Cheboygan Democrat*, March 3, 1911
23 *Michigan State Gazetteer and Business Directory,* 1907-08, 1909-10, Cheboygan City Directory, 1908.
24 *Memorial Record of the Northern Peninsula of Michigan,* Chicago: The Lewis Publishing Company, 1895, p. 349.
25 *Cheboygan Democrat*, May 15, 1884
26 *Cheboygan Democrat*, November 8, 1907.

Cheboygan Brewing and Malting Company buildings in foreground along the Cheboygan River c. 1911, just before it closed.
Collection of the Historical Society of Cheboygan County, Inc.

other regional communities including Mackinaw City, Indian River, Petoskey, Harbor Springs, Onaway, Rogers City and Mackinac Island.

In 1911, after 29 years of beer production, the Cheboygan brewery closed its doors for the last time as a result of a declining local economy, the impact of local prohibition laws, and competition from larger breweries. Cheboygan's sawmills kept humming as long as there was enough white pine to feed the demand for lumber, but timber production in Michigan dropped by almost 70% between 1889 and 1905 as the state's forests were cleared.[27] Mills were closed, jobs were lost, and the community's population began to stagnate. The problem in Cheboygan was compounded by the 1898 fire that destroyed Duncan City and it lumber production facilities. The county population peaked at 17,872 in 1910 but began to fall soon after and by 1920 had dropped 22%. It wasn't until the 1970s that the county population once again reached its level of 1910.[28] While a growing tourism industry provided some seasonal relief to employment decline, it could not replace the losses suffered from the timber industry decline.

The brewery also suffered from the growing prohibition movement that was gathering momentum in the early twentieth century. Although the sale of alcoholic beverages was not banned across the country until the passage of the Eighteenth Amendment in 1919, substantial pressure from the temperance and anti-saloon movements impacted ordinances in northern Michigan communities a decade before.

In April 1909 Emmet County went dry, closing that market to the brewery. The following year the City of Cheboygan voted to restrict the number of saloons in town to one for every 500 residents. As a result, the number of local bars dropped from 30 to 14. The ordinance took effect in 1911, the same year that the brewery closed.

The rise of large beer companies that shipped their products across the country beginning in the 1890s, also spelled doom for the Cheboygan brewery. Typical of the variety of beers available to Straits of Mackinac area residents was the situation on Mackinac Island where 1890's soldiers at Fort Mackinac enjoyed Schlitz of Milwaukee in their post canteen and the island's local taverns were serving Anheuser Busch beers. In Cheboygan, grocer Cornelius Gallagher met the demand for national brews by offering Pabst Blue Ribbon beer in his store just south of the brewery on Main Street. Gallagher's placed large advertisements in the local paper touting it as the "Best Beer Brewed." [29]

As the number of beer drinkers decreased and competition grew, the owners of the Cheboygan Brewing and Malting Company had no choice but to cease operations. In September 1911, company president Dietrich Thoma shuttered the brewery, mothballed the brew kettles, and began selling Chicago's Schoenhofen beer from the company's cold storage plant.[30]

27 Friday, Op. Cit. pp. 95-106.
28 Correspondence from Sally Eustice Humphrey, September 27, 2010.
29 *Cheboygan Democrat*, December 2, 1910.
30 *Cheboygan Democrat*, September 15, 1911.

South Main Street, Cheboygan, Mich.

By 1915, the Cheboygan Brewing and Malting Co. brewery buildings had vanished and the only remnant of the company was the office and bottling plant across the street where Joe Moloney was bottling soft drinks (at left).

Embury-Martin Mill 1900
Cheboygan, Mich.

Embury-Martin Lumber Company located on the West side of Cheboygan on Lake Huron. Company owned by S. Harris Embury and William L. Martin. Logs delivered to the mill during the winter by the steam powered locomotive running on caterpillar treads. Embury-Martin was the last lumber mill to operate in Cheboygan running until fire destroyed it on November 1928. Collection of the Historical Society of Cheboygan County, Inc.(6)

The Crown Chemical plant located on West side of Cheboygan near the old Embury-Martin Lumber Mill. The plant was constructed around 1905 and operated to around 1920. The building was destroyed by fire on May 15, 1925.

Store and Flouring Mill of the W. & A. McArthur Co., Ltd.   CHEBOYGAN, Mich -1898

McArthur's Store and Flour Mill, with the smoke stack in the background from his paper mill.

The Hub Livery and Simpson J H & Co. Livery, located on the NW corner of Main and Elm Streets. Later the Adams Standard Service occupied this spot until recently when the First Community Bank constructed their new office building here.

Located at Water and First Streets, the house and tanks have long been removed. The building on the right is still standing and is currently owned by Ryba Marine Construction of Cheboygan.

Cheboygan Tannery
Largest Sole Leather Tannery in the World
By Sally Eustice Humphrey

For many years a smokestack and some old pilings along the riverbank were the only signs of the thriving tannery industry Cheboygan once hosted. Today even the smokestack is gone and memories have faded, so the story must be told before it is all forgotten. In December of 1891 Edgar Roselle Hinkley came to Cheboygan to build a tannery. He was joined in the spring by Charles Orlando Shaw of the Shaw Tanning Company, and they commenced to lay out the grounds and began to build the buildings that would one day cover twenty-five acres and include over thirty buildings plus numerous housing units. Both men had experience in tanneries, their family histories tracing back to generations of tanners.

Charles Shaw descended from the Fayette Shaw family of Boston, Massachusetts, which at the time was the largest sole leather tannery in the world. Charles grew up in Dexter, Massachusetts, where his father managed a branch of the com-

---

1 Photo from Patricia Wight Geyer post card collection, courtesy of her family.

pany. He attended business classes at the Phillips Exeter Academy which was a very prestigious prep academy that fed students into Harvard University. After attending this school he went into the family tanning business, and at the age of 28 came to Cheboygan. He remained here about four years, leaving soon after the birth of his son in 1895. The Shaw's sold their remaining portion of the tannery to Phister & Vogel and Charles left for Huntsville, Ontario. The Shaw's later established tanneries in Montreal, Roxton, Waterloo, and Farnham in Canada. By 1912 their Canadian companies were producing eight million pounds of sole leather, much of which was exported to England. Charles expanded into rail and ferry transportation, the hotel business, and entertainment as well as tanning.

Edgar Hinkley, the son of Nathan Hinkley, grew up in Sandisfield, Berkshire County, Massachusetts, where his father worked in a tannery. He learned his trade in a very progressive mill. The son of the mill owner, Edwin Burt, went to Hartford, Connecticut where he was the first to make shoes by machine. The Hinkley family then moved to Stephenstown, Rennselaar County, New York which was the home of another expert tanner. Zadock Pratt, born in Stephenstown, built a large town of 2,000 inhabitants around his tannery that was later renamed Prattville. Edgar grew up surrounded by tannery life. It appears he moved away from his family by the time he was 17 and was probably working at the tannery in Johnsburg, Warren County, New York, where his future wife, Lavina Steele, was born. He married in July of 1875, and by 1887 had moved to Leetonia, Pennsylvania, home of the Cedar Run Tanning Company. His son Lloyd Hinkley was born there. The family moved to Cheboygan in December of 1891. Edgar's obituary stated that he and Mr. Shaw were the first two men to start on the erection of the tannery and he worked there ever since.

Lloyd Hinkley

Cheboygan was looking to put in a tannery business. Much of the original pine forest had been cut, but there was plenty of hemlock which could be cut for bark. There had been a former hemlock extraction plant in Mullet Lake Village and there were men still willing to supply the bark. This had been known as the Newton-Ellis plant and was running from the mid 1870's until about 1890, when the property was sold to John Rittenhouse.[2] This hemlock extract was the chemical agent used to tan the hides. Cheboygan also had a railroad and a port which could bring in hides. The men who formerly cut wood were looking for jobs and available for labor.

The newspaper reported:

A few days ago, the junior member of a big Boston firm of tanners and leather dealers slipped quietly into town, made a thorough investigation of our bark supply, proposed a sight for a tannery, facilities for shipment and manufacture, and after satisfying himself, made a proposition to the Business Men's Association, and at a meeting at the City Hall Tuesday night the proposition was promptly accepted, and a guarantee at once signed by our business men, which will secure the much sought for and desired improvement. The proposition of the Boston firm was very favorable, and was based upon the splendid natural advantages of our location for such an institution as the gentlemen propose to establish. In brief, the proposition was that if Cheboygan would give the firm a site and the right of way for a railroad to connect with the Michigan

---

2 Guth, Fred E. and Eleanore, *A Bit About Mullet Lake Village*, 1975, p 216.

Central road they would at once build a tannery with a capacity of about 10,000 cords of bark per year, the site to be given them in fee simple one year after they had got out the tannery in operation. The site picked out by the firm is the John F. McDonald farm just over the city limits to the south of town, opposite Robinson's mill, which is a splendid location, furnishing ample ground for the works and can be had at a very reasonable price.[3]

Leather had more importance in the nineteenth century than it does today. Boots and shoes were all made of leather as were belts, wallets, and gloves. Leather was used in clothing as vests and jackets. These garments protected the wearer from wind and weather much better than woven wool, cotton, or linen material. Leather harnesses for horse buggies, leather saddles and upholstery for buggy seats and furniture were in demand. Blacksmiths and other craftsmen wore leather aprons to protect their bodies from heat and sharp objects. Men carried knives in leather sheaths. All kinds of straps and buckles were made of leather—it was the Velcro and bungee cord of the 1900's. Machinery that was belt driven—everything from a treadle sewing machine to a huge steam thresher-required leather made into long strips.

Tanneries were set up to produce certain kinds of leather. Some of the vegetable-tanned leather was very soft, and they used goat and calf skin to make items such as gloves. The upper parts of shoes had to be flexible to be comfortable, and they needed to be made softer and of different kinds of hides. The soles of shoes needed to be thick and tough. They were best tanned with hemlock and that is what was made in Cheboygan.

The Cheboygan plant was first built and run by the Shaw Tanning company. These clips from the *Cheboygan Democrat* tell of the progress in building the mill.

May 1892 Mr. Shaw is overseeing now in person. He is boarding with several of his men at Mrs. F. Cummings. Mrs. Keen and Mrs. Rhodes have their houses full of boarders. There are several families moved into the tenement houses on the river bank. The store and office is about completed and ready for paint and plaster.

June 1892 The exterior of the leach house has been completed. The store is also being filled with goods. Several teams are kept busy hauling material such as lumber, timber, and old gas pipes, the firm having purchased a lot of brass pipe from F. H. Stinchfield, which were formerly in use in the old Newton & Ellis extract factory. The tenement houses are all filled. The firm's old horses are not gaining in flesh very fast but Cheboygan's fresh air is making them more spirited.

June 8, 1892 The family of Mr. Shaw, of the tannery arrived Monday, including that gentleman's father. They came from Montreal via the Soo. Mr. Shaw will be settled in his new home on Huron Street in a few days.

August 20, 1892 Work at the tannery is going right along. The engineer who is to superintend the building of the trestle over the gulley for the railroad arrived Wednesday and will push the work. There are a number of cars loaded with bark on the switch.

October 8, 1892 *The Tannery Now a Go with Lots of Capital.* The unfortunate and unforeseen business embarrassments of the

Leather from the tannery was used to make a variety of goods including clothing items like belts, gloves, vests, jackets and shoes.

senior Shaw of the tannery firm, paralyzed for a time the attempt to start a tannery here. For several months the firm has been in the soup, but now Fred Vogel, of Milwaukee, has purchased an interest, and the firm will be made a stock company, we hear, with $300,000 capital. Messrs. Shaw & Vogel are in Bay City prepared to close the matter of a side track with the Michigan Central Railroad, and men have been sent outside to close up and pay up on all bark contracts, and a large force of men will be put on next week to finish the tannery at once.

Nov 12, 1892   The spur track to the tannery will be completed Dec 1. The tannery folks are receiving 10 to 15 carloads of bark per day, and several carloads of hides. They have settled up all their contracts for bark down the road. Jene Hartig, city surveyor of Bay City, is working on the plans for the trestle for the spur track to the tannery.

June 1894   C.O. Shaw is making great improvements to his property. The barn has been raised and improved, the house is being painted, new cement sidewalks are being laid, and everything put in nice shape.

NOTE: A BOSTON SHOE COMPANY WHICH BOUGHT LARGE AMOUNTS OF TANNED LEATHER FROM THE SHAW TANNERY WENT INTO BANKRUPTCY AND THEY DIDN'T PAY FOR THE GOODS THEY RECEIVED FROM THE SHAWS. THIS PUT A STRAIN ON THE SHAW COMPANY WHICH WAS BUILDING THE TANNERY IN CHEBOYGAN AS WELL AS ONE IN WISCONSIN. THEY ALSO HAD A DOZEN OTHER TANNERIES IN MASSACHUSETTS , NEW YORK AND CANADA. THEY FORMED A STOCK COMPANY FOR THE CHEBOYGAN TANNERY AND THE PFISTER VOGEL COMPANY BOUGHT A LARGE SHARE, PUTTING CAPITAL INTO THE COMPANY AND ALLOWING THEM TO FINISH BUILDING IT. SHAW SOLD OUT TO PFISTER & VOGEL IN JUNE OF 1895.

TANNERY

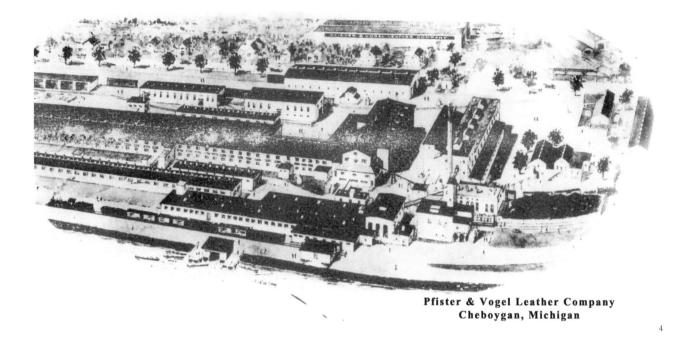

**Pfister & Vogel Leather Company
Cheboygan, Michigan**

4

Oct 9, 1907 *Cheboygan News* Somewhere about midnight Sunday night the two safes in the office of the Pfister & Vogel Leather Company, were blown open and about $200 in currency is gone. From the general appearance of the office it is evident that it was the work of experts. The first intimation that the place had been burglarized was when the night watchman went to the front door of the office and found one of the lights of glass broken. On entering the office he found the floor strewed with papers and the doors of both safes open. The steel chests were also open and the contents removed. Superintendent Herman Georges says that in one of the safes were checks for various amounts but three were found on the floor; the burglars satisfying themselves with what currency was there. It amounted to in the neighborhood of $200. They never keep a large amount of money in the office safes as their business is done with checks.

Nitroglycerine was used to blow open the safes and in order to confine it in the vicinity of the combinations used a quantity of soap which was scattered all over the walls and ceiling of the office. It was a stormy night which gave them a good opportunity to carry on their work. The men in the boiler room heard a muffled sound about midnight, but did not think anything of it. The burglars came and went leaving little or nothing that might lead to their arrest. However, the company has offered a reward of $50 for information that will lead to their apprehension.

The land platted for the tannery consisted of a forty and a twenty. One half of the twenty was between the highway and the river and this is where the tannery buildings were built. This land was located where Spies Auto Parts and the Citizen's National Bank south branch are located in 2011.

The Tannery's first building was a tool shed. It was probably build in 1891. Harris Emory supplied the lumber and it was delivered by Mark Thompson.[5] A large office and general store were then located in the center of the main buildings. The

4 Drawing from Phister-Vogel Company Brochure, courtesy of Ellis Olson.
5 Ramsby, Eva Lowe, "The Old Tannery", Cheboygan Observer, February 2, 1950.

Photo of the tannery bark sheds. The water level is very low, so this photo might be dated to 1909 when the river water lever was lowered to allow for removal of trees and stumps which blocked the river channel.

Photo ©Johnson Studio, from collection of the Historical Society of Cheboygan County, Inc.

general store was a two-story building that housed a post office for the employees, a meat market, a furniture and shoe department, a first aid station, and a grocery.

George Rittenhouse was the store manager for a long time. Charles Ramsey, Arthur Rawsin and Victor Fisher were among the other store employees and Carrie Crump was clerk for seven years. Here the employees received their mail as well as everything they needed. The company employed in the neighborhood of 200 men. On pay day they came in and stocked up with supplies to last until the next pay day. When they left, the store usually had eaten up all their wages.[6]

There were three housing units for employees called tenement blocks. The Store Tenement Block was located between the store and the river. The second one was built at the south end of the plat and was called the River Block. The third

block was on the second street west of the highway and was called the Woods Block. Each tenement block housed ten families. Each family had two large upstairs bedrooms. Downstairs there was a living room, a dining room, a kitchen, and a pantry. Rent in a tenement block was two dollars and fifty cents a month. There were also at least two rows of separate houses and they could be rented for four dollars and forty cents, while larger ones cost five dollars and fifty cents per month. These rentals included paper and paint as well as the labor to put it on for you. Yesteryears Antique Shop, 10871 Straits Highway, is located in one of the tannery homes (2011) so stop by and visit their shop and see the inside.

Water was piped to the homes from a ten- inch well that was between 700 and 740 feet deep. This well was located near the old chimney. This ice-cold water was needed to process the hides. They had a sewer system made of wooden planks which served both the houses and the plant. There was

6 Ibid.

Tannery School from the collection of the Historical Society of Cheboygan County.

a tank house that held water for fire protection. They also stationed sand bags in various locations to aid in fire protection.

A Tannery School was also built on the east side of the property. This was to accommodate the children who lived in the tenement houses. That building is still in use today as a commercial building.

East of the store bark shed and toward the river was the blacksmith shop and the machine shop. They had a large barn to house the eight to ten teams of horses. An accident to one of the teamsters was told in the local paper.

7 1910 panoramic photo of Tannery employees, on display in the Cheboygan History Center.
8 Ramsby

PER & VOGEL LEATHER Co. MARCH. 22-1910
CHEBOYGAN MICH

7

John Galbraith's Skull Crushed by a Big Iron Wheel

At 7:30 yesterday morning the startling news of an accident at the Tannery was brought to the city. John Galbraith whose age was 17 or 18 years worked at the Tannery as a teamster and at 5 o'clock yesterday morning he started with a load of machinery and scrap iron from one of the buildings where repairs and alterations had been made. He was directed to drive with the load to the barn and some men would be sent to help unload. John drove down the lane and Otto Weiland the first man who was sent to help unload, found him lying in the lane with his skull crushed by a big wheel that had fallen on him. A messenger on a bicycle attracted attention by riding at headlong speed along Main Street heedless of the mud that spattered wheel and rider. He was on his way to notify the dead boy's mother who walked back with the messenger. Coroner C.B. Marks with Sheriff Ming went out to the scene of the accident and impaneled a jury: A R. McKinnon, Fred Springfield, Jacob Zurcher, Francis Sullivan, Wm. Taylor, Charles H. Nuite. The evidence of Mr. Smith the outside foreman showed that the load was not a big one. The wheel had a 10 inch face, was four feet in diameter and weighed 250 pounds. There are 2 roads to the shed where the iron was to be stored and John took the one least used when hauling loads. He was not directed to take that road. Scarcely 10 minutes elapsed between the time of starting the load and finding the body as he started to send men at once. John was lying between the wheels and was breathing. He was struck on the right side of the head. The verdict rendered was that "John Galbraith came to his death by falling out of the wagon with an iron pulley which struck him on the head causing instant death. We attach no blame to any person other than himself in the cause of the accident." The funeral will be from St. Mary's church Sunday afternoon about 2 o'clock.

9 *Cheboygan Democrat* December 4, 1899.

Illustration from a 1897 book, The Manufacture of Leather by Charles Thomas Davies, published by Henry Carey Baird & Co.

A major reason the tannery was built in Cheboygan was the amount of hemlock bark that was available locally to produce the tannic acid necessary to dye the leather. The bark was removed from the trees and processed, and the extract or "liquor" was used to process the hides. Those who have visited Tahquamenon Falls in the Upper Peninsula will recall the rust color of the water. This is also caused by tannic acid from the hemlock and cedar which has leached out into the soil and ground water, and colors the river water to look like tea. Much of the bark was supplied by the lumber camps, and some was supplied by private citizens who were clearing trees from their property.

The bark peeling season was from mid-May to mid-August when the sap running through the trees made the bark easier to peel. The men would cut the trees with a one-man or two-man saw.

The bark was cut in four foot, four inch lengths. The men ring-cut around the tree with the axe at the desired length and split a straight line lengthwise on the tree through the bark. Then they took a bark spud, a sharp rounded cutter blade with a twelve to eighteen inch handle, which could be managed with one hand. They helped moved the sheet of bark with one hand and used the spud with the other hand. They often wished they had two more hands to fight off flies and mosquitoes.

The bark peelers worked long hours and earned their money. When the bark dried, which took about twenty four hours in dry weather, they put it in piles of one, or three quarter, or one half cords. In order to preserve bark it was necessary to place good skids on the ground to pile the bark on, and good end sticks to keep the pile straight up and down. When piling bark it was necessary to lay out the wider and unbroken sheets until finishing the pile, then put on a couple of layers of the good sheets for top cover. When bark was piled right it would keep a long time. . . Bark peelers were required to pile the bark four to six inches over the four foot high and eight foot long pile to be scaled as a full cord. It was also necessary to see that the bark didn't get too dry before piling or the thinner sheets would curl up like a stove pipe. When piled, it might be four feet high but would only contain about two feet.[10]

Once the men were through cutting bark, they were ready to haul it to the tannery. They loaded it on wagons or sleighs and drove it there with teams of horses or oxen. If the hemlock was cut near water, it was brought in by boat. You can still see remnants of the old pilings and docks where they used to tied up and unload. Once the bark was measured it was piled in a bark shed to keep it dry and ready to use. They had to buy enough bark in a summer season to get them through to the next bark peeling season. There were two bark sheds near the river, one near the general office and three more across the highway behind the tenement houses. Some of the bark came by railroad and was stored in those sheds. Art McGinn measured the bark when it arrived at the tannery and after it was unloaded the seller went to Herman George, the German business superintendent, to get paid. Some of the farmers chose to get their pay in supplies from the general store. Others, especially the larger lumber companies, were paid cash.

The tan bark came in four foot lengths as it was peeled off the hemlock trees. It was a coarse red bark. From its

pile in the bark shed it was loaded on the tram cars and taken to the **bark mill**. Here it was ground or pulverized. It then went to the leech house. The "**leech house**" had many big round vats. Coils of copper pipe wormed their way around the bottoms of the vats. Through these coils passed live steam to keep the leech's maw full of pulverized bark and water, boiling. A hood covered each vat to keep the liquid from evaporating. It required forty-eight hours of cooking to make the hemlock extract. A trap was in the center of the bottom of the leech vat. When the cooking was done, the trap door was released and the mass was carried through into an elevator which carried it to the "**tan-press**", where the water was extracted. This hemlock extract was removed for future use and the dry bark pulp was carried by another elevator to the "**fire hole**" to be used for fuel. The fire hole was really the boiler room or steam plant. Here, Joseph Leising kept the boilers lined with brick. Here too, was the great smoke stack which was later replaced by a 200 foot chimney made of tile which is said to have cost the company $3,000.[11]

In 1893 the factory used 20,000 cords of hemlock bark a year to tan hides. The 1914 Polk Directory said that $100,000 was distributed in the county for the purchase of the 14,000 or 15,000 cords of hemlock bark required in the tanning processes. The February 13, 1897 *Democrat* said the Tannery "is proving its usefulness in another way. The sawdust from the McArthur pile is being used as fuel."

Many of the local farmers cut hemlock bark off their property and used the proceeds to pay the taxes and buy seed for the next year. This was a

---

10 Corrigan, George A., *Calked Boots and Cant Hooks*, Northword Inc, Ashland Wisconsin, p 18.
11 Ramsby, Eva Lowe, *The Old Tannery*, Cheboygan Observer, February 2, 1950.

dependable "cash crop" for them. Many of the lumber companies also cut hemlock bark to sell to the tannery. M. D. Olds had a large tract of hemlock forest which was burnt in the October 15, 1908, Metz fire. This fire destroyed a large amount of forest –starting near Millersburg and burning to the Lake Huron shore, destroying forests near Rogers City and reaching as far as Alpena. This was a "crown fire" burning only the treetops. Olds send in crews to cut down and remove the bark from the hemlock trees, and was able to sell this to the tannery.

The hides arrived in Cheboygan in railroad cars. Most were cow and pig hides from the packing companies in Kansas and Chicago. They also used other hides such as horse, water buffalo, and camel. These were imported from South America, China, Russia and India. They were weighed and then taken to the hide house. These hides were in large bundles and had usually been sprinkled with salt or immersed in a salt solution to help prevent spoilage.

The process of tanning a hide required about three months. The hides came into the **hide house** either as dry hides or green hides. Here the hides were placed in vats or pits of cold water to soak out dirt and salt. This took from two to seven days, and then they were rinsed to get rid of the salt and loosened dirt. The next step was to remove excess flesh and fat. They used a special "fleshing" knife which had a sharp blade for removing fat and meat and a toothed edge for removing any hair from the flesh side of the hide. The men who did this work were called **beamsters**.

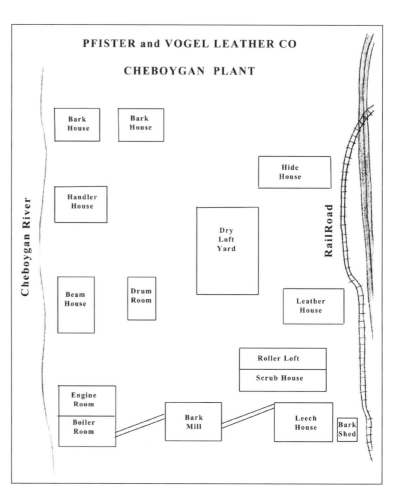

Hide house. Most hides processed at the Cheboygan Tannery were cow or pig hides shipped from stockyards in Kansas City and Chicago. The tannery also processed horse, water buffalo and camel hides shipped from all over the world.

Photo of Wilcox Tannery at www/Jonestownship.com(4)

Beamsters at work at Wilcox Tannery remove excess flesh and fat from hides using a special "fleshing" knife.

Hides hanging in a "dry loft" located in a long wooden building. The hides were later tanned with dye made from local hemlock bark. [13]

In the **beam house** these hides were hung on poles which could be lowered, and then they were soaked in pools. As many as 200 hides were soaked in one pool. Lime was added to the pool with the dry hides, and sulfide was added to the green hides. This soaking loosed the hair, after which the hide was put through a machine with a roller which removed the hair. Next, the hides were washed. For years the waste from the hides was thrown into the river, but eventually this practice was stopped.[12]

From the beam house the hides went to the "**handler house**." Here they were placed in a light solution of sulfuric acid which caused the pores to open up. After a week they were taken out of this acid and put into a weak liquor of hemlock extract. It was approximately three weeks before they were taken to the "**yard building**" and put into a liquor of hemlock extract which was gradually strengthened. This building was 900 feet long and contained 100 vats. Each vat held 50 hides. These vats were clay lined pits, which had been dug into the ground.

Several months later they came to the "**scrub room**." All hides were scrubbed by hand from wood shavings bound to a handle. Anybody could make the brooms from black ash or ironwood and the Tannery would buy them. The hides were then

placed in drums containing sugar and Epsom salts and twirled to open the pores and fluff the hides, after which they were moved upstairs to the "**drying loft**."

When the hides were dry, they would be ready to be oiled. In the early years, the oil was put on by hand with a brush. Later, it was done by machinery. In a few days the leather would be taken to the "**rolling loft**" to take out the wrinkles and soften the leather.

The hides were graded according to size, weight, and quality. They were then sent to the "**leather house**" where they were sorted into two divisions, (backs or bends), folded into three folds,

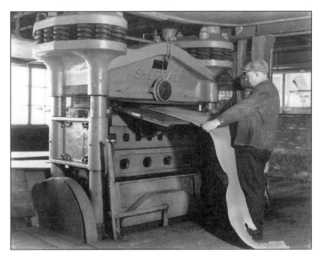

Rolling Mill at Wilcox Tannery.

---

12 Description of tannery taken from two sources—CMU term paper by Eunice Hansen, Cheboygan Tannery: Pfister & Vogel Leather Co, 1895-1926. Also Eva Ramsby, "*Tannery*" as printed in the *Cheboygan Observer*, Feb 2, 1950.

13 Drying loft of Wilcox Tannery, www.jonestownship.com (Photo used as we have no interior photos of the Cheboygan Tannery.)

"The men usually worked a ten hour day with two shifts. They started at 7 a.m. and worked till 6 p.m. with an unpaid hour lunch break."

Finished hides being loaded for shipment. Much of Cheboyan's leather production was shipped to shoe plants.
Photo of Wilcox Tannery at www/Jonestownship.com

packed flat, and tied into bundles. From here the hides were shipped to various shoe plants including foreign countries such Russia and Switzerland.

There was a danger in handling the hides. As seen in this article.

JOHN J. MURRAY DIED AT THE TANNERY OF THAT FATAL DISEASE, ANTHRAX MALILGNA

In April last John J Murray came from Dickinson's Landing, Ontario, to work at the tannery. He brought with him his wife and four children. Sometime last week he was taken ill, but did not have a physician's care until Friday. He was found to be suffering from anthrax maligna, a disease among cattle known as splenetic fever.

Mr. Murray was handling hides brought from China. He wore gloves, but must have rubbed some portion of his face, probably his nose, as that was affected and his face was swollen out of shape. He was an Odd Fellow in good standing in Fellowship Lodge, Dickinson's Landing. Temple Lodge, I.O.O. F. took care of him, furnished a nurse and buried him. He died Tuesday at 10 o'clock. The tannery company, we are informed, paid him wages while sick, and besides being very kind to him,

bore the expense of his illness. Mr. Murray was also a member of the A.O.W. in Canada, with a benefit of $500. Fellowship Lodge has a burial benefit.[14]

The men usually worked a ten hour day with two shifts. They started at 7 a.m. and worked till 6 p.m. with an unpaid hour lunch break. During the peak World War I years they ran three shifts and kept it going around the clock. They were supplying the army with boot leather for the soldiers who were marching across Europe. Some of the workers lived in the tannery housing. Others lived as far away as Duncan and walked to work daily. For a while, in the 1890's Cheboygan had a horse- drawn street car that made trips out to the Tannery.

Eunice Hance wrote a term paper in 1967 and interviewed several men who told about working at the tannery. Her interviews tell the following:

• Frank Johnston started to work at the tannery unloading bark when he was sixteen years old. He was paid seventy five cents an hour for a ten hour day. Later he worked in the shipping department. After Mr. Johnston became foreman in this department, he would have to go whenever or wherever the company received a complaint of sole

14 *Cheboygan News*, Sept 8, 1900.

Phister & Vogel Company.   Collection of the Historical Society of Cheboygan County, Inc.

leather. Having seen the needs of the various manufacturers, he knew and understood their needs. One leather company ordered first grade leather and because Pfister and Vogel were out of it, Mr. Johnston sent second grade quality, knowing that it was suitable for this companies need. They returned this shipment, however and Mr. Johnston was fired. After several years passed, the supervisor went to Detroit to persuade him to return to the tannery, which he did.

• Henry Sova started to work at the tannery at an early age, working in the yard for fifteen cents an hour. He served as a spare and worked wherever there was a vacancy. One of his jobs was in the scrub room where he worked for many years. Another job that he did regularly was to go to Cheboygan with a team of horses for the payroll every second and seventeenth of the month. Art McGinn usually went with him

• Pat Gouin went to work at an early age and worked at the tannery for about twenty five years.

His first job was the construction of a cinder sidewalk from the Tannery store to the police post. Later he worked in the bark mills and at various other jobs. One of the most tedious tasks was hauling the hides out of the coloring vats onto the tram cars which took them to the yard.

• Mr. Ludwig, the foster son of the Vogel's who owned the company was the supervisor when he started working for the company. Mr. Ludwig knew all the tanning processes, but the business grew to greater heights under the supervision of Mr. Ludwig. Approximately 700 sides were colored by the older method and 1400 sides when using the chromating process.

• Herman Georges was the company bookkeeper. He paid the people who sold wood to the tannery as fuel for the boilers. The wood, which had to be cut in four foot lengths, sold for $1.25 a cord. Many local farmers cut wood to sell to the tannery. They stopped at the store where Art McGinn measured it and then took it to the shed attached to the building that housed the boilers.

Eva Ramsby's term paper of 1950 mentions these men who worked at the tannery and their jobs.

Ed Ranville—bark mill

Lloyd Hinckley in the rolling house

Mr. Grigsby in the leather house

Mike Samp in the handler house

Alvie Roberts –drums

Mr. Sangster—yard

Roscoe Smith-outside foreman

Frank Johnston—shipping

Mr. McKinzey –head carpenter

E.J. Smith bought bark and stumpage

Art McGinn—bought bark and stumpage

Herman Georges—Company Bookkeeper

Pat Gouine—bark mills

Henry Sova–took team to town to get payroll

Mr. Crump—foreman of hide house

Joseph Leising—boiler room

George Rittenhouse—store manager

Charles Ramsey-store employee

Arthur Rawsin-store employee

Victor Fisher-store employee

The 1914 *Polk Directory* said this about the men who were employed at the tannery. "The Pfister & Vogel Leather Company, whose headquarters are in Milwaukee, operates a tannery at Cheboygan which is one of the most extensive industries of the kind in the west. Its force of men averages one hundred and fifty, to whom fully $75,000 is annually paid in wages and salaries." Some of the men who worked in the tannery were listed in the 1914 *Polk Directory*. This also gives their residence and position in the company. When it says "boards" it means either they were in a rented room or boarding house or that they were an adult child living in their parent's home.

Pfister & Vogel Leather Co
Fred Vogel Jr. President
Charles F Pfister, Vice-Pres.
August Helmboltz Treasurer
Frederick A Vogel, General Manager
Herman George, Agent, Main s Tannery Set

Ayotte Louis, beamster, bds 4 Tannery set
Bellant, Sherman laborer, bds 1109 Mackinaw
Berk, Andrew, laborer
Charbonneau, Felix (Bertha) teamster, res 7 Tannery set
Cools, Emil, laborer
Curran, John (Ellen), laborer, res 1068 Main S
Curran, Wm, fireman bds 1068 Main
Cyprys, Valentine (Cecelia) foreman, res 225 C N
Davison, Parker (Julia), roller, res 38 Tannery set
Dawson, Robert, watchman
De Loy, Edward, laborer, res Benton Township
Demara, Archie, laborer
Denewitt, Henry (Emma) laborer, res 57 Tannery set
Doe, Joseph, W (Mary), steamfitter, res 512 Lincoln Ave w
Doroski, Flavius, laborer
Elliott, Wm (Lenora) lab, res ns Mill 1 w of Main s
Falowitz, John (Margaret) laborer, res 5 Tannery set

Feeney, Wm J (Ida), tanner, res 34 Tannery set
Fisher, Harry, D (Fannie) laborer, res 60 Tannery set
Fisher, Victor, (Denise) teamster, res 51 Tannery s
Frederickson, Carl A, beamster, res 825 Huron S
Fuller, Charles E , foreman, bds 48 Tannery set
Fuller, Fred G ((Emily S), carpenter, res 48 Tannery set
Fuller, John, laborer, bds 4l8 Tannery set
Furlow John B, (Minnie) teamster, res sw cor Lincoln Ave w and Cuyler
Geoffrey, Frank, laborer, res 757 Spooner
Geoffrey, Jacob G (Delia) laborer, bds 727 Spooner
Georges, Herman (Mary J) agent, res 31 Tannery Set
Gouine, Patrick,H , laborer
Gubota, Philip (Agnes) laborer, res 1 Tannery set
Heizer, Joseph, laborer
Hilla, Richard laborer
Hinkley,Charles F, laborer, bds 36 Tannery Set
Hinkley, Edgar R (Della) foreman, res 36 Tannery set
Hinkley, Lloyd B (Katherine) laborer, res 35 Tannery
Jana, Frederick (Alvina) foreman, res 109 F s
Johnson, Edith C, clerk
Johnson, Frank J, foreman, res es Main s, 1 s of limits
Johnson, Milford, laborer,

Klemens, John, dryer, bds 1 Tannery Set

Kujala, Joseph, fireman

Lannoo, Ernest (Zoa) carpenter, res 6 Tannery set

Lawler, Frank T (Catherine) supt , res 32 Tannery set

Lawler, Leo, tanner, bds 32 Tannery set

Locke Gustaf, laborer, res 160 Harrison Ave

Locke, Paul W, laborer, bds 160 Harrison

Loeffler, Otto, (Caroline) laborer, res 881 Main s

Loeffler, Frank C (Henrietta) electn, res es Mullet Lake rd, 3 s of D & M RY

Loeffler, Paul O, laborer, bds 881 Main

Loiselle, Andres (Phoebe) laborer, res 419 D

Lucier, George W (Bessie) carpenter, res ws Mullet lake Rd 4 s of Old Petoskey State Rd

Lucier, John A , laborer,

McCombs , John H (Mary) laborer, res 119 D

McCombs, Malvin, engr,

McCombs, Robert (Ruth), beamster, res 855 Main s

McKinder, Irwin, laborer, bds 43 Tannery set

Maciejewski, Thomas (Anna) laborer, res 364 Harrison

MacKenzie, James, millwright

Mainz, Andrew, foreman

Mann, George E L (Maude C) mngr of Pfister & Vogel Leather Co Store, res 52 Tannery set

Mason, Edward, engr,

Mason, John, fireman

Metivier, John, laborer

Meyer, Thomas, laborer

Muschell, Theodore, beamster, res 184 Harrison Ava

Nalippa, John (Catherine), laborer, res 2 Tannery set

Nalippa, Louis, laborer

Nalippa, Michael, laborer

Olson,, Barney, clerk, bds 37 Tannery set

Passino, John laborer, res Inverness

Patch, Norman, laborer

Quaine, Albert, laborer

Quaine, Filbert, laborer

Quaine, Jeremiah, laborer

Ramsey, Charles A, clerk

Robcrts, Wm, laborer,

Roberts, Sherman, appr

Sapp, Michael (Isarah) foreman, res 42 Tannery set

Schall, Emil F (Hester G) carpenter, res sw corn Old Petos key and Mullet Lake rds

Schall, Walter, blacksmith, res ws Mullet Lake Rd 1 s of Old Petoskey State Rd

Schramm, Lawrence, laborer, res Inverness

Schramm, Walter (Polly_ tanner, res 215 D s

Shields, Joseph (Edith) fireman, res ws Mullett Lake rd 3 of D & M RY

Shimkowitz, Wm F (Martha) laborer, res 46 Tannery set

Sigman, Wilford (Rebecca) laborer, res 215 Center Ave

Slack, Frank (Eliza) fireman, res 5 Tannery set

Slack , Oscar, lab

Socha, Henry, laborer

Sova, Epraim (Loretta) laborer, res 58 Tannery set

Spinkowski, Stanley (Virginia) laborer, res 715 Western Ave

Still, Augustus A (Edith) beamster, res ns Old Petoskey State Rd 2 w of Mullet Lake rd

Still, Edward, beamster

Sullivan, Frank (Mary) beamster, res 40 Tannery set

Swiderek, Michael (Katherine) laborer, res 2 Tannery Set

Teachout, Wm (Beulah), beam hand, res 3 Tannery set

Theunick, Joseph L, laborer

Trudeau, Herbert, beamster

Trombley, Romeo, carpenter

Van Horn, Charles (Mary) watchman, res 11 Tannery set

Wagner, Henry, laborer

Wait, Henry, (Mary) millwight, res 30 Lincoln Ave

Williams, Peter, beamster

Williamson, Charles (Malinda) Fireman, res ws Loomis 1 s of North

Willis Clark, beamster

Wood, James W (Margaret M) liquormaker, Pfister & Vogel Leather Co, res 53, Tannery

Zenzen, Jacob M (Anna) beamster, res ws Loomis 1 n of Lincoln Av w

After World War I the demand for shoe leather sharply decreased. The tanneries lost government contracts to supply the soldiers with leather for boots. When the soldiers returned home the economy was in poor shape and people weren't buying any extras. Also, farmers were starting to use more tractors and needed less leather for harnesses and farm equipment. The many tanneries throughout the country became very competitive with each other and prices dropped. Also the hemlock bark was running out in many areas, and they began to experiment with come chemical tannins such as chromium sulphate. Technology was also changing, and composite materials to make shoe soles had been invented, thus decreasing the need for sole leather.

---

15 Note: The term "fireman" means a man who worked in the boiler room. They kept large fires going to produce heat to extract the tannin from the hemlock bark in the leech house. Steam produced also operated other equipment.

This photo shows some workmen from the tannery, including Otto, Frank and Paul Loeffler.

Photo courtesy of Sharon Singleton, descendent of the Loeffler family.

A sign of problems to come came with this notice.

TANNERY TO SHUT DOWN

This is an alarming piece of news to a great many men in our city and community who have worked at the big plant for so long and without any breaks in time. The plant has been one of the most consistent workers of any plant of any nature in the country and it is shutting down at this time if it is obliged to do so; is not a surprise to those who are acquainted with the leather situation throughout the country. The local tannery has manufactured leather when there has been no market for it until everything and everywhere the company can pile the product is filled. Thousands of dollars are tied up and this product is mostly manufactured at a very high cost of production. A loss must be sustained before the stock is disposed of but the company is ready to take that loss and anxious to get back into normal working conditions again, but cannot possibly be expected to pile up more stock at high cost on a falling market. This is one of the few tanneries of the country that has kept operating in the face of market conditions, most of the others have been shut down long ago. An announcement that has been looked for all winter, never came until this week, and that was to the effect that the tannery would close down. Notices were posted on Wednesday to the effect that the big plant would close down on May 1st.[16]

---

16 *Cheboygan Democrat*, March 18, 1921.

AUCTION SALE

Having purchased from the Pfister-Vogel Leather Co., of Milwaukee, their tannery and all real estate in connection, at

CHEBOYGAN, MICHIGAN

(The largest sole leather tannery in the world)

We will offer at public auction starting promptly at 10:00 a. m.

FRIDAY, MARCH, 26th, 1926

the following described property:

-Entire Contents Of A General Store-

including stock anud fixtures, large office safe, big cash register, number of counters, show cases, etc., and good stock of general merchandise. including Clothing, Boots, Shoes, Rubbers, Yard Goods, Groceries and hundreds of other items included in the stock.

Miscellaneous lot of Sleighs, Farm Implements, Wagons, Harness, Tools, etc. Approximately 400 tons Soft Coal, Fully equipped Modern Machine Shop. Fully equipped Woodworking Plant, 15 Tons of good Hay, Motors of all sizes and kinds. Large quanty of small tools, Big lots of good used lumber, Big quantity of all kinds of good pipe, Big lot of windows and doors, Several good Fire Extinguishers.

34 Good Dwelling Houses Go to the Auction Block **34**

at 2 p. m., Saturday, March 27

Houses can be purchased either with or without land. See representative before sale about details.

TERMS—All store merchandise, cash. Terms can be arranged on other items.

For particulars see F. L. Midgeley at Pfister-Vogel Leather Co., Cheboygan, Mich.

This notice reads as follows:

Indications are that this tannery will probably be shut down May 1st and remain so until October 30th, However we will post confirmation of the same ten days previous to taking such action. Pfister Vogel Leather Co.[17]

The plant did reopen but by 1926 the hemlock bark had run out.

Pfister and Vogel Leather Company closed the Cheboygan plant in 1926. They sold the buildings to a wrecking company which salvaged the lumber and other salable goods. The homes went for $75 and the people who lived in them were given first chance to buy them. The following ad appeared in the March 18, 1926, *Cheboygan Tribune* advertising the auction of the tannery equipment, houses, store merchandise, tools, etc.

The houses were auctioned off and many are still in use today. You can see them on the west side of US 27 and along Tannery Road. The factory buildings were sold off for lumber, dismantled and leveled off. For many years the only remains were the old docks along the riverbank and the smokestack. The old smokestack was deemed a hazard and in 1986 it was dynamited, thus removing the last marker of a once thriving Cheboygan industry.

17 *Cheboygan Daily*, March 16th, 1921
18 *Cheboygan Daily Tribune*, March 18, 1926

MEDICAL CARE BEFORE THE HOSPITAL

By Sally Eustice Humphrey

What did the early residents of Cheboygan do when they got sick or were injured? Most would have performed simple first aid at home. They would apply bandages and perhaps stitch a large cut with a sewing needle and thread. They might have applied a poultice of comfrey root to a sprain or broken bone as well as binding it with a splint. For upsets of the stomach they would have purged (vomited) or perhaps prepared a mint tea. A willow bark tea might bring down a fever or relieve aches and pains. For poison ivy they would apply some bloodroot. For croup or cough they could boil a kettle of water and make a steam tent to breathe moist air. If the disease was more serious, they were in trouble.

The closest help would have been Mackinac Island, if the patient could be taken there. Transportation to the Island was often a problem when the lake was too rough to go by boat or an ice bridge had not yet formed. The fort had a medical officer stationed there and he also took care of patients in the village. Dr. Joseph Bailey was assigned there in 1852. He served there until 1854, when his son, Dr. John Reed Bailey was appointed Acting Assistant Surgeon, U.S. Army, Fort Mackinac and Indian Physician, Michilimackinac Agency. Dr. John Bailey left to serve in the Civil War and later returned to Mackinac Island, had a private practice, operated a drug store and lived there over fifty years, dying January 26, 1910.

One of Dr. John Reed Bailey's sons, Guy Bailey, born in 1868, grew up, went to medical school and returned to the area setting up a practice in Cheboygan. A notice in the *Cheboygan*

Dr. John Bailey

Democrat on August 22, 1895, says.

Dr. Guy G. Bailey, formerly of Mackinaw Island, and more recently of Pueblo, Colorado, has opened an office for the practice of his profession in the Gerow Block, and is ready to answer all calls. Professionally, Dr. Bailey has received all the advantages of the best colleges in the country, and has for several years practiced in the west and is a student at all times. We have no doubt he will meet with the success his merits deserve.

A newspaper interview of Charles Sammons, son

---

1 Photo from John Reed Bailey, Mackinac, Formerly Michilimackinac, R. Smith Printing Company, Lansing, 1899.

of Jacob Sammons, tells of some of his memories of early Cheboygan when no doctor was available.

Lorenzo Backus had a sawmill and gristmill where the south range light stands. In the days before Cheboygan had a doctor, he used to do some surgery. Bob Mickeljohn had his feet frozen. Gangrene threatened, so Backus operated. He cut off the feet at the insteps, and Mickeljohn got around with two canes.

Mr. Backus owned the first mill in Cheboygan. Mrs. Backus, was the village doctor at that time. Once day as she was watching for her husband to come to dinner, she listened and could not hear the mill running, so she went over to the mill and found that Mr. Backus had been caught in the machinery and had stopped the mill. She assisted him in freeing himself. She and my mother doctored and nursed him as best they could. But he was always bent over and a cripple afterwards.[2]

Mrs. Backus died in 1879. She is remembered by the early settlers in connection with pioneer life. For some time she was the only physician in the settlement. Being an excellent nurse she obtained some information of the use of medicine and was enabled thereby to be of much service.[3]

Childbirth did not require a doctor at that time. When a woman began to feel labor pains usually a midwife or neighbor lady was called in to assist. What better help could there have been than Amanda Smith who had borne 15 children herself!

Thursday, January 5, 1900, there was laid to rest in Pine Hill Cemetery a lady pioneer who was the sixth white woman to come to Cheboygan. Mrs. Amanda Melvina Smith, widow of the late Nathaniel Smith. Mr. and Mrs. Smith came to Cheboygan June 19, 1849, almost 50 years ago. At the time Cheboygan was a cedar swamp with no indication of being the bright and spacious city, it now is. She was born May 8th, 1816, and was married in 1834. Fifteen children were born to her, six daughters and two sons surviving. Three daughters, Mrs. Charles (Martha) Bellant, Mrs. George Carter and Mrs. Frank (Eva) Enault were with her when she died, also her brother, the well-known veteran John Marshall. Mrs. Smith was prepared for burial by Mrs. Julia Carter who was one of the first white children born in Cheboygan, and who was assisted into the world by Mrs. Smith 46 years ago.[4]

"The first pioneer physician and surgeon who administered his patent medicines and cared for the sick was Dr. Strong of Duncan City in 1854. After he left, Cheboygan and Duncan were without a medical man until Dr. Arthur M. Gerow hung out his shingle at the corner of Main and Third (State) Street." [5]

Dr. Arthur M. Gerow   Minnie McDonald Gerow

Collection of the Historical Society of Cheboygan County, Inc.

2 *Cheboygan Daily Tribune*, Golden Jubilee edition 1939.
3 *The Traverse Region, Historical and Descriptive, with Illustrations of Scenery and Portraits and Biographical Sketches of some of Its Prominent Men and Pioneers*, Chicago, H.R. Page & Co., 1884, p 114.
4 *Cheboygan Democrat*, January 14, 1900
5 Judy Ranville, "*Memories of Mackinaw, "Cheboygan County—Early Settlement*" by Ellis Olson, p. 23.

Collection of the Historical Society of Cheboygan County, Inc.

Dr. Gerow was an interesting character who added much to the development of early Cheboygan. He was a doctor, real estate developer, banker, politician, and farmer, and spent a great deal of time promoting the growth of Cheboygan. Arthur Martin Gerow was born in Nappanee, Ontario, Canada, on March 7, 1845, and was the fourth of seven children. He grew up on a farm, attended a village school during the winter and worked in a saw mill during the summers until he was seventeen. He taught school, saved his money, and went to the Toronto Normal School in 1863, and then again taught school for two years. He passed his vacations studying medicine with Doctors Parker and Bradley in Sterling, Ontario. He entered the Royal College of Physicians and Surgeons in Kingston, Ontario, and then went to the Buffalo New York Medical College where he graduated in 1868.

Dr. Gerow came to Cheboygan in the autumn of 1868, with $40, his medical case, and diploma, and was the first physician to settle there. His first

wife, Josephine Bradley, and infant daughter died in Cheboygan in 1873. In 1874 he married Mary McDonald, daughter of John and Amelia McDonald and they had a son, Allen. Mary died November 23, 1922, six months after Arthur died May 25, 1922, age 77.

"As a practitioner Dr. Gerow was of the old school and one of the most thorough our city has ever had. He was conscientious in all of his work and administered to the rich and poor alike, drawing no lines and showing no favors. He was always ready to respond to the call of the sick and needy whenever it was in his power to do so."[6] An example of a surgery he performed was found in the newspaper. "Dr. Gerow, assisted by Drs. Hayes and Steffins, successfully removed a tumor from Mrs. J. Arnold, of Mackinaw City, Tuesday afternoon. The tumor weighed over two pounds, and was cut from the lady's breast."[7]

The following account from Perry Power's *History of Northern Michigan* shows how he was respected in the community.[8]

He found at Cheboygan about two hundred residents, but all so sound and vigorous in bodily health that they had little need of a doctor. As a consequence of these conditions his finances were soon exhausted and he was forced to either seek employment outside of his profession or leave the town. At this juncture he was offered a place as a clerk and salesman in a store, and he determined to take it and perform its duties until he could get money enough to take him to Kansas City, Missouri. His pay was about sixty dollars a month in the store, and his work there gave him acquaintance with the people, so that in a short time he was able to add to

6 *Cheboygan Democrat*, May 25, 1922, obituary
7 *Cheboygan Democrat*, November 31, 1901.
8 Powers, *History of Northern Michigan*, pp. 939-942.

Dr. Gerow opened his Ottawa Hotel in March, 1911 with a splendid banquet by the Chamber of Commerce. It was named to honor the Ottawa Indians.
Photo courtesy Patricia Wight Geyer Collection

his income the receipts from a small but growing practice of medicine. By 1869 he had accumulated enough capital to open the first drug store in the village. This was a small affair, but it proved to be a healthy acorn, and from it has grown the sturdy oak of his present prosperity and extensive worldly wealth. His management of the drug store brought him additional practice, and in time this became so extensive that he was compelled to sell the store, which he did in 1883, and give his whole time and attention to his professional work.

In the meantime he had invested all his surplus capital in building lots in the town and when the financial crash of 1873 came he found himself very much embarrassed financially, and at one time faced the probable necessity of letting all his property go for what it would bring. He managed to hold on to it however, until the dull times passed and it has steadily grown in value until it is now some of the most desirable and valuable in the city, especially the portions which he has improved with good business houses. He

now owns nearly a whole block of stores and buildings devoted to other than mercantile business, and from this alone he receives a comfortable income. Dr. Gerow's last and most imposing addition to the building improvements in Cheboygan is the Ottawa Hotel, named in honor of the Ottawa Indians, which was formally opened to the public with a splendid banquet on the night of March 15, 1911 under the auspices of the Cheboygan Chamber of Commerce. In the speeches that followed the banquet, Dr. Gerow was highly complimented for his enterprise in giving this fine hostelry to the city and for his general spirit of progressiveness in using all his means to promote the development and improvement of the community in which his faith is firmly fixed. . .

Last week Dr. A. M. Gerow completed a contract for the sale of all apples on his many thousands of trees to a Chicago commission house, just as they hang on the trees, and the firm will send expert pickers and packers here to harvest and ship the crop at their own expense and are to pay the owner cash for the crop, relieve him of all worry over storing them and marketing next winter or spring, according as prices go. They will all be shipped south and kept in cold storage until wanted. Thus has another industry come to the profitable point, and it is an industry that bids to be of the greatest benefit of the whole county.

Not only will Dr. Gerow reap a well-deserved reward, but like Columbus and the egg trick, he has shown them how and he will have a lot of imitators who will go ahead and do likewise for the rewards that nerve and faith promise the doctor. In this connection it is curious to note that when Dr. Gerow got his idea of apple raising at work, and began to buy farms and set out thousands of trees most of the farmers who had a few trees and found difficulty in realizing half price for fruit began to growl. "We might as well cut down the trees," they said, if the few trees we have now produce more fruit than we can sell, the doctor will have to give them away!"

This is where the farmers were not business men and could not see through a mill stone that had a big hole in it. The fact is they raised so few apples that they had no market but the local market and that was overloaded by summer and autumn fruit that would not keep and could not be shipped. There were not enough winter apples of the first class to justify the big commission houses coming here after the fruit. Now that Dr. Gerow has created a market by producing enough fruit to bring the buyers here to solicit the privilege of having it on the trees all will benefit.[9]

Dr. William Perry Maiden was born on March 15, 1841, in Quebec, Canada. When he was very young he learned telegraphy and served as a telegraph operator for the Grand Trunk Railway. He then went to The Queen's University Medical College, graduating in 1861. He also got a degree from Bellevue Medical College in New York City. He served in the Civil War as a surgeon. During this time he was thrown from a horse and his hip was severely damaged. In 1865, after the war, he settled in Alpena where he started the first drugstore. He was burned out in 1868, rebuilt, and then sold out

his drug business in 1870 and moved to Cheboygan. He only stayed in Cheboygan one year. He went to New York for surgery on his hip joint. He then returned to Alpena and practiced in that area.[10] While in Cheboygan he issued the first newspaper—thirteen editions of the Manitawauba Chronicle starting January 28, 1871. The first edition of this paper had this story about Dr. Maiden.

A sad accident occurred on Tuesday last at D. Smith's upper camp on Black River, whereby two men named Mathew D. Chapman of Maine, and Wm. Greer of Cheboygan were injured, one of them fatally. Tuesday afternoon about 4 o'clock Greer was finishing the felling of a tree; Chapman having broken his axe, was going away for another, after admonishing his companion "be careful of the tree, for it looks as if it might split." Greer had only struck the tree twice when it split up some 30 feet, and with lightning speed shot back upon the men, who were running out of its way fast as the deep snow permitted. The butt of the tree struck Greer upon his left side and arm, bruising him badly but breaking no bones; poor Chapman was not so fortunate, though farther away, the tree came crashing down upon his abdomen, breaking his hip and inflicting fatal internal injuries; the tree rebounded and this time fell upon his legs fracturing his left one shockingly. Greer, hearing the piteous screams of Chapman, raised himself and staggered towards him, but fainted and fell helplessly before reaching him. Assistance came from neighboring choppers, and the men were made as comfortable as possible in camp, while a messenger immediately started for Dr. Maiden. The Dr. made all possible

---

9   *Cheboygan Democrat*, August 11, 1905
10   Ellis Olson, *Old Rivertown Cheboygan Centennial Booklet*, p. 66.

haste, travelling all night Wednesday, and having changed horses at the lower camp, ten miles distant, reached the upper camp Thursday at daylight. After attending to the sufferers, Dr. M decided that Chapman's chances for recovery were better in town than in camp and a conveyance was arranged that brought them without further suffering to town, but notwithstanding he was rendered comfortable by proper attentions. Chapman sank and died the following morning, from his internal injuries.[11]

J. W. STEFFINS, M. D.,

Physician, Surgeon and Obstetrician.

Office in Golden block.

15Jul94.   CHEBOYGAN, MICH

John W. Steffins was born in London, Ontario, in May 1856. He studied medicine in Canada and held a certificate from the Toronto General Hospital. He moved to Cheboygan in the early 1880's. He was a teacher in one of the county schools and later was principal at Central School. About 1884 he resigned and went to Chicago and again took up the study of medicine, graduating from the Chicago College of Medicine and Surgery. He returned to Cheboygan and opened an office. When he died in 1909 he left a widow and a stepson. He had been a member of the Masons, Maccabees and Elks. His obituary said "No man in Cheboygan will be more greatly missed than Dr. Steffins. This is especially true among the poor people, being ever ready to respond to their call for medical aid. He was generous to a fault and a kinder hearted man never lived." When you visit the Logmark Bookstore (on Main Street at the intersection of

Backus) in downtown Cheboygan today, notice the name "Steffins 1904" on the face of the building.

Egbert D. Sutherland was an early doctor in Cheboygan. He was also the Superintendent of the Public Schools. In 1884 he boarded at the Grand Central Hotel. The following story was found on Dr. Sutherland.

About 4:30 Monday morning an alarm of fire was sounded and dense masses of smoke were seen pouring from the rear of Sutherland & Forsyth's drug store. There had been some delay in giving the alarm, and the fire was as well under way. Fortunately there was no wind blowing at the time and after the hose companies once got to work they soon drowned the fire out, though the building was a sad wreck. The fire is supposed to have caught from the chimney of Eberhardt's which adjoins the store of Sutherland & Forsyth. Dr. Sutherland was asleep in the rear of the store and the roar of the fire awoke him. He only had time to partly dress and save a few of his books when the smoke drove him out. Very little of the drug stock was saved, and besides that Dr. Sutherland lost his clothes, several hundred books, surgical implements , etc. Loss was about $2,000 on stock with an insurance of $1,200.[12]

[Editor's Note: In the early days of Cheboygan very few men had professional degrees or college educations. Physicians and Surgeons did have that training and were often called on to guide local government by serving on various boards and holding office. Many doctors were involved with the schools—some as teachers and others as board members. They generally had a classical education and were some of the most well-read men in town.]

---

11 *Manitawauba Chronicle,* January 28, 1871
12 *Cheboygan Democrat,* December 24, 1885

T. A. PERRIN, M. D.,

Physician and Surgeon

All calls attended to both day and night.

Office on Main Street, above Elm, CHEBOYGAN, MICH.

Thomas Abraham Perrin, M.D. a prominent physician and citizen of Cheboygan, was born October 27, 1844, in Mt. Vernon, Ontario, Canada. He spent five years studying medicine, and then came to the United States in 1864. In 1866 he came to Cheboygan and engaged in the mercantile business which he continued several years. By 1873 he graduated from the University of Michigan and engaged in the practice of medicine. He married Francis Viola Mattoon on January 1, 1870, in Cheboygan, and they had six children: Charles, Freda, Fred, Arch, Maud and Thomas.

In 1881 Thomas' brother, Charles A. Perrin, became associated with him in practice, and the firm became known as the Perrin Brothers.[13] The Perrin Brothers had their drug store on the corner of Main and Elm Streets. "They keep a full supply of drugs, chemicals and all the leading patent medicines and are manufacturers of the Lumberman's Bone Liniment." Thomas's medical practice began to grow and he needed to give it his full attention. He gave up his part in the drug business and George Case went into partnership with his brother Charles instead. This was called "Case and Perrin, People's Drug Store." [14] The first surgeries in Cheboygan that are known were by Dr. Thomas A. Perrin. Dr. Perrin operated in what was later the Murphy home on East State Street.[15] Later he operated at the Northwest Hospital that was built on the NW corner of Main and Court Street.

Dr. Perrin did not spend all his time working as seen in this social clipping from 1886. There was a horse racing track off Mackinaw Avenue, just west of where the Mackinaw Apartments now stand. In the winter, they raced out on the frozen ice. Later a racetrack was built at what became the Cheboygan County Fairgrounds on lands donated by the Spies family.

Thomas Perrin and his family moved to San Jose, California in 1889. His brother left for California about the same time.

Dr. Stanislaus Alcide St Amour was born February 12, 1863, in St. James, Quebec. He went to the Victoria Medical College in Montreal. He opened an office in Ishpeming, Michigan, but moved to Cheboygan in September 1886. "He established St. Mary's Hospital at Cheboygan, intended especially for the lumbermen and to this institution he gave the most thoughtful attention, the patients receiving skilled treatment under his personal supervision." He was the vice president of the Cheboygan County Medical Associates, a member of the pension board, and a member of the Cheboygan Board of Education. He belonged to St. Mary's Catholic Church. He married Alphonsine Durrand on April 28, 1890. He purchased a number of lots in Cheboygan as an investment in real estate. He went to Chicago in 1915 for a postgraduate course in surgery and died there. His death certificate states he had a cerebral hemorrhage. The body was found robbed of all money and valuables.[16] The 1914 Polk Directory lists him in the Frost-Kessler Block, residence at 115 N. Huron Street. His children were Hector, Armand, Aurelie and Gabriel.

---

13 *The Traverse Region*, 116.
14 *Cheboygan Free Press*, January 27, 1876.
15 *Cheboygan Daily Tribune*, Golden Jubilee, 1939.
16 Powers, p. 235.

Dr. Charles B. Tweedale

Charles B. Tweedale[17] was born at Vienna, Elgin County, Ontario on August 2, 1866. His father was a doctor. Dr. Charles B. Tweedale graduated from the University of Medicine in Buffalo, New York, in 1888, took advanced classes, and then worked with his father in St. Thomas, Ontario, and then four years in Washtenaw County, Michigan. He moved to Cheboygan in 1895. He specialized in blood, kidney and nervous diseases. He was secretary of the Cheboygan Medical Society for at least fifteen years. He was county coroner two terms, county physician one term, and city health officer 1909-1911. He was also surgeon for the Detroit & Mackinac Railroad.

He was also surgeon for the Detroit & Mackinac Railroad. He was medical examiner for several insurance companies. He was also the examining physician for numerous fraternal orders and beneficial societies. He belonged to the Cheboygan Lodges of Elks, Odd Fellows, Knights of Pythias, and Eagles.

This story about a patient of Dr Tweedale and Dr. St Amour tells of a difficult but successful case.

BEAUGRAND SAVED AFTER LOGGING MISHAP

Oliver Beaugrand (whom Beaugrand Township was named after) was working in Bray's Camp on the Little Pidgeon. A big pine tree that he was felling slipped about twenty feet. Being in a swamp, it was hard to get out of the way and the tree caught Mr. Beaugrand, falling on his left leg. The tree was so large that it had to be chopped away from him and it took an hour and a half to release him. The nearest team was eight miles away. The injured limb was bleeding freely. After being bound up, Mr Beaugrand was taken across the lake to Topinabee, and lay there waiting for the train to Cheboygan. Arriving at Cheboygan he was taken to his home on the east side and Dr. Tweedale was called and found a compound fracture. Dr. St. Amour was also called and when the bandages had been taken off a careful examination showed that the bone of the ankle and just above the ankle was crushed in pieces. The next day, it was found necessary to cut off the foot. The leg was then taken off midway between the ankle and the knee, the patient have been put under chloroform. The operation was successful and the patient stood it well.[18]

Oliver Beaugrand

---

17 Powers, *History of Northern Michigan* pp. 707-709
18 Photo of Oliver Beaugrand from Hist. Soc. of Cheboygan County. Story from Ancestry.com; family history, accident occurred in 1897.

George Goddard Family—(left to right, top row) Marion, Frank and Clara Goddard (Front Row) Fred, George (the father) Charles, Julia (Mother) William.   Photo from "Our Yesterdays, Volume I" by Gretchen Sumerix

Dr. Marion Goddard was the first woman physician in northern Michigan. Her father and brothers came to Wolverine where they were in the lumber business. Marion, along with her sister Clara and brother Frank, trained in medicine in Battle Creek. From there she went east to complete her training and then came home to Wolverine to open an office on Main Street. "House calls were made with horse and cutter or buggy, cost $1.00, and that included medicine. Among her patients were the two little daughters of Sheriff George Darling. He was a widower. A romance budded and grew, and in a couple of years, the lady doctor gave up her practice to become Mrs. George Darling."[19]

Dr. Willis Earle Chapman was born December 25, 1867, in Sparta, Michigan and died May 19, 1950, in Cheboygan. He married Mary MacArthur in Cheboygan on April 28, 1898. She was the daughter of John MacArthur and Nancy Judson and she was born in Cheboygan on September 16, 1876, and died December 21, 1967, in Grosse Point. His obituary tells a lot about his life in Cheboygan.

One of Cheboygan's outstanding citizens Dr. W. E. Chapman died at 9:30 this morning at his home on Sammons Street, from effects of a stroke with which he was stricken Monday evening. His death is mourned by a host of friends who knew him during his career

19 Gretchen Sumerix, "*Our Yesterdays*", Volume 1, p. 27.

in Cheboygan as doctor, army captain, city health officer, coroner, and mayor. A Republican stalwart he was mayor of Cheboygan for three terms and initiated progressive municipal developments that are still helping Cheboygan today. But for a host of people his service in official life was overshadowed by his connection as personal physician and as a neighbor and friend. Dr. Chapman practiced medicine in Cheboygan for over 50 years becoming a life member of the Michigan Medical Society. He was 86 years old, born on Christmas Day, 1865, at Sparta, Michigan. He was ill for several months. Several years ago he was stricken with a heart attack, since which he has engaged in only limited practice.

Educated at Michigan State College and the University of Michigan Medical School, Dr. Chapman, on getting his doctor's degree, came directly to Cheboygan and opened practice in what had been office of the late Dr. Berdan. The building has since been torn down, and the lot is now the site of the Step Inn. For most of his practice, Dr. Chapman was located in offices over the Sangster & Leonall Drug Store. When he came to Cheboygan, this city had 11 doctors of medicine. Despite the competition, he made good, as proved by over 50 years of practice in the city of his choice.

He served his country with distinction by taking part in two wars. In the Spanish American war, he was sent to the Philippines Islands, where he was acting Assistant Surgeon with rank of Captain, working in three hospitals. He saw active service and was under fire. After the war, he continued his connection as

a reserve officer, and when World War I opened he went to camp at Battle Creek for six months, examining recruits as they enlisted.

Dr. Chapman was surgeon for the New York Central Railroad for over 30 years. He was medical consultant for the Michigan Bell Telephone Company. Until last January he continued as acting Assistant Surgeon for the United States Public Health Service, his duties including care for members of the Coast Guard of the Cheboygan area.

He was elected mayor in 1924, then re-elected in 1925 and 1926. During his administration Main Street was widened and the project to reclaim wasteland at the foot of Huron Street for a city park received its inception (Now Gordon Turner Park). Dr. Chapman was one of the first and most zealous workers in an early movement to secure a modern hospital in Cheboygan. When it seemed funds might be secured from a foundation to establish the hospital, he made several trips to New York City, in Cheboygan's interest. Choice eventually was made between Cheboygan and an Ohio city, the hospital was awarded to Ohio.

The doctor identified himself with fraternal life in Cheboygan by membership in the Elks and Masonic lodges. He was at one time exalted ruler of the Cheboygan Lodge of Benevolent and Protective Order of Elks, In Masonry, he was a life member, with affiliation in the Cheboygan Lodge, besides being a member of the Shrine at Bay City. Brothers of his profession throughout north Michigan honored him and acknowledge his interest in health of the area by electing him president of the Northern Michigan Medical Society. He held this office three years. The same interest in public health was shown in his service as Cheboygan city health officer.

He is survived by his wife, his two children Mrs. Edward Trowbridge of Grosse Pointe and Dr. Earle N. Chapman of Boston and three grandchildren, Steve Trowbridge of Grosse Pointe, and Duncan and Judith Chapman of Boston. Burial will be in Pine Hill Cemetery.[20]

W.F. REED M.D.,
Physician and Surgeon.
Office hours—10 to 12 a. m., 1 to 3 and 7 to 9 p. m.   Office in Howell block
Special attention given to Diseases of Eye and Ear.   aug12-89

"When Dr. Wilber Reed came to Cheboygan it was by boat. To make sure he would have a way to get around to see patients he bought a horse and buggy with him. His first operations were performed on a dining room table. In the days before autos, he rode a bicycle on calls, or got out his buggy and steed. Sometimes he drove as far as he could in the countryside, and then hitched his horse to a tree and walked the rest of the way on a trail to a farmhouse."

(*Cheboygan Daily Tribune*, February 7, 1946.)

Dr. Wilber F. Reed was born in Pontiac, Michigan, on November 4, 1850. He attended the University of Michigan and graduated in 1874 with a BA degree. In March, 1877, he got his Medical Degree at Michigan. Before coming to Cheboygan he was a physician at Ionia Prison from 1877 to 1881. He worked at Maple Rapids from 1881 to 1887. His wife, Sarah Miner, was born in Champlain, New York, on October 15, 1857. She married Dr. W.F. Reed on October 11, 1883 at Hubbardston Michigan, and they moved to Cheboygan four years later, in 1897. Children were Seth Reed of Cleveland, Ohio, and Harry Reed of Hamilton, Montana. In 1939 Dr. Reed was living at 504 Pine Street and his office was at 221 N. Main. After Sarah died Oct 20, 1921, he married Mrs. Minnie Pennell of Cheboygan on December 1, 1922.

Dr. Reed was city health officer for 18 years, county corner, and a lieutenant in the Cheboygan militia company. When he died at the age of 94,

he was Michigan's oldest Mason. His father had lived to 100! He was Secretary of the Cheboygan Lodge of Mason's for 41 years and was head of all three Cheboygan Masonic Orders. On July 6, 1943, he celebrated his 50th anniversary of becoming a member of the Masonic Order.

Dr. William R. Stringham was born October 27, 1858, in Berlin Township, St. Clair County, Michigan, on the Stringham homestead. He was the youngest of six children, his mother dying when he was two years old. He graduated from Romeo High School, taught for a while and then studied medicine and pharmacy at the Detroit College of Medicine, graduating from the medical course in 1884. He later qualified as a registered Michigan pharmacist.

Dr. Stringham practiced medicine for a few months in North Branch, Michigan and then heard of the need of a physician in Wolverine. He

20 *Cheboygan Daily Tribune*, May 19, 1950.

Sign from collection of the Historical Society of Cheboygan County, Inc.

moved there in the fall of 1884. He was the first doctor in the town and also opened the first drug store. At that time the Wolverine school was unable to get a teacher, so in addition to being a doctor and druggist, he was called on to teach. He got an assistant for the store, while he worked in the school room. When a call came for a doctor, he turned the school over to some of the older girls to superintend while he visited patients. He was in Wolverine for a year and a half and then moved to Mecosta where he met and married his wife, Ida Mai Pattison, on March 22, 1886.

Dr. Stringham moved to Cheboygan in 1907. He developed a general practice as well as working as a surgeon. Dr. Will R. Stringham had a hospital here in 1915-17 on Backus Street near their home. His office in 1914 was at 516 North Main Street. William returned to school in 1914 for a postgraduate course in surgery. He performed much of Cheboygan's early surgery, aided by his son and by Dr. St Amour.

Dr. Stringham was a county doctor for years. At the time of his death, in 1935, he had the county contract for all the contagious cases and was the official doctor for the Cheboygan County Poor House, as well as the railroad physician for the D & M. Railway. He was a member of the Michigan Medical Society and the Northern Michigan Medical Society of which he served as president. He was a staunch Republican and served as a delegate to the Republican convention. He was also a member of the Masons, Oddfellows, and Eagles lodges.[21]

Dr. James R. Stringham was born February 22, 1887, in Mecosta County, son of Dr. William Stringham. He graduated from Marquette Normal College and then attended Detroit College of Medicine, graduating in 1911. While attending college he worked in the dispensary of St. Mary's Hospital in Detroit. He immediately went into practice with his father in Cheboygan. He married Adeline Belting on Dec 9, 1913, in Cheboygan. She was born June 21, 1890, in Ishpeming, Michigan, and died December 6, 1976, in Cheboygan. He was in practice for 59 years, retiring in 1970. He was the physician for the D & M Railroad following his father's death in 1935. He was appointed city health officer until the office was abolished in favor of a district health department. He was elected a vice president of Community Memorial Hospital in December of 1948 and later was Chief of Staff. Dr. James Stringham was a member of the Michigan State Medical Society. He died January 22, 1971, in Cheboygan.

Have you ever wondered what people did before you could call 911 for help? "In 1934 Theodore Amiott drowned in the river near the DNR dock, just south of the State Street Bridge. He and his mother were in a small wood rowboat which tipped over. Several men dove in to recover the body and by the time they had him ashore they had five men from the Michigan Public Service Company, ready to do artificial respiration. "Dr. J.R. Stringham was first on the scene. Dr. E A. Christie arrived shortly. Dr. F.C. Mayne and Dr. H.G. Morrow arrived later, and all did what they could. Miss Florence Holbern, a nurse from the Cheboygan General Hospital, assisted them. For nearly two hours, the work continued, without a moment's stop." [22]

21 *Cheboygan Daily Tribune*, February 1, 1935
22 *Cheboygan Daily Tribune*, September 8, 1934.

F. C. Mayne

PHYSICIAN & SURGEON

Masonic Temple Building

Office Hours: 1:30-5 p. m.

Also 7-8 p. m. Saturday

Phones:

Office 380-F1

Residence 380-F2

Dr. Frederick C. Mayne was born June 15, 1889, in Charlevoix, the first son of Judge and Mrs. F.W. Mayne. He attended Charlevoix Public Schools and Albion College before entering the University of Michigan where he received his Bachelor of Science degree. He graduated from medical school in 1915 from the University. He interned at Harper Hospital, and received further training at Michigan Mutual Hospital, both in Detroit. He served on the staff of Traverse City State Hospital for one year before enlisting in World War I. He married Miss Meta Hintz in Traverse City in May, 1918, and soon after was assigned to duty at Camp Dodge, Iowa, before going overseas with the 88th Division. He served as lieutenant in the Medical Corps in France, then as Captain until his honorable discharge in May, 1919.

He came to Cheboygan in late 1919 to begin the general practice of medicine and surgery. After the death of his wife in 1925, he married Miss Edith Harbron of Cheboygan on October 17, 1927, in Charlevoix and they made their home in Cheboygan. He was a member of St. James Episcopal Church. He also served on the school board and was a former member of the Rotary Club. He held memberships in the Northern Michigan Medical Society, American Academy of Family Physicians, and the American Medical Association. He retired in June 1956, and spent several winters in southern Texas and California, always returning to Mullett Lake. He died May 1, 1980.[23]

Dr. Jack R. Georges was born May 23, 1904, on Dresser Street, Cheboygan, son of John and Edna Georges. He graduated from Cheboygan High School where he played football, basketball and baseball. He attended Kirksville College of Osteopathy and Surgery at Kirksville, Missouri, and graduated in 1929. He married Susan Goodrich, born on May 13, 1906, in Fort Fairfield, Maine, in 1931. He first set up practice in Maine. In 1944 they moved to Cheboygan, where he opened an office in the Fleischman Building, at the corner of Main and Division Street. Between 1944 and their retirement in 1960, the Cheboygan couple delivered 2,500 babies as home deliveries without losing a mother. In 1958 Dr. Georges and his wife received an award from the Cheboygan County Dairy Association at its annual banquet for going into every township of the county on their many calls. He was chosen as the 1973 recipient of the Cheboygan High School Hall of Fame by the National Honor Society. He was a longtime member of the First Congregational Church and served on the Board of Trustees. Dr. Georges died on August 1, 1977. Their only son, Carleton, died at the close of World War II, in 1946, while serving in the U.S. Navy. Susan later married Karl Heilman in 1992. She died, age 98, on June 14, 2004 in Cheboygan.[24]

---

23 *Cheboygan Daily Tribune*, May 1, 1980
24 *Cheboygan Daily Tribune*, August 1, 1977

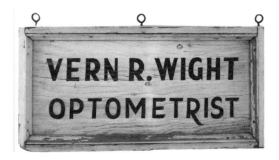

The Wight Jewelry Store was owned by **Vern Roland Wight**, the author's maternal grandfather. He had an optometry shop in the back of the store where he fitted glasses. His wife, Doris Wight, ran the front end of the store, selling china and jewelry. Bob (Robert) Hudson was the watchmaker and he did clock and watch repair. For many years Vern was the only optometrist in the area, and he kept very busy fitting glasses. His exam chair, eye charts, and optical equipment were donated to the Cheboygan County History Center.

DENTISTS

Dr. Albert E. Sangster, D.D.S. He was born at Stouffville, Ontario, Canada, on August 3, 1867, and had nine brothers and sisters. He attended the Toronto University and Temple University in Philadelphia. He came to Cheboygan in 1894 when he bought the Packard Drug store and opened a dental office on the second floor.

Dr. Sangster became partners with Dan Gahon. Miles Riggs was a clerk in the store. When Gahon was murdered, Riggs then went into partnership with Sangster. Carl Leonall than began to work for them as a clerk, and he later succeeded Riggs as a partner, and the firm became Sangster & Leonall. He was a charter member of the Cheboygan Golf and Country Club and the Rotary. He was in the Masons, holding many offices. He was also in the Elks. At the time of his death he was survived by his wife, his son Al, who was mayor, a daughter Vera, who was the Countess de Chap-

"Before the days of disposable syringes for shots, the glass syringes and needles were reused. Dr. McCarroll, a local physician, used to bring his syringe needles into the Wight Jewelry Store to have the needles sharpened by Bob Hudson, the watchmaker. Bob would sharpen the needles several times until he felt the ends were too blunted and thick. When he though they were too dull and he wouldn't want a shot with them himself, he threw the needles out and told the doctor they were "broken."

plaine of Montreal, and another daughter, Mrs. Roy A. Gexzelius of Walford, Pennsylvania.

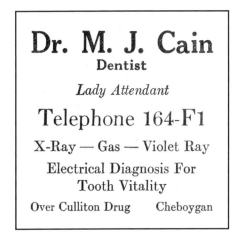

Dr. Martin J. Cain was born April 23, 1873, in Cheboygan, a son of John Cain. He went to the Detroit College of Medicine, graduating in 1907 as a dentist. He married Agnes Richards of Alpena in 1912. He had a dentist office in the Paquette building, the Frost-Kesseler building, and later in the Gerow building. He practiced dentistry for 46 years in Cheboygan. He was also active in promoting Cheboygan. He purchased the Duncan City property from the First National Bank and tried to develop it. Some of his projects were the American Music Camp, Camp Knight of the Pines, a National Youth Administration Camp and a Boy's Club camp. Martin also served ten one-year terms as mayor. He died November 10, 1954.[25]

FIRST HOSPITALS IN CHEBOYGAN

Photo © Johnson Studio,
from Historical Society of Cheboygan County, Inc. Collections

This building was located on the NW corner of Court and Main Street, prior to the building of the courthouse there in 1900. It was known as "*St Mary's Hospital*," the "Cheboygan Sanitarium" and also as the "*Northwestern Lumberman's Hospital*." According to Ellis Olson, local historian, it was a former hotel operated by George Starr. It was meant specifically for the woodsmen who often suffered serious injuries and had no one to care for them. The first lumbermen's hospital was St. Mary's in Saginaw. There were soon others built in Bay City, Big Rapids, Flint, Grand Rapids Alpena, Cheboygan, Oscoda, Marquette, Menominee, and Manistique. John Fitzmaurice of Cheboygan wrote a book called "The Shanty Boy, Life in a Lumber Camp" in 1889 and he wrote of his time selling subscriptions or insurance for these hospitals. He said the Northwestern Hospital Co., of Cheboygan, Bay City and Marquette were the most important.

Certificates are sold to the men, entitling the holder to care, board, lodging and medical treatment, for one year, and whenever sick or hurt, these tickets open for them a good home. The men fully appreciate this great blessing, and buy readily from the agents visiting the camps.... Possibly the most successful hospital agent in Michigan is Mr. George Starrs, agent for the Northwestern Hospital Co., of Cheboygan. Starrs is a born mimic, a good comic singer and dancer, and as a storyteller is simply inimitable. These are the social requisites for a Saturday night in camp, and frequently the fun grows so fast and furious that all restraint is cast aside, and free license given to every description of monkey shine and horse play. . .

As one goes out cured, another takes his place, with his broken fragments of humanity tied up in a dirty rag, just as when he left the battle field. When he arrives at the haven of safety, on which he fortunately holds a ticket, he is in good hands. Men who have risked their professional reputation as being both kind hearted and skillful, take charge of him. If at all possible, the first thing is a bath, then clean clothes, then into a soft, clean, comfortable bed, and under the watchful care of an experienced nurse, acting by the strict directions of a skillful surgeon, the man gets a fair start back to the realms of health again, and all for the tax

---

25 Ellis Olson, *Old Rivertown Cheboygan Centennial Booklet*, p. 69.

of nine cents per week, for a year, which he assumes when he buys his ticket—not for the price per week of a good cigar.[26]

The *Northwestern Hospital* had a good reputation as seen in this notice in the Cheboygan Democrat of November 1888. "The *Northwestern Hospital* is so popular that sailors will endure untold agonies uncomplainingly in ports where there are Marine Hospitals, so they can get into the hospital here, and if the collector insists on sending them to Detroit they get up on their ear (complain).[27] This story in April of 1891 tells of more unfortunate incident. This article also shows the power the press used to preach morality.

Tuesday morning a sick sailor named Frank Mercer, was put ashore here (Cheboygan) from a Detroit vessel and left very ill and penniless on the docks. He made efforts to get hospital relief from the Deputy Collector of the Port, but failed, and finally was taken to the poor house for treatment. The laws of the United States provide for the relief of sick seamen, and ever since the establishment of the office of Deputy Collector of this port until the present incumbent was put in charge of the office to give Mr. Perkins a chance to collect his rent, sailors have been given the relief they are entitled to under the laws. But the present Deputy Collector is a law unto himself, and does not care for such a little thing as a U. S. statute; consequently sailors are given no attention. There is no doubt that part of the trouble is caused by the red tape of the Marine Hospital service, which makes the granting of relief a matter of great incon-

venience and doubt, frequently saddling the costs of relief upon the unfortunate collector, who fails to make out the papers properly. But this is no excuse for a lazy collector refusing to grant relief which the law entitles him to.[28]

The *Northwestern Hospital*, which ever since it was established, through its superior management, has maintained a high standing, has changed hands, and the new proprietors, Starrs & Boyce are the gentlemen who will continue to make a success of the business. Dr. Boyce is a man that stands high in the profession and in the short time that he has been here he has secured the confidence of those he has had occasion to meet. Of the other member, Mr. Starrs, suffice it to say that he is a man who understands the business thoroughly. Mr. Starrs will continue on the road in the interest of the hospital. It has received a thorough overhauling and put in shape to receive private patients. Tom Shaw will continue to be resident manager of the institution. As before it will be run in connection with the hospitals of the same name at Bay City and Marquette.[29]

This *Northwest Hospital* was closed by May 21, 1892, when the *Cheboygan Democrat* placed a notice that "N.W. Lyons has rented the building on Main Street, known as the Northwestern Hospital, and it will be fitted up as a residence for his family." By 1900 the building was torn down and the Cheboygan County Courthouse was built on that location. The city saw a need for a hospital and was seeking help.

Two years or so ago, the sisters of the *Big Rapids Hospital* came here to see about starting a general hospital but the Great Northern Protective Association had the same project in hand and so noth-

26 John Fitzmaurice, *Shanty Boy, Life in a Lumber Camp, Cheboygan, 1889.*
27 *Cheboygan Democrat*, November 1888
28 *Cheboygan Democrat*, April 1891
29 *Cheboygan Democrat*, March 13, 1889

ing was done. January 1 of this year the association made a good start toward the establishment of such an institution by the purchase, on contract, of the elegant Rice residence. But before anything could be done the building was destroyed by fire and all plans were spoiled. We understand that negotiations are now pending for a union of forces, the sisters to start a hospital and to get the patronage of the G.N.P.A. which would make it better for all concerned. We hope it may succeed.[30]

This hospital never seems to have gotten off the ground. About 1915 Drs. William and James Stringham rented a house at 238 Backus Street and equipped it for hospital use. They used it two years and then closed it.

CHEBOYGAN'S PRIVATE HOSPITALS

After the attempts to arrange for an institutional hospital failed, the residents of Cheboygan relied on private hospitals within the homes of local residents. Many of the health care providers were often self-taught or were nurses who trained under physicians. Cheboygan had a number of these hospitals before Community Memorial Hospital was built in 1943.

Walker Hospital--Estelle Walker (Mrs. Richard) had turned her home on Duncan Avenue into a private hospital. She took a correspondence course in nursing and received her diploma. She then went into hospital work at the Backus Street building the Stringham's had formerly used for their hospital. It was not large enough so she moved into the old Mould home on Cuyler Street. This is the large house next to Cheboygan Co-op, on the corner

of Cuyler and Taylor. The county started to contribute thirty dollars per month toward the hospital and she then took care of county patients at a reduced rate. The Woman's Club furnished one room and did some fundraising for hospital linen.[31] She had to close this hospital in 1922 because of illness. Mrs. Walker's obituary said she slipped and fell down the steps of her home and was later taken to the hospital at Detroit for a serious operation. A year later she was again rushed back to St. Mary's hospital in Detroit, accompanied by Dr. Chapman's wife, for an operation for peritonitis. She died there November 8, 1923. The newspaper said "During the time Mrs. Walker conducted her hospital, she made a number of very warm friends as being always willing to do everything possible for the comfort of her patients."

Whenever a major operation was performed, Dr. W. J Cassidy of Detroit was called and he came and operated, assisted by the local doctors. The first major operation performed at the Walker Hospital, by a local doctor was an emergency appendicitis operation performed by Dr. F. C Maine, assisted by Dr. J. R. Stringham and his father. The patient was Chester Wixon.[32]

Next Dr. Cayley rented a house on South Huron Street and, with the help of his sister, took care of a few patients there. Before it was fully equipped for a hospital, the house was destroyed by fire. The patients were all rescued, but that was the end of the **Cayley Hospital.**

The next known home hospital was at the corner of Pine and Bailey Street, north and across the street from the where the Cheboygan Public Library is now located. The newspaper made this announcement.

30 *Cheboygan Daily Tribune*, March 8, 1902
31 *Cheboygan Daily Tribune*, Golden Jubilee, 1939.
32 *Cheboygan Daily Tribune*, Golden Jubilee, 1939

A **Community Hospital** has been established in the commodious home of Mr. and Mrs. Will Trudo at corner of Pine and Bailey Streets. At the present time accommodations have been made for eight patients and arrangements are being made whereby fourteen patients can be cared for at the same time. The home is nicely located with all modern conveniences. The ladies in charge of this much needed establishment are Mrs. Alta Betterly of Detroit and Mrs. Elma Bannister also of Detroit. The ladies are no strangers to our people.

The author's mother was born in 1927 in this home hospital. The home was later purchased and lived in many years by the Carl Leonall family.

In 1929 Mrs. Ruth Nordman opened the **Cheboygan Medical Home** on Duncan Avenue. She remarried in 1933 and became wife of Perry Ritter, a local funeral director. In 1935 she made many improvements, including the installation of a well-equipped operating room, and the Cheboygan Medical Home was renamed the **Cheboygan General Hospital.** It was run under the supervision of Mrs. Ritter until she died in 1936. After that time, it was under the supervision of her daughter, Mrs. Ruby Brooks. They increased the number of beds from six to twelve. They had a fully equipped operating room, an X-ray and fluoroscope, and had a registered nurse in charge.

Another home hospital was the **Hubacker Hospital.** Mrs. Fred (Clara Milmine) Hubacker was born on June 3, 1883, in Cheboygan. Her first husband was Louis Hubacker, and he died

---

HUBACKER RECEIVING HOSPITAL

Diagnostic and X-ray equipment available.

Registered nurses in charge.

419 Court Street   Phone 286-M

---

in 1917. She then married Fred Hubacker in 1919. For about ten years, Mrs. Fred Hubacker carried on hospital work in her home on Court Street where the Cheboygan County Museum Spies Hall is located today. In 1935 it was legally opened as the **Hubacker Receiving Hospital.** She started with four beds. By 1939 she had sixteen, which were in use most of the time. She had a well-equipped operating room, an X-ray and fluoroscope, and could handle emergencies. She had a nursery in a pleasant room with six tiny baby beds. She also had a large screened- in porch upstairs, which was for convalescing patients in the summer.[33] "She was known for her nursing skills. She will long be remembered for opening a hospital on Court Street during the period before the Community Memorial Hospital was built. She operated this health service for several years." [34]

The story of Cheboygan's hospitals and doctors continues in the publication "Cheboygan Memorial Hospital Celebrating 65 years of Caring" compiled and edited by Rich Adams and published by the Cheboygan Memorial Hospital in 2007.

Photo courtesy of Cheboygan Memorial Hospital

---

33 *Cheboygan Daily Tribune*, Golden Jubilee, 1939
34 *Cheboygan Daily Tribune*, April 14, 1960 obituary

COUNTY HEALTH CARE

Before the days of the district health departments, the county chose a county health officer. It was his duty to oversee epidemics of contagious diseases. We must remember that smallpox, diphtheria, and typhoid were common causes of disease in those days. Cheboygan was a port city with many outsiders coming into the community so contagious diseases were a big concern. These duties seemed to have rotated throughout the medical community, with the new members all taking their turn.

The County Health Department evolved from the earlier "county health officer" system. One of the most remembered parts of this program are the school shots that were given by the county health nurse. How many of you remember lining up in long lines at school to get your polio shot? They used a glass syringe and students were lined up and expected to go through without any fuss. Doris Reid coordinated many a school inoculation programs.

Doris Reid, County Nurse—Doris received her Registered Nurse Degree in 1936 from Traverse City State Hospital. She later received a scholarship and attended the Frontier School of Midwifery, in Wendover, Kentucky, where she became a certified midwife in 1943. Doris returned to the Burt Lake area in the 1950's and was northern Michigan's only certified midwife. In 1951 she became a public health nurse for District Health Dept. # 4 and retired in 1973 as nurse coordinator and nursing supervisor. She wrote a book called *Saddlebags Full of Memories*. She was a member of the Burt Lake Christian Church since 1929, and died at the age of 86.[35] In 1992 the Health Department dedicated its new building in Cheboygan as the "Doris E. Reid Center."

Doris Reid, R.N., County Nurse
Collection of the Cheboygan County Historical Society, Inc.

PEST HOUSE

At the turn of the century most towns had a "Pest House." The term stood for the word "pestilence" and was meant for those who were suffering from contagious diseases such as typhoid, cholera and smallpox. All of these diseases occurred in Cheboygan during its early days. In fact, the first recorded deaths in the county were Emma Jane Sammons on November 25, 1846, and her sister, Martha Sammons on December 12, 1846, who both died of smallpox, just a few months after the family moved here. Small pox vaccinations were not yet common, and many epidemics traveled through the pioneer and Indian populations.

Typhoid and cholera are spread through contaminated water and food. At the time Cheboygan was first settled, people got their water from springs or the river and wouldn't have known to boil it first. Bathrooms were outhouses or the nearest bush and, even after sewers were built, many

35 *Straitsland Resorter*, 2004

drain pipes ran to the river. The author's father, born in 1927, talks about swimming in the river as a kid. He said that those who swam below the dam were called "turd dodgers" because of the raw sewage that emptied into the river. When reviewing the county microfilm death records, typhoid and cholera were often mentioned. There were also reference to consumption, diphtheria, "brain fever" and "spring complaint" as well as the expected heart and childbirth causes of death.

There were a number of smallpox cases in the Cheboygan area in the early 1900's. An example is "John Diekman is over the small pox and is out again, but his own dog can't track him yet, as there is a cross smell of carbolic acid and sulphur. Eight of his family had the disease." [36] The newspaper published the active cases and also told when the families were recovered. When a family had smallpox in their home, they were quarantined and could not go out in the community where they might spread the disease. There were many cases reported between 1902 and 1905. There are references to a "pest house" in Cheboygan. There was also a complaint by Arthur Watson of Cheboygan, who had a lumber camp near Mackinaw City. While he came to town for supplies, the health officer in Mackinaw took over his camp and quarantined several smallpox patients there!

J.J. Donnelly the well-known main street saloon man, was ordered taken to the pest house Thursday morning suffering with a slight attack of small pox. Mr. Donnelly's many friends hope he will not be long in quarantine, as everyone misses his genial presence. [37]

T.A. MacDonald was taken to the pest house Thursday suffering from

smallpox. There are five men confined there now all from the city. J.M. Donnelly, Henry Jana, Miller and another man whose name could not ascertained. [38]

The author questioned local historian, Ellis Olson, as to the location of the pest house. Ellis thought it was near Joe Mel's Bay, near the back of the County Fairgrounds., but was never able to locate an exact site.

Senator Fred Ming, from Cheboygan, had a major influence on the health of northern Michigan. Ming had three brothers die of consumption while in their twenties, and this motivated him to get a tuberculosis sanatorium located in northern Michigan. He was

FRED R. MING, Representative.

trying to get it established in Cheboygan but was not able to accomplish that. However, it was built in Gaylord and able to serve the residents of Cheboygan. There was a movement to name the sanitarium after him because of his efforts. Ming declined that honor although he accepted a position as a member of the State Tuberculosis Sanitarium Commission. Senator Ming convinced the Legislature to fund the sanitarium through a tax on malt. He fought the prohibitionists and was quoted as saying "I don't care a hoot about what malt is being used for. All I want is the sanitarium." This Sanitarium was built in 1937 and operated until 1963. It later became the "Alpine Center."

36 *Cheboygan Democrat,* January 1902
37 *Cheboygan Democrat,* April 7, 1905
38 *Cheboygan Democrat,* April 7, 1905